A FRESH LOOK AT
EASTER

Seeking a Deeper Understanding of This Festival

PETER RUSSELL-YARDE

Printed in the United States of America
Library of Congress Control Number: 2025917152
ISBN: Softcover   978-1-969213-00-7
          e-Book   978-1-969213-01-4
Republished by: TwinVerse Prime
Publication Date: 09/01/2025

To order copies of this book, contact:
TwinVerse Prime
Phone: (725) 257-6538
clients@twinverseprime.com
www.twinverseprime.com/

DEDICATION

To the God who called me to serve Him
and who has inspired me to write on His word

Contents

BOOK PUBLISHED BY PETER

Biblical Comment:
The Origin of Life : God's Relationship with Man in Genesis
God Rescues His People : Birth of Nation According to Exodus
The Wilderness Training School : Powerful Lessons in Numbers
Seeing Into the Future : Understanding the Revelation of John
The Path of Wisdom : A Study of Proverbs Chapters 1 to 4
Proverbs 5 to 12
Hosea
Deuteronomy
Epistle to the Ephesians
Epistle to the Colossians
Epistle to the Romans
Epistle to the Hebrews
Epistle to the Galatians

Matters of Faith:
Are There Demons? & Other Matters of Faith
Letters to the Seven Churches in Revelation
Lost Souls : The danger of losing sight of God
Covenant & Testament : God's rules for God's people to obey
Belief and Faith : Understanding the Essentials
Ordinary People : Extra-ordinary faith
So You Think You Know About Faith : Learning to Trust God
A Fresh Look at Easter
You Will Receive Power
Assuredly God IS!
Truth & Doubt

Christ IS King : A Guide for Doubters
Law & Grace (Lessons from the Kings of Judah & Israel)
The God Who created Us

Autobiographical:
A Tale of Three Men (Provides background information about how these books came to be written and distributed)

What our faith is all about
The Tent of the Meeting : Illustrating God's Plan of Salvation

PREFACE

About This Book

I am reminded about what Paul said to the Corinthians, *"For now we see through a glass, dimly, but then we will see face to face. Now I know only in part; then I will know fully, even as I have been fully known." (1 Cor. 13:12).* Not one of us knows the whole truth, only what we have been given by God through His Holy Spirit and according to our God given gifts to handle that knowledge.

What I have written is to my knowledge the best teaching I can give on this subject of Easter and according to the guidance I have received of God along with many years of research and much reading and prayer and giving of myself into God's service. Those who read it should be equally as prayerful in order for them to try to understand what God is teaching them through this book.

I tend to be a very definite person and as a Technical Author in industry where risk must be kept to an absolute minimum, the Operating Instructions and Maintenance Manuals and training material I wrote over the years had to be correct and written in such a way that the reader knew exactly what they were being instructed to do or taught. This was done as a result of my need to know exactly how things worked and the proper way for the operator to approach and use the equipment or process effectively and safely.

Undoubtedly one of my failings is that the exactness of my writing, as described above, in a religious context might suggest a fundamentalist approach. However, nothing could be further from the truth. One reviewer on Amazon wrote:

"Your way of writing is very precise, this makes it difficult to absorb sometimes, "not easy to read" said your reviewer.

God is not easy to understand at all and most of his communications were written down by people so what we think we know is written by Men. Your work explains God but the reader has to work very hard to understand all the finer points and definitely has to look up the references and pray. Researched facts.

1. If someone believes in God and reads your work they are not sure.

2. If someone believes in God and reads your work and looks up the references they are reasonably happy.

3. If someone believes in God and reads your work and looks up the references and prays they either say, "sorry Lord", or "that's really good", while they look faintly embarrassed.

I spend months reading your work. Have some really good times with the Lord; thank you Peter."

What has become very clear to me over the years is that God's word is His word and not ours, and reading what has been written throughout scripture it is clear to me that He does not take kindly to any man amending His word:

> "I warn everyone who hears the prophetic words of this book: if anyone adds anything to what is written here, God will add to that person the plagues described in this book; if anyone takes away from the words of this prophetic book, God will take away that person's share in the tree of life and in the holy city described in this book" (Rev. 22:18, 19).

Undoubtedly the best way to even begin to understand scripture is to read the Bible from cover to cover, at least once, just like any book written by man, then everything begins to make sense. Certainly one important fact comes to the fore, and that is the goodness and severity of God, for He blesses those that are obedient to His will and statutes and are fully focused on pleasing Him, and severe to those who rebel against Him because time and again when reading about the reigns of the various kings of Judah in the books of Kings and Chronicles, it becomes very clear that God is only prepared to work with those who have a heart for Him and willingly submit to His guidance, but withdraws His support and protection from those who reject Him, thus allowing trouble to engulf them.

Consider the problems experienced by the Jewish people after the rejection of their Messiah. Using their own intelligence the leaders tried to govern the nation themselves without any reference to God. The First Testament gave them sufficient information for them to realize not only that the Messiah would come at that time but, reading Isaiah 53 (which many rabbis and leaders of the Jews have been ordered to avoided for centuries), they would have learned that He was to come as the suffering servant.

At the time of Christ's coming it was necessary for the leaders of the day to be against Him, although it was their decision entirely because they had drifted so far from God. Thus it was that God's choice of timing fitted in very well with the waywardness of those governing the nation so that they opposed and finally murdered Him. This became advantageous to the Gentiles because, as most of the people of Israel rejected Him, God's only option was to open the gift of salvation immediately up to all who believed to the Gentile nations, which was not only prophesied but also made possible by the persecution that erupted in Jerusalem and the rest of Judea thus dispersing Jewish believers in Jesus as missionaries around the known world.

In Romans 11 Paul speaks of the cultivated olive tree that represented Israel. Throughout the First Testament it becomes very clear that when the people rejected their God He withdrew His protection and help. Because of their rejection of the one man who came to save them from their sins, God withdrew His protection and help but in so doing He opened the way for the Gentiles to be given the chance of receiving that salvation instead of them. Spiritual Israel came into being through Christ their Messiah. Paul stated in chapter 9 that just because a person can trace his lineage back to Abraham does not mean that they belong to Israel, because unless they are children of the promise they are not of Him. It was not Ishmael who was promised to Abraham but Isaac and then Jacob. Why was that? Because God promised Abraham a son and that son was Isaac, then from Isaac came Esau and Jacob, but it was Jacob who was chosen because his heart was right with God.

So what has this got to do with us? Gentiles have been made right with God not because of their efforts in obeying the letter of the law of God, which they did not know, but because of faith in God just like Abraham even though they were not seeking Him; whereas the Jews, except for a remnant, were seeking to be saved through their own efforts by obeying the law of God, which is impossible because of sin. Therefore those Jews who reject God can no longer be part of the cultivated olive tree, but those Gentiles who receive the word of God and believe in Him by faith are grafted onto the cultivated olive tree even though such a grafting of a wild branch onto a cultivated tree is considered by horticulturalists as impossible.

The Jews had got to the state in which they believed they were saved by being obedient to the law of righteousness without reference to God in whom they had no faith. Therefore we Gentile believers are privileged to be saved by responding with faith in the Lord Jesus, and by so doing have been grafted onto the cultivated olive tree that is spiritual Israel, which will be explained later in this book. But of this matter we cannot boast, rather we must ensure we do not lose faith in God and be removed from our position in the new spiritual Israel, just as Jews have been, rather we must pray that they will come to believe in their Messiah through faith.

Let us be in no doubt, just as the laws of the country in which we live are applied by our judges, so at the time of the judgement, God will interpret His laws in the way He meant them to be interpreted and apply them to all who go before Him, not in the way you or I might prefer them to be interpreted. He is the One who has saved us and not the other way around, His grace is sufficient for us no matter in what situation or what state we find ourselves, therefore we must get as close to our loving and gracious God as possible and be guided by His Holy Spirit for we are reminded by scripture that:

> *we do not have a high priest who is unable to sympathize with our weaknesses, because he has been tested in every respect as we are tested, yet without sin. Let us, therefore, approach the throne of grace with boldness, so that we may receive mercy and find grace to help us in our time of need" (Heb. 4:15, 16).*

God is not an ogre of whom we must be in fear of our lives, rather He is a God that wants to bless us if we put ourselves into His loving and capable hands and obediently follow His guidance.

The feedback received from many sources from a draft copy of this book has been very encouraging, which is why I have felt the urge to continue my writing in the belief that God will continue to bless it. In fact my writing has led a rabbi to meet with his Messiah and enjoy his epiphany moment, which is most encouraging. He is now serving his Lord as a missionary.

One criticism received was that there is no bibliography of books from which quotes have been taken. However no direct quotes from the writings of other Christian writers have been used in this or any other book that I have written. Although I read a great deal, particularly bible commentaries and Bible notes and spend time meditating on them, I always seek for inspiration from God, sometimes waiting for a little while before writing anything thus what is written is original, for why reprocess what others have written, especially the ancients when it is much better to put forward fresh teaching on spiritual matters? Certainly my experience has been that as I type away what appears on the screen is often new to me as though God was guiding my hands; the experience of seeing text appear that is full of teaching for me is very exciting and stimulating. This book therefore contains my understanding of what the

Bible tells us of what happened at Easter all those years ago when the Son of the Living God died for us, as I have been inspired by the Holy Spirit. Even the scriptural verses used are my interpretation of the verses after consulting the various translation at my disposal as source material.

Another point made was that there seemed to be no reliance on the thoughts and understanding of writers that have gone before. One of the reasons that the religious elite at the time of Christ did not believe He was the promised one was that they relied more on the writing of the ancients, than seeking a personal understanding of the scriptures for themselves. The question we must ask ourselves is, "Why rely so much on the writings of men, however inspirational they might be and useful for encouragement, when it is possible, by opening our hearts to the work of the Holy Spirit, to receive inspiration and knowledge direct from God?" Do we need to be reminded that it is the word from God that provides us with true spiritual food? Therefore what is the point in depending solely on the fast and not necessarily nutritious food of others? After all so much depends on the quality of their relationship with the living Lord, and I have read some confusing and indistinct writings in my time. Read their work by all means but form your own opinion of what the scriptures mean by referring directly with scripture and meditating upon it.

And thirdly it was suggested that I am a fundamentalist. If being a fundamentalist means all I write is strictly according to scripture, then I admit to being a fundamentalist. Why pollute our spiritual food with modern ideas which are ever changing according to the whim of society, could that not be the reason many churches die through disillusionment? Is not God the same yesterday, today and forever and His word never changes? Therefore it is essential that the Word of God is treasured and meditated upon so that we might learn more about God's word to man as the Holy Spirit reveals its message to us.

My prayer is that what has been written will bring inspiration to all those who dare to read it and generate a desire within them to study the subject further. However, it is up to the reader to check the references and satisfy themselves that what I have written is in accordance with scripture.

May God bless you and inspire you as you read this book.

What This Book Is About

The message of eternal salvation to those who believe in the life changing sacrifice of Christ Jesus is totally unique, causing the Christian faith to stand out from all other religions in the world. It is important, therefore, that all true believers must be unique in the way in which they live their lives and witness to the living God, which can only effectively be done by relying on the Holy Spirit to inspire and motivate them in that witness; a witness that should be quietly inspired, open and clear. Unless true believers stand out as being different from everyone else, then the impact of their witness will be reduced and no one will be attracted to the faith, therefore the harvesting of souls in that area will fail for the lack of workers, as has become evident in so many places where churches stand empty or have been given other uses.

There is a very real danger amongst Western believers to lose the crucial and very much deeper meaning of Easter because of the lack of emphasis on the inerrancy of the Bible, the reality and true person of God, the origin and historical meaning of the Jewish Passover and on the person of the Jewish Messiah; that is who He really is and what He came down to do, the reason for the conflict between the Messiah and the leaders of the Jews during His short ministry, along with the final prophetic information of His future role in the final stages of the life of the creation and the promise of a future spiritual life with Him for eternity for those who belong to and willingly serve Him. Any watering down of the gospel will detract from the full impact of its message and render it useless.

The very fact that we have eye witness accounts of His arrival, life and teaching, along with his suffering and death, His resurrection and ascension with the relevance of all that information to man's spiritual relationship with God, is to our benefit and opens up to us all that God has to say to man. What is more it was written by ordinary people, with the exception of the apostle Paul who went to a Jerusalem university, who would not normally be able to provide a written record because of their lack of schooling. The message, which is included in the gospels and the letters written to churches, has provided so much of the church's Christian doctrine, which is remarkable enough, but its true power lies in how it has influenced millions upon millions of individuals around the world and changed their lives for the better. It has been that effect which is nothing short of miraculous. No one can be bullied into the kingdom of our Lord, they can only be persuaded that Christ is the answer to all their problems and needs.

In the First Testament scriptures we see God in action but confined to His chosen people Israel. In the Second Testament we see God fulfilling the First Testament's prophetic announcements of His plan of salvation in the form of His Son. The coming to earth of the Son also enables us to clearly identify the individual members of the triune God, their individual roles within the godhead which enables us to begin to understand why the emphasis has always been on the fact that God is one. The total unity of vision and purpose amongst the three members of the godhead cannot be more clearly defined than in the activities of the Son, assisted by the Holy Spirit under the authority of the Father. At no time in all that is said and done by the Son can any suggestion of division be detected, thus emphasizing the uniqueness of the Oneness of God.

There can be no doubt that Easter must be considered as a whole. It is the pinnacle of Christian celebrations. From Genesis, where the true nature, character and supreme power of God is first fully disclosed, to Revelation where the need for, and the purpose and achievement of the Messiah's activities during Easter, are explained in detail, along with the fulfillment of the prophetic utterances of the Messiah that have occurred and will most definitely occur in the future, clearly emphasize the supreme importance of this celebration.

It is this 'whole message' approach that brings all the various parts of the story into perspective rather than merely focusing on the events at the centre of the Easter message alone (see Appendix A) which give an incomplete and incoherent message confounding those who have considerable theological expertise (even doctorates and professorships) but have no spiritual ability to communication with the Spirit of God about these matters and are thus prevented from hearing what the Holy Spirit has to say about it. In one programme I saw on television doctors and professors of theology spoke much about certain events involving the Christ but it was obvious that there was no certainty about what they said because it was made clear that they did not know why certain things happened when logically they should not have happened. This is exactly like the religious leaders in Israel at the time of Christ's visitation. Only when taken in the context of the whole of the Biblical text, together with the guidance of the Holy Spirit, can the full impact of all that the Son of God accomplished during the Easter period be properly understood.

Now some will argue that the style of writing used throughout scripture, often called the *'genre'* or the style or category of writing, which changes from prose to poetry to picture or descriptive language such as in parts of Genesis and certainly in Revelation, needs to be accounted for when seeking to understand the scriptural text. Whilst it is true that the style of writing within scripture is so diverse that it is almost impossible to treat the message each writer is offering in exactly the same way, yet there is one consistent theme running through the whole of scripture which identifies the fact that from Genesis, where we have recorded what happened 'In the beginning …', to Revelation where John writes, "… *even so come Lord Jesus"*, all scripture is not the word of man: rather it is the word of God and must be treated as such.

Because of this one vital factor, that all scripture is the Word of God and not of man, it is essential that it is interpreted as the Lord gives inspiration to those who have been baptized in the Holy Spirit, as was Paul, so that the meaning is spiritually discerned, rather than having a university degree in theology, which is of man. Paul as Saul studied the Hebrew scriptures under the respected Gamaliel, yet did not recognize the Messiah. It was not until his experience on the Damascus Road, which we will deal with later, and the work of the holy Spirit to open his eyes to the truth that he finally understood the true message of God in Christ.

The commission to teach and preach must come from God not man because it is God who provides all the gifts necessary to serve Him in the way he has chosen for them to serve Him (1 Cor. 12:4 – 11). Unless God is in charge of one's life and work there can be no spiritual revelation, making the message given dead of all real meaning.

Now some will ask "how will those listening to the teaching of others or reading the books that others have written, such as this one, know what is true or false?" Simply by each person asking God to open their eyes to the truth and checking everything that is said or written against referenced scripture. God knows how to teach each one of us according to our abilities providing we are willing to seek Him and listen to what He has to reveal to us. If God can teach me deep spiritual truths with my poor educational background and lack of theological training, then He can teach anyone.

It is important to point out, however, that all those who write, teach and preach will be judged far more harshly than those who receive instructions from them, which means that it is the responsibility of all those who seek to teach or lead others, by whatever means, to ensure their calling is definitely of God and not of man. Consider carefully what Paul wrote to the Ephesian church:

> *"With all wisdom and insight God has made known to us the mystery of his will, according to his good pleasure which he purposed in Himself, by his own will, as a plan for the fullness of time, when he will gather up all things under the authority of Christ, that is all things in heaven and things on earth. In Christ we have received an inheritance from God who chose us from the beginning, and predestined us according to the purpose of him who accomplishes all things according to his counsel and will, so that we, who were the first to set our hope on Christ, might live for the praise of his glory. Now in him you also, when you had heard the word of truth, the gospel of your salvation, believed in him, and in so doing were marked with the seal of the promised Holy Spirit; who is the guarantee of our inheritance that he will give us the promised redemption as God's own people, to the praise of his glory" (see Eph. 1:9 – 14; cf.*

Heb. 1:1 – 3).
And in chapter 3 of his letter Paul says:

> *"… for surely you have already heard of the commission of God's grace that was given to me to teach you the mystery that was made known to me by revelation, which I have written above in a few words (Eph. 1 quoted above), a reading of which will enable you to perceive my understanding of the mystery of Christ (see Eph. 3:2, 3).*

When he was a young man Saul, as he was at his conversion and commissioning, had been thoroughly trained by Gamaliel, the leading teacher on the Hebrew scriptures in Jerusalem, which afforded him a university degree, however what he was taught was of man. After his experience on the Damascus Road when he met with the risen Christ, he spent three days blind in Damascus fasting and praying. During that time the Holy Spirit caused him to go over the scriptures he had learned so thoroughly during his university training revealing to him how they spoke of the coming and ministry of the Messiah. As we shall see later Isaiah 53 was all about the life of the Messiah, and the Messiah was Jesus of Nazareth. From that point on God continued to reveal to him the mysteries hidden in those scriptures, which he had thought he knew so well, and the revelations he received he was then able to pass on to the churches through his writing and teaching.

To the elders of the Ephesian church Paul said, *"… for I did not shrink from declaring to you <u>the whole counsel of God</u>." (see Acts 20:27 – 32)* alerting them to their responsibility to continue to teach and lead the flock of God's people in the ways of God that he had so painstakingly taught them:

> *"Therefore take heed to yourselves and to all the flock, of which the Holy Spirit has made you overseers, to shepherd the church of God which he purchased with his own blood. For this I know, that after I have departed, savage wolves will come in among you, not*

sparing the flock.

*Some even from your own group will come distorting the truth
in order to entice the disciples to follow them. Therefore be alert,
remembering that for three years I did not cease night or day to
warn everyone with tears. And now I commend you to God and to
the message of his grace, a message that is able to build you up and
to give you the inheritance among all who are sanctified.*

This warning Paul gave to the assembled leaders is as relevant today
as it was then, for over the years I have heard erroneous teaching from
preachers and teachers that I have found very disturbing. The ignorance
of ordained ministers and lay preachers to the true spiritual meaning of
the scriptures has led to the closure of many churches. With the people
being deprived of wholesome spiritual food they are unable to grow
spiritually unable to find and enjoy a relationship with Christ Jesus
Himself and therefore, being a shadow of what a true believer should
be, unable to live a life worthy of God. Unless a church has within it
believers who are filled with the Spirit of God and living the life of true
dedication, then that church is unattractive to none believers or even
those searching for an answer to life. Unless the preachers and teachers of
the word of God have experienced that epiphany moment when they met
with the risen Christ causing their lives to be dramatically changed like
a rabbi I had the privilege of leading to his Messiah, then what hope do
their hearers have of becoming true believers in the living Lord? Unless
the words uttered from their mouths is Holy Spirit empowered, then
what they say is of no real worth. That has certainly been my experience.

It is also up to the reader to read all the quoted references, including
the verses before and after the reference, to understand the context of
what was written, and study them because it is the personal responsibility
of the individual to assure themselves of the truth of what has been
written and only obey the truth. And God will be faithful to all those
who truly seek Him.

In Revelation, the last book God caused to be written, we have recorded visions of God in triumph, with the Lamb of God identified as the only one who has the authority to break the seals of the scroll He received from the Father who sat on the throne in heaven (Rev. 5:6 – 10). With regard to the scroll and what John saw:

> The scroll "is full, with writing on both sides, declaring completeness, there being nothing else to add to what has been written. It is the mystery which God, who created all things through Christ Jesus (Eph. 3:9, 10) planned and recorded concerning what was to happen in the end times, knowing full well what would happen to His creation. And this record was kept hidden from the beginning of all ages (Heb. 1:2, 3), the title deeds if you like to the inheritance He wanted to make available to all those who would become worthy because of their willingness to become His committed servants."
>
> [*An extract from my book 'Seeing Into the Future'*]

This is the mystery hidden in God, who created all things through Christ Jesus, that He had kept secret from the beginning of the world which He revealed to Paul, who became a man 'in Christ', so that he could tell the Gentiles about the endless treasures available to them though their commitment to the Lord Jesus Christ. It was God's purpose to reveal His manifold wisdom in all its rich variety to all members of the Church, founded on the work of His Son, the members of which had given their hearts fully to him, and would be found worthy (see Eph. 3:8, 9, 10).

So what was the important message Paul was commissioned pass on to the Gentiles:

> So then, remember that at one time you Gentiles by birth were considered outsiders, being called 'the uncircumcision' by Jews who were proud to be called 'the circumcision' — which was a physical circumcision made in the flesh by human hands, which has nothing to do with the circumcision of the heart proposed by Moses and other

prophets.

In those days you were living apart, without Christ, excluded from God's chosen people Israel, ignorant of the covenants of promise made to them. As a result you lived with no hope and without God in the world.

But now, by belonging to Christ Jesus, you who were once far off have been brought near to him by the power of the blood of Christ. For he is our peace; in his flesh he has made both Jews and Gentiles into one and has broken down the dividing wall, that is, the hostility between us.

(Eph. 2:11 – 13)

The new church, far from being merely for those Jews who had come to believe in Jesus as their Messiah, was immediately opened up to the rest of the world by God Himself through the act of leading Peter to Cornelius (Acts 10) and baptizing him and his household with the Holy Spirit, as He had done to the disciples and other close followers on the day of Pentecost. Since that moment, just as with those Jews who now believe in Jesus as their Messiah have become part of spiritual Israel, so we who were born Gentiles have that same opportunity to be part of the new commonwealth of spiritual Israel, the church which is the bride of Christ. The whole purpose of God choosing Abraham then Isaac and then Jacob and his offspring was to speak to the world through them, so now all who come to believe in the Lord Jesus Christ have become part of that missionary people, not in a nationalistic human sense, but in a spiritual sense.

So then you Gentiles are no longer strangers and aliens, but citizens with the saints and also members of God's family. His house built upon the foundation of the apostles and prophets, with Christ Jesus himself as the cornerstone. We who believe in him are carefully joined together that we might become a holy temple in the Lord; in whom you also are built together spiritually into a dwelling-place for God. (Eph. 2:19 – 22)

This is the essential message of what happened that Passover which was transformed into the first Easter, and was God's intention all along. That we, who were once outside the chosen nation of Israel, have been included with them through Christ's sacrifice allowing us to enjoy all the promises of God to Israel, for we are encouraged to press on and learn more about the Lord God of Israel, under whose authority and reign we now live.

Paul wrote to Timothy that scripture has but a single author because:

> *"All scripture is inspired by God and is profitable for the teaching of doctrine, for reproof, for correction, and for training in righteousness, so that everyone who belongs to God may be proficient, equipped for every good work" (1 Tim. 3:16, 17).*

Paul wrote these words by inspiration of the Holy Spirit and they have been included in holy writ. That inspiration of the Holy Spirit did not stop with the death of the disciples; rather it was just the beginning of an outpouring of the Holy Spirit over the centuries since into believers of successive generations.

This means that if what has been written is of and from God, even though it is written down by men, then accepting what our Saviour said to His disciples regarding the Holy Spirit (Jn. 16:13), who inspired those who wrote down what we have in the Bible, then we must seek that very same Holy Spirit to interpret the scriptures to us, in order for the man made complications of seeking to understand the writing style and knowledge of those writers of scripture to disappear as mist disappears with the heat of the noonday sun. It is undoubtedly true that the closer we get to God in spirit, the greater the revelation of truth we receive. No wonder the Psalmist said that only a fool was willing to state with conviction that there is no God.

If we are to accept that the Bible is the word of God, then we must accept it as it is and not put objections in the way by saying, "yes but we cannot accept it in this or that way because…." Or "we don't really know if this or that text is true or a story to illustrate a morale point" which was stated on the BBC by a religious writer about the birth of the Messiah. Yet the virgin birth is crucial in understanding the legalities of the crucifixion.

If we say such things, then we are also saying that it is impossible for the Holy Spirit to interpret the scriptures to us. To put it another way, if we say that those who wrote it might have got it wrong, or the translators did not do their job very well, then we are limiting the almighty power of God to present His message to us in His way, yet the only way man has changed is in his reputed degree of sophistication. If we interpret a section of scripture in such a way that it is made incompatible with other parts of scripture then we err, not knowing the Spirit of God who alone is in charge of the safety and integrity of the word of God on earth for men.

To interpret scripture properly to others needs much prayer, the inspiration of the Holy Spirit and the willingness of the teacher to come fully under His influence.

Consider this. The coming of the Messiah to the earth was crucial in God's plan of salvation, yet the eternal Spirit that is the Son of God came to earth in the form of a new born and completely helpless baby, was born of a mother who was engaged to be married, arrived on earth after spending time in the womb of a very young woman into the place where cattle were kept, and, after being offered up to His Father in the prescribed manner in Jerusalem and acknowledged as the Messiah by two poor people completely dedicated to God, some wise men from another nation and some shepherds, who were at the bottom of the social order along with dung collectors, He had to be carried into exile into Egypt to save Him from the wrath of a human king; yet the eternal Spirit within the body of a baby boy had within Him the same all encompassing power that He had as the author of all that had been written, along with His Father and the Holy Spirit, the creator of all things that are seen and unseen.

God the Son arrived on the earth in the only way He could to ensure that no human authority was able to boast of having taken any part of His birth and subsequent ministry, and which gave Him legitimacy when He died in man's stead. No palace or hospital is able to display a plague stating "The Messiah was born here"; no midwife, no school, no local authority is able to claim they helped the Messiah in any way. It was God on His own authority causing thing to happen according to His own will and purpose.

I read in a book where the writer had noticed that sermons where the name of the Lord Jesus is central were effective and brought results, whereas those sermons where the name of Jesus was either rarely mentioned or not mentioned at all were completely ineffective and did not satisfy the hearers. So it is with books. Where the Spirit of God is allowed to control the thoughts of the writer and the name of the Lord Jesus is glorified, then that is the book to read and its message carefully considered.

Consider the second verse of Genesis chapter one where it says:

The earth was a formless void and darkness covered the face of the deep, and the Spirit of God hovered over the face of the waters.

The Jerusalem Targum[1] says:

"And the earth was vacancy and desolation, solitary of the sons of men, and void of every animal; and darkness was upon the face of the abyss, and the Spirit of mercies from before the Lord breathed upon the face of the waters."

There was nothing on the face of the embryonic earth except, hovering over the surface as an eagle hovers in the air over the land, was the Holy Spirit of God overseeing the miracle of the transformation of the earth from that cooling molten piece of debris that had been

---

1. Targumin (plutal) — spoken paraphrases, explanations and expansions of Jewish scriptures by a Rabbi in the common language during a time when it was mostly Aramaic. This was just before the Christian era, when the common language was in transition and Hebrew was used for little more than schooling and worship.

projected into space by that initial explosion where from nothing came the embryonic planets.

Therefore it had to be God who told the first receptive man what had happened at the very beginning - so that from the total chaotic, and empty item of debris, God formed a spherical spinning planet by His spoken word alone which was enacted by the hovering Spirit of God. Thus solely by the word of His mouth the earth was made into a sphere, then light came, then the separation of the land from the water (where did the water come from when the explosion produced only rock?), and ultimately day and night, vegetation and all living beings. Each one was a miracle of God.

The Bible is full of miraculous happenings accredited to God and performed by His servants working in conjunction with the Holy Spirit. But the first and major miraculous events ever recorded were those that happened, *'In the beginning...'* when only God existed and through the word of His mouth (*God said and it was done*) from that formless mass cloaked in darkness, void of any features with the enveloping atmosphere still clinging to the earth, God miraculously caused the earth to develop in such a way that it was able to support vegetation, animals, insects, fish, birds and finally man.

This is the wonder of it all; at sometime God told men what He had accomplished when memory was at its height and then caused it to be finally written down as a record. The word is of God and about God for man's physical and spiritual benefit.

Surely all this demonstrates as nothing else can, just how important Genesis is to our understanding of the greatness of our God.

Easter cannot be viewed in isolation. During my research, the importance of the history of the Hebrew people in relation to the God who chose them and the meaning behind the annual celebration of the Passover became very clear, as did the immediate history of the two nations of Israel and Judah which had a major impact on all that happened during the life of the Messiah and the events surrounding His crucifixion.

Thoughts about Easter have just recently (2015) so challenged me that it seemed God was calling me to write a book on the subject. The reaction to an initial draft copy of this book by someone who knows their Bible was sufficient to persuade me to continue my efforts.

There is one last point that I would emphasize and it is this. 'If we do not experience God we will never really know Him.' King David wrote, *"O taste and see that the Lord is good; blessed is the man who trusts in Him!"* *(Ps. 34:8).* Experience leads to knowledge and knowledge leads to trust and faith, and without true and unconditional faith we are far from God. Many have given up on God when faced with an extremely challenging moment in their lives, and yet if you ask them if they had prayed to God and sought His help and guidance in the matter the chances are that they have never really considered God or truly believed in His reality. God is no man's debtor. *"O taste and see that the Lord is good ... "* wrote David, and that can only be done when you treat God as a real person with whom you can converse.

To experience God initially means searching for Him with your whole heart and determination, just as you would for lost treasure (Matt. 6:21; 13:44 – 46) and asking Him to respond to you, and then when He knows that you really do want to commune with Him, He will respond and your experience of God will begin.

Peter

2023

ACKNOWLEDGMENTS

To God who is ever my source of inspiration

To Revd. Mary Tucker who is not only a joy to hear preach but who took up the enormous task of checking through my manuscript (first edition) and did it exceedingly well, reminding me of my frailty and inadequacies.
I am indebted to her for challenging me to the extent that she did because the final result is a hundred times better than it would otherwise have been; indeed it is through her efforts that this book is in any state to be published

Derek who first got me writing on scripture and has continued to encourage me. His comments on this book have been invaluable.

INTRODUCTION

Whilst celebrating Easter Sunday (2015) at the prison chapel where my wife and I were regular worshippers and where I used to be a prison visitor, God laid on my heart the need to write a book on the meaning of Easter. As few believers seem to study the deeper truths hidden in the Biblical text, which is the source of our spiritual food, there is a tendency for many to quote scriptural passages in isolation as a mantra, which introduces the potential for wrong teaching to creep into the minds of believers and for them to gradually grow away from Christ.

Sadly, a friend once told me that there was no need to consider the Old Testament and just concentrate on the New Testament and particularly on the four gospels. Yet that is like trying to build a house at bedroom level, ignoring completely the ground floor, which of course is physically impossible. But the New, or as I prefer to call it the Second Testament, is the fulfillment of the Old or First Testament. By getting rid of the term Old and New the sense that one has no relevance because it is 'old and passed it' can be dispensed with. Another way is to consider the two testaments as part 1 and part 2 of the gospel, the good news of salvation.

It is not always easy to understand the early scriptural texts because there may be moments in the First Testament where the factual is bound up in pictorial rather than plain language, with the moment man is recorded as being warned about eating the fruit of just one of the two trees in the middle of the garden being a particularly powerful example. The two trees represents the choice we have between being obedient to the will and statutes of God and being disobedient, which is the way of sin. The main reason the word of God is essential reading is because it chronicles man's relationship with God from his creation to the present day and into the future, and clearly teaches not only how man can relate to and communicate with God but also the importance of so doing.

It is important for man to not only realise he is a sinner before God, which is why he no longer has the uniqueness of intimacy Adam and Eve once enjoyed with God, but also the ways God has provided for man to ask for and received forgiveness.

The whole matter of sin and salvation must be taken seriously and fully understood by all those who are persuaded that they are saved by the blood of the Lamb. As Peter tells the believers in his letters, it is essential for all of them to not only know what they believed but also to be able to explain it to others who might ask them about their faith. What everyone must ask themselves is, "Do I understand why I am saved sufficiently for me to explain it succinctly enough to others for them to also believe, or at least be interested enough to search for God for themselves?"

The teacher obviously needs to know and understand their subject in sufficient depth to be able to respond to any questions the enquirer or student might ask, or at least have sufficient confidence in their knowledge of the subject to be able to discuss it with those who find it difficult to understand. As far as the believer is concerned a suitable response to any challenge to what they believe from a genuine seeker after the truth depends on their own understanding of the word and maturity of spirit and experience of listening to the Lord. There is nothing to be ashamed of if the question is so searching that they are not able to answer it so long as they are prompted to find out the answer for future use.

What is not good is to pour doubt on any part of scripture. Someone who wrote on scripture on being asked about the authenticity of the account of the birth of the Messiah suggested it might only be a story written by two of the gospel writers to explain the birth of the Lord Jesus, but that its accuracy was questionable. What is so interesting about that remark is that certainly one of the writers of the account of the nativity was Matthew who, with the other disciples, had been baptized in the Holy Spirit sent to them to reveal to them the truth, and therefore he would not have included a made up 'story' just to explain an event; also, and of far greater importance, is the fact that if the Messiah had not been born of a virgin under the control of God the Father, then the salvation He earned for mankind would be false, and therefore nullify the whole message of the Second Testament as my book "The Tent of the Meeting" fully explains.

What was especially disturbing about the comments made on the BBC's radio 4 programme on Monday morning of December 28th 2015 was that the man being asked about his thoughts on the subject was doing Satan's job for him by casting doubts on the authenticity of the essential facts of the nativity. *"Did God say, 'You shall not eat from any tree in the garden?'" (Gen. 3:1b).* Is the account of the nativity real or made up, and does it really matter? Surely all we need to do is accept it as a story with a moral content, don't we? But such an approach is both devious and destructive

It is because of the scripted and organized nature of the annual remembrance that there is the potential danger of worshippers merely going through the motions and not appreciating in some way just how traumatic and painful the death of the Son of God was when He presented Himself as the Holy and Perfect Lamb of God on Good Friday, followed by the more celebratory remembrance of His resurrection on the third day of Easter, a Sunday. The whole aspect of God becoming man and then experiencing torture and death in human form is almost impossible for the human mind to comprehend. Providing the liturgy is used as a guide to stimulate the thoughts of the worshipper, encouraging them to meditate on the events, particularly by researching the account in the Bible for themselves, then the liturgy, which was written by those who had a heart for God, is more likely to have a more positive outcome.

The true meaning of Easter can only be fully understood in the light of the prophetic messages and instructions from God throughout the whole of the First Testament, from Genesis to Malachi. The accumulated information contained in the Bible provides the essential background knowledge and basic criterion to enable the believer to understand, each in their own way, the deeper meaning of all that happened during the birth, life, death, resurrection and ascension of our Lord.

Merely to rely on the Second Testament narrative means that there is a danger the importance of the virgin of birth of our Lord, the Divine nature of His life and immense cruelty but necessary death by crucifixion, along with the work of the Father and the Holy Spirit at the time of His crucifixion, are at best ignored and at worst believed to be of no importance.

Such unwitting ignorance also has the effect of disconnecting the believer from the inter-relationship of the annual Passover celebrations, the Last Supper the Lord had with His disciples, and the Communion service as it is celebrated in churches today.

Consider carefully how it all began, the original idyll:

> *The Lord God took the man*
> *and put him in the garden of Eden*
> *to till it and keep it.*
> *And the Lord God commanded the man,*
> *'You may freely eat the fruit of every tree of the garden;*
> *but of the tree of the knowledge of good and evil*
> *you shall not eat,*
> *<u>for in the day you eat of it you shall die.</u>'*
> *Then the Lord God said,*
> *'It is not good that the man should be alone;*
> *I will make him a helper as his partner.'*
> *(Gen. 2:15 – 18)*

That was the purity of the creation and the relationship between God and the man He had created from nothing, albeit the man was formed and fashioned to perfection over a period of time. Man is not an animal, in the way some thinkers would suggest. Because God breathed into his nostrils the breath of spiritual life, man was elevated above all animal life and was given the gift of being able to communicate with his creator God.

To better understand what the Easter celebrations are all about it is essential to go back to the beginning and look into what made the sacrifice of the Son of God essential to our future well being in the first place. Why do we need to be saved? From what do we need to be saved? For what purpose? Three questions that rightfully need as full and truthful an answer as is reasonably possible to provide within the limitations of our understanding. That is the purpose of this book.

God spoke to the man Adam directly concerning the forbidden tree before the appearance of the woman. Some time after God spoke to the man came the moment when God created the woman, not as a separate entity but from a physical part of the man:

> *So the Lord God caused a deep sleep*
> *to fall upon the man, and he slept;*
> *then he took one of his ribs*
> *and closed up the flesh in its place.*
> *The rib the Lord God had taken from the man*
> *he made into a woman and brought her to the man.*
> *Then the man said,*
> *'This at last is bone of my bones*
> *and flesh of my flesh;*
> *this one shall be called Woman,*
> *for she was taken out of Man.'*
> *(Gen. 2:21 – 23)*

Thus, when Satan tempted Eve, he was targeting the softer option because the man had been actively engaged with his maker and with tending the garden sometime before his wife-to-be was created from one of his ribs. Adam knew full well that eating of the fruit of the tree was to be avoided at all costs. In life there are many things that we might like to do for a challenge but know it is best avoided because not doing so would lead us into trouble with unfortunate results.

Because of the woman's reply to the 'serpent's challenge' it is clear that she had at sometime received a warning about eating the fruit of the forbidden tree from the man. The text is extremely brief so we have no idea of exactly what Adam said to Eve. As it is the woman's reply to Satan's challenge regarding the eating of the forbidden tree was none too accurate, although the meaning of the test God put upon the eating of the fruit of that tree was still basically understood by her (Gen. 3:1 – 7). The significance of the event was that Adam seemed to do nothing to stop her and then directly sinned by also eating of the fruit of the forbidden tree; that was blatant disobedience to the command of God, which is sin.

This is not a fairy story, because not only did Paul take it seriously through his preaching and letters, but God also took it seriously (1 Cor. 15:22) because He allowed His Son to die in the place of sinners. What happened in the beginning of the human race is true because God, by His actions says it is true.

The celebration of Easter is undoubtedly a significant moment in the Christian calendar because it is the moment when the payment of the death penalty for sin, incurred by Adam, was finally and legally paid in full. Our Lord Messiah, God incarnate, died on day the Jewish Passover was celebrated in accordance with God's instructions to Moses and known as the Haggadah, and then rose from the dead according to prophecy three days later, and ascended into heaven before the day of Pentecost when the Holy Spirit was sent to the earth to commence His ministry amongst believers, which is also a significant day both for Jews and Gentile believers (see my book, "You Shall Receive Power …").

The purpose of this book is to provide an overall picture of the deeper spiritual meaning of Easter as it fits within the earthly life of our Lord and Saviour Jesus Christ, the Messiah, Yeshua to the Jews, culminating in His resurrection and then His ascension which event initiated the coming of the promised Holy Spirit in power in order that through His ability to enter into each individual He would empower all believers, Jews and Gentiles alike to live a new God focused life.

Hopefully it will provide encouragement to many to enter into further study in order to enhance and build upon the effect of this book on their knowledge and understanding of the extent and implication of the salvation God is offering to all those who are seeking for a more fulfilling and purposeful life on earth and on into eternity.

Note that the use of the words man and men refer to both sexes except where they might be used in connection with the Messiah.
No book, however well written or inspirational, is of any use unless the information and challenges it contains are acted upon by the reader. Please check everything against scripture.

THE HOLY SPIRIT

The biblical text starts with God the Trinity (Father, Son and Holy Spirit). This is made evident in John 1:1 where it reveals that in the beginning the Word was not only with God but was God and in Genesis 1:2 it says that before the earth had any form or life, the Spirit of God moved, or hovered, over the surface of the embryonic sphere of this newly formed planet through which God had chosen to reveal His creative powers in physical form (see Appendix C).

What is so special about the Gospel according to the disciple John is that of all the disciples it was he who was closest to the Messiah. From the start there was a greater spiritual awareness within him than was evident in the other disciples, just as with Joseph who of all the sons of Jacob was the only one who knew God and was therefore chosen by God to become second only to Pharaoh in Egypt to save that area from the forthcoming famine. John's spiritual sensitivity developed over time to the point where it was he who, in his spirit, was allowed the experience of meeting with the risen Christ in heaven resulting in the writing of the book of Revelation.

John was part of the Lord's inner circle of disciples, a triumvirate (God is three and three is a holy number) of Peter, who had that necessary air of authority and leadership skills that was required by the early church (Jn. 21:15 – 19), John and his brother James. But John's special relationship with the Messiah was clearly displayed when he reclined next to the Lord at table, the place of honour, the bosom-place where he laid on his saviour's chest (Jn. 13:23), and a number of times he refers to himself as the disciple whom Jesus loved, which, because of his intimacy with the Lord, he could not have written on his own authority (Jn. 20:2; 21:7; 21:24).

John's status was confirmed when the Lord Jesus committed to him the care of His mother, a considerable honour. Just as Jacob saw in Joseph a man after His own heart with regard to his love of his God, which was completely proven during his time as a slave in Egypt, and the manner in which he handled the meetings with his brothers when he was Viceroy of Egypt, so there seems to have been a strong spiritual relationship between John and his Messiah, no doubt confirmed by God the Father through the Holy Spirit, that led to such a closeness, that the other disciples may not have seen, that enabled John to be specially inspired by the Holy Spirit in his writings, which are far more spiritual than those of the other disciples.

The reason for giving the above information is to explain how it was that John recorded what the Lord said about the need for the disciples and all those who would be saved to focus their attention on being obedient to Him and why the gift of the Holy Spirit was not just important to them but vital (Jn. 15 through 17). Indeed, it is through the writing of John that we read about Nicodemus and the way in which the Messiah explained the importance of the new birth through the actions of the Holy Spirit to anyone who wants to get close with God. Just as flesh gives birth to flesh John tells us, so Spirit gives birth to spirit (Jn. 3:6) and that new birth in the spiritual realm is the first stage of entry into the kingdom of God, an absolutely essential first step for all those seeking to get close to God and enter into spiritual communion with Him.

To a Gentile, and a female member of the despised Samaritans at that, the Lord Jesus spoke a truth that the Jews had conveniently ignored. Not only must we be born again, but if we want to be a true worshipper of the one creator God, who is Spirit and the source of all truth, then we can only do so in spirit and in truth (Jn. 4:23).

How can we know truth? By being reborn spiritually and being open and sensitive to the instructions of life that only the Holy Spirit can provide us. After all it was the Lord Jesus Himself who said that it was that same Holy Spirit who would lead the disciples and those who followed them into all truth (Jn. 16:13, 14).

It is, therefore, through the writing of John that we are able to learn how we can enter into a deep spiritual relationship with our Saviour God, and how we can serve Him in newness of life. Be assured, we are only able to enter into a meaningful spiritual relationship with God, and become true servants of God according to the degree of commitment we are willing to make with regard to the depth of spiritual communion we have with God and our willingness to serve Him and be obedient to His laws and statutes that have the most impact on our daily lives and how we view the manner of life of those around us.

Unless we realize there is a clear distinction between the way of life of non-believers and the way of life decreed by God, such as the first and second commandments where we are instructed to put God first and foremost in everything we do, and then consider our neighbour as ourselves without living as they do, then we will not succeed in our walk with God.

From the perfection and purity of God's initial creation, almost immediately comes the corrupting influence of Satan, the most senior angel in the spiritual realm who was able to reveal himself in physical form, the result of which was the corruption of God's creation and the necessary separation between God and man. It was the rebellion of Satan and his ability to appear as an angel of light to Eve that initiated the corruption of man and then inevitably the earth itself.

Immediately God initiated His long term plan to bring as many souls back to Himself through sacrifice as were/are/will be willing to respond. Thus the whole idea and purpose of sacrifice takes centre stage. As my book "The Tent of the Meeting : Illustrating God's Plan of Salvation", deals with the subject of God's plan of salvation through sacrifice, there is no point in replicating it here.

However, it is important to initially focus on the work of the Holy Spirit, because He has been an essential feature in the work of God amongst men throughout the history of mankind in conjunction with the other members of the Trinity of God throughout scripture. Although the focus for salvation must be on the Lord Jesus Christ, the Messiah to the Jews, who took upon Himself the sins of all mankind and won the battle over sin and death, it is also important the work of the Holy Spirit is not overlooked or hampered, but rather understood and acknowledged and allowed to influence our own lives.

It was the Spirit of God, through breathing into man's nostrils the *breath of God*, that not only elevated man out of the animal kingdom to bring him to the point where he was transformed into God's own image, but also introduced a spirit within man's body that enabled him to commune with God directly. Indeed it can be said that, *"the spirit of God has made me, and the breath of the Almighty gives me life" (Job 33:4)*. That is life not just in the physical sense, but also in the eternal spiritual sense, which is that part of the image of God who is the Eternal Spirit.

The fact that the Lord said to Satan, *"man shall not live by bread alone but by every word that comes from the mouth of God"*, means that physical food may be necessary, as with all earthly creatures, although it is true that man can live on very little food and water in certain circumstances as those who have experienced torture and extreme living conditions in prison have proved, but the word of God is even more important to those who truly believe in Him because *"it is spirit and it is life" (Jn. 6:63)* and man, certainly spiritually alive man, cannot live (in the sense of him being created in the image of God) without the food that sustains his spiritual life, even in extreme prison conditions. It is the neglect of spiritual food that has caused many believers to drift away from God with the potential of finding that heaven is closed to them on the day of resurrection and judgement. To hear the phrase, "I never knew you" would be devastating.

This point is illustrated by the parable of the ten bridesmaids (sometimes referred to as virgins), five of whom were wise and five foolish, and it is all to do with the second coming of the Lord:

'Then the kingdom of heaven will be like this. Ten bridesmaids (virgins) took their lamps and went to meet the bridegroom (the Lamb of God, bridegroom of the church or spiritual Israel). *Five of them were foolish, and five were wise. The foolish took no oil for their lamps; whereas the wise took flasks of oil with their lamps. As the bridegroom was delayed, all of them became drowsy and slept. But at midnight* (an hour when he was not expected and when their lamps would be needed) *there was a shout, "Look! Here is the bridegroom! Come out to meet him." Then the bridesmaids got up and trimmed their lamps. The foolish asked the wise, "Give us some of your oil, for our lamps are going out." But the wise replied, "No! there will not be enough for you and for us; you had better go to the shop and buy some for yourselves." But while they went to buy oil, the bridegroom came, and those who were ready went with him into the wedding banquet; and the door was shut. Later when the other bridesmaids returned, they stood outside calling, "Lord, lord, open to us." But he replied, "Truly I tell you, I do not know you." Keep awake therefore, for you know neither the day nor the hour of the Lord's return." (Matt. 25:1 – 13)*

The foolish bridesmaids were lax in their reading of the word of God and prayer life with God, therefore they were not prepared when the bridegroom appeared to receive Him because they did not know Him, neither did He know them. It was not a case of missing the arrival of the Lord so much as being indifferent to Him altogether. It is now as we wait for His second coming that we need to be very vigilant and be persistent in our preparation for His return, even though it might not be in our lifetime.

There is a subtle difference between those who know the Lord intimately and those who only know *of* Him; that is they might be stalwarts in the local church community and regular attendees at church services and midweek meetings, but their personal, spiritual relationship with Christ is lacking, relying as they do on appearances not on a genuine relationship with the living Lord.

Talk of things of the Spirit and they do not know what you are talking about. I know because it has happened to me when I have spoken to other lay readers. So many are ignorant of the things of God because they are not diligent in their search for God and an understanding of the true meaning of His word. The Lord Jesus Himself differentiated between the true believer and those who played at being a Christian when He said, *"not everyone that says to Me "Lord, Lord" will enter into the kingdom of heaven."* Let those who sound religious beware, because the critical issue is not the saying but the doing, for the Lord went on to say, *"but only those who actively do the will of my Father in heaven" (Matt. 7:21).* James in his letter calls on believers to be *"doers of the word"* and not merely hearers who deceive themselves by their play acting (James 1:22).

It can be added that when faced with physical death, believers and non-believers alike will sleep until the return of the Lord to receive His own unto Himself, when according to Paul the dead in Christ will be called first and then those that are living, but only those who are spiritually alive will be accepted into His eternal kingdom. The word of God, all of it, is our spiritual food, both light snacks and full three course meals, and all of it must be accepted and consumed into our spirits, none of it being rejected and replaced with worldly food. Unless we meet with God through the word and prayer then we cannot expect God to have anything to do with us. Even those who are unable to read or write can be spiritual inspired by listening to the word read by others and seeking God with all their hearts and receiving Him into their hearts; no one need be excluded. The Holy Spirit is available 24 hours a day, seven days a week, 365 days a year, for God never slumbers or sleeps.

Nicodemus learned the importance of being born again, not physically but spiritually, when the Spirit of God rejuvenates the spirit within a man that had died through the lack of spiritual food. Indeed the Holy Spirit is the one person of the Trinity of God whose task it is to work with the spirit that He breathed into man at the very beginning of human history and is now dispersed amongst all mankind. This is because, when a believer is baptized in the Holy Spirit, the Spirit alone is able to enter into the body of the believer, breathe spiritual life back into that individual spirit and then commune with the believer Spirit with spirit in an intimate and amazing way. As one of a multitude who has experienced this baptism in the early years of my life, I am completely assured of its truth and relevance to human life (1 Cor. 14). Indeed God has bestowed on me the gift of tongues and of prophecy (both foretelling and forthtelling which has resulted in my books and many years of preaching and teaching and mentoring).

Baptism

Before certain worship ceremonies were enacted before God, the Jews were required purify themselves by washing themselves in running water. The high priest had to wash before putting on his holy robes. Thus baptism is a form of ceremonial washing.

Through Isaiah God called on His people to, *"wash and make yourselves clean, put away the evil of your thoughts and activities from before My eyes, cease to do evil, learn to do that which is good ... "* He wanted them to acknowledge and repent of their sins, to refocus their attention on Him their God, who had rescued them from the land of Egypt and saved them from their many enemies and for them to become faithful and obedient to their Saviour, Lord and King. Repentance and faith have always been key to individuals entering into a relationship with God.

Surely that is what water baptism is all about. It is giving witness to the fact of a change in heart, a symbolic dying to self in repentance of personal sin, and rising again out of the waters to a new spiritual life of faith in God. That is why, when I had the privilege of baptizing seven individual believers, once they had been brought up out of the water I laid hands on each one asking God to fill them with that portion of His Holy Spirit they would need to serve Him faithfully. Each one had a spiritual experience during their baptism and the laying on of hands that stayed with them and changed their lives and thinking.

Going through the waters of baptism is a recommended fruitful first step for the believer in acknowledging their new found faith in the Lord Jesus as a means of symbolically becoming clean through repentance. It is the process by which a believer says publically that they have asked God to forgive them their sins and want to enter into a new life in Christ. A symbolic gesture of compliance, of dedication and submission of their will to God. It is then necessary to progress in that new relationship through the study of the word of God and an opening of themselves to the work of the Holy Spirit.

At this point it is important for me to admit that I was christened in a Methodist church when a baby (my mother's brother was a Methodist Minister), but then in my early twenties I felt the need to be baptized by full immersion in a little Brethren assembly in Fareham in Hampshire. The verse I had given to me on that occasion was prophetic, confirming to me that I had done the right thing (Joshua 1:9).

It is not up to churches to dictate what individuals can and cannot do, although there is always a need for orderly conduct. Rather it is up to the individual to considered the matter with much prayer and to assure themselves that that is what God wants them to do; after all it is not the church that saves an individual from eternal spiritual death, but the blood of the Lord Jesus. It is the cry of the sinner to our Lord and Saviour for forgiveness as they repent of their sins that brings spiritual cleansing through the application of the blood the Saviour shed at Calvary by the Holy Spirit (Heb. 9:14, 15).

Having been personally called by the Lord, the disciples had entered into three and a half years of training with their Messiah, but there came a time when He would leave them which meant they would ostensibly be left on their own to fend for themselves. However, just as the Lord was filled with the Holy Spirit without measure, so the disciples would also need that empowerment by the Holy Spirit to enable them to preach the good news, particularly in times of intense opposition, and be reminded of all that their teacher had said and done.

Being immersed in something is to use the word 'baptize' in a figurative sense. When the disciples James and John approach their Lord to ask if they could sit one on each side of Him when He was in His glory, Jesus challenged them about the matter of baptism. Were they prepared to drink the cup He would have to drink and be baptized with the baptism of suffering that He was being baptized with? That is being immersed in suffering.

When the Children of Israel walked on dry land through the Red Sea they were referred as being baptized with the baptism of Moses because they were immersed in that activity.

The disciples were Jews, called by their Lord Messiah to follow Him, which they did, giving up everything to do so. However, after the Lord's death and resurrection they felt alone and powerless. This situation was dramatically changed when they received the baptism of the Holy Spirit according to the promise made to them by the Lord Jesus.

But what is the baptism of the Holy Spirit, and what does it mean for the believer today?

Fifty days after the Lord's resurrection and then His ultimate ascension back to His Father, the disciples were together hoping against hope that the authorities would not find them. Suddenly there came a sound from heaven like that of a mighty windstorm in the sky above them that filled the house in which they were meeting. Then there appeared what looked like tongues of fire which rested on each of them and everyone present was filled with, immersed in, the Holy Spirit and they involuntarily began to speak in tongues as the Lord gave them utterance. What the disciples said in what was to them a foreign language were so accurate that those within hearing distance could understand what was being said in their own language. Quite remarkable.

The baptism, of the Holy Spirit also gave them boldness to witness to the salvation of God through Jesus Christ their Messiah, but more than that, having the Holy Spirit dwelling within them He was able to lead them into all truth

> *'If you love me, keep my commandments, and I will ask the Father, and he will give you another Helper/Counsellor/Advocate/ Comforter, to be with you for ever. This is the Spirit of truth, whom the world cannot receive, because it neither sees him nor knows him. You know him, because he abides with you, <u>and will be in you</u>. (Jn. 14:15 – 17)*

The Lord Jesus was boldness itself when confronting those religious leaders, who did not have a personal spiritual relationship with the God of Israel because He had the power and wisdom of God within Him. Many times He was challenged because the authorities wanted to trip Him up so that they could bring legitimate charges against Him, but with the power of God and the Holy Spirit with Him He was able to see through their scheming and embarrass them rather than be embarrass by them. It is essential that the Divinity of the Lord Messiah is recognized because He was, is and ever will be a member of the one God who cannot change, He is ever the same, yesterday, today and forever.

Whilst on earth the Lord Messiah could not separate Himself from the Godhead. When He came to the earth on that mission to save mankind from eternal spiritual death, He was still an integral part of the Trinity. As a demonstration of that oneness, the Holy Spirit appeared at His baptism by John in the form of a dove, indeed we are told that He was filled with the Holy Spirit without measure; in fact as it is impossible for the Father, the Spirit and the Son to be separated, thus the Spirit was always with the Son, which means the falling of the dove on the Son at His baptism was symbolic as will be explained in detail in a later chapter. Because of this fact, consider what John says in his gospel:

> *The one who comes from above is above all; the one who is of the earth belongs to the earth and speaks about earthly things. The one who comes from heaven is above all. He testifies to what he has seen and heard, yet no one accepts His testimony. Whoever has accepted his testimony has certified that God is true. He whom God has sent speaks the words of God, for He does not give the Spirit by measure. The Father loves the Son and has placed all things in His hands. Whoever believes in the Son has eternal life; whoever disobeys the Son will not see life, but must endure God's wrath. (Jn. 3:31 – 36)*

For the Son of God to do His work, the Father and the Holy Spirit had to be part of it, because the one God cannot be separated, being unique in itself, in its complete unity. God has to work as one with each member playing their intrinsic part. The only time there was a separation was when the Lord Messiah took upon Himself the sin of the world and as a result the Father could not look upon Him. But the Father was in the heavenly places nonetheless and the Holy Spirit was with the Lord at all times.

As reassurance for the time He knew He was due to leave the disciples in physical form at His ascension, the Lord Jesus told them that they would receive the baptism of the Holy Spirit. This meant that just as the Holy Spirit had provided the Lord with information about what was going on around Him in the hearts and minds of individuals, and be able to cause physical things to happen such as stilling the storm and returning the soul and spirit of a person back to the body so that they would come back to life again, or even to cause an evil spirit to leave the body of an individual, that same Holy Spirit would enable them to achieve the same thing or even greater things.

> 'When I send the Counsellor/Advocate to you from the Father, the Spirit of truth who comes from the Father, He will testify on my behalf. (Jn. 15:26)
>
> When the Spirit of truth comes, He will guide you into all the truth; for He will not speak on His own, but will speak whatever He hears, and He will declare to you the things that are to come. He will glorify me, because He will take what is mine and declare it to you. All that the Father has is mine. For this reason I said that He will take what is mine and declare it to you. (Jn. 16:13 – 15)

It was through the Holy Spirit coming upon them and immersing them in Himself that they became the future leadership of the church Christ the Lord Messiah had started with them being the first members. Also it was the Holy Spirit who initiated the arrival of the Messiah by causing the last of the First Testament prophets to be born to a barren Elizabeth and causing Mary to become pregnant with the embryo of a boy child into which the Spirit of the Son of God would enter to become the Son of Man.

It was the Holy Spirit, working with the Messiah under the authority of the Father, who caused miraculous things to happen, people to be raised from the dead, blind the eyes of those who would seek to murder the Messiah before His appointed time and then be a witness to the crucifixion and fulfil the sacrificial requirement for full salvation.

TRUE MEANING OF SIN

The Mystery of the Creation

The why and how of the appearance of the heavens and the earth is a compound mystery that human kind finds impossible to understand because it was God's decision to create it all. All man's increasingly sophisticated research has focused on trying to find out how the world and the heavens surrounding it came into being. After the theory of evolution came the theory of the big bang as a means of explaining the vast distribution of matter evident in the heavens and, with the introduction of giant telescopes above the earth's visually restricting atmosphere, came amazing pictures in full colour of stars previously unseen beyond our own galaxy.

The study of the cosmos has accumulated vast amounts of images and data that has been poured over by the brightest minds of men giving mankind a picture of what surrounds us on the earth, with distances between planets and the size and numbers of galaxies that strain the understanding of most men.

Much to the frustration of the researchers, the frontier of the heavens and how it all came into being in the first place is as illusive as ever. Although the theory of the big bang is accepted by most researchers, the how and why the big bang occurred is beyond them and discarded as impossible to fathom.

The one who wrote the first book of the Bible was, in comparison to the scientists of today, extremely simple, lacking the accumulated knowledge, and understanding, and sophistication of today. Yet since the book of Genesis was first written down, surprisingly it alone has provided man with the information he needs to know, not only about how (God spoke and it was done) the world and the surrounding heavens came into being, but about the God who created everything that exists over a period of time (evolution), finally developing man and making him God centred by breathing His own spiritual breath into the first man.

That condensed but essential information identifying just who God was, is and will be, had to last mankind until the appearance of the Messiah when, with the fulfilment of the prophetic utterances and prophetic knowledge of the prophets of old, more descriptive and explanatory information was provided by the Son and by the Holy Spirit, through the disciples.

Through experience many believers have been enabled to do amazing things for God in His service, this is because God has the ability to empower those that are truly His and cause them to rise above their natural abilities. Consider Philip who, after he had baptized the Ethiopian eunuch, was transported in the Spirit from the desert to the city of Azotus (Acts 8:26 – 40).

To better understand the importance of Genesis concerning our knowledge and understanding of God, especially accepting the greater simplicity and slow pace of life in the days in which it was written, it is important to consider the first verse of the Bible to give us a taste of the knowledge that was contained in the opening text:

In the beginning God
created the heavens and the earth

In the beginning God - is an incredibly pregnant statement to use as the opening line of the Bible. All authors are conscious of the importance of the opening lines of any book they are writing because the readability of the book is often dependent upon the very first sentence or paragraph.

It needs not only to capture the imagination of the reader, but also to take them by the hand and lead them quickly into the body of the book. Certainly from the enquirers point of view, the first few words say a great deal about the writer and what they have to say.

In the case of the opening chapter of Genesis we have, in a very few words a very powerful statement of what existed before the advent of time. Indeed we are told that before anything existed that exists God was present. This means that everything that exists has come from Him.

Think about it. If '*In the beginning*' only God existed, then everything that has appeared and become reality since must have come from Him because He is the unique source of everything that is because there was no one else. It also tells us that He is the source of all power, indeed it is quite legitimate to say that His power and authority exceeds that of everyone and everything that exists and has ever existed because all the power on the earth and in the heavens comes from Him alone.

But consider another aspect of the statement *In the beginning God created the heavens and the earth.* How do we know that? It is no good saying that someone wrote it because '*In the beginning* only *God* existed. So who else was around at the time to witness it? The truth is no one existed except God. So how come this first sentence came to be written?

This leads us into another remarkable fact. God is able to speak to man and man is able to hear Him. Nothing we have is of ourselves. Everything we have is a gift from God, in fact Paul says concerning the faith of those who have faith, even that it is a gift from God:

> *For by grace you have been saved through faith, and this [faith] is not of your own doing because it is the gift of God, neither is it the result of works, so that no one may boast about having attained to it. For we are what he has made us, created in Christ Jesus for good works, which God prepared beforehand to be our way of life. (Eph. 2:8 – 10)*

Therefore, at some time God told man that '*In the beginning I AM*', that is '*before anything existed, I was alive*', and the first man that heard

God say that to him and was able to keep a mental record of it did so and it was passed on from generation to generation until it could be written down for the benefit of the rest of mankind. Is that not amazing?

But this point about God speaking to man and man hearing what God has to say is not impossible because not only is nothing impossible to God but by the Holy Spirit breathing into the first man's nostrils the breath of spiritual life (see my book The Tent of the Meeting : Illustrating God's Plan of Salvation' or 'The Origin of Life : God's Relationship with Man in Genesis for a fuller explanation) God specifically made man God-focused and God-conscious enabling man to communicate with Him. Indeed a man without God has a spiritual emptiness within him that cannot be filled in any other way which will cause him to constantly search for an alternative to fill that spiritual void that is within him but will remain forever unfulfilled.

And this gift of being able to hear and communicate with God has not been restricted to the earliest days of man, when man was less distracted by all the technological achievements of mankind that we have today. Many true believers have heard, are hearing and will hear God speak with them directly, to think otherwise puts restrictions on God's abilities that are not there because nothing is impossible to Him. In fact being able to commune with God, to be able to share one's most intimate thoughts and feeling with Him, is an essential part of believing in Him and living in union with Him.

Now to those who question my claim about the importance of the book of Genesis in providing man 'with all the information he needs to know about God and the creation', what better place to establish a vital truth than right at the very beginning of the only book, the Bible, that provides us with all the information we need to explain to us all that we need to know about God, the creation of which we are a part and God's relationship and activities through and with man throughout the history of mankind.

That one vital fact in the first verses of Genesis is then the subject of reminders to the chosen people of God, both Jews and believing Gentiles, throughout the Bible. Those reminders confirm and develop the authenticity of Genesis in a positive way. Consider what Isaiah said:

"For thus says the Lord God,
who created the heavens
and put everything in its place
and formed the earth to be lived in,
not a place of chaos
'I am the Lord, and there is no other'".
(Isa. 45:18)

In providing man with an albeit cryptic yet remarkably complete written record of the manner in which God created the heavens and the earth, the book of Genesis gives an important insight into who God is and all that He did, of and for Himself, in the very beginning.

What is made clear in the first chapter of Genesis is that as God existed before the heavens and the earth appeared, He must be other than physical, which means that being a Spirit, He cannot be seen and therefore is invisible to the human eye. Also, as there was nothing before the heavens and the earth appeared, He must be infinite which the finite, restricted, worldly programmed mind of man finds almost impossible to accept, yet that is what faith is all about, accepting what is difficult to accept because of the witness of the Holy Spirit within us.

It is later in the narrative of the Bible that God is fully revealed as three separate individuals who act in complete, loving, unity, without the hint of disagreement yet have different tasks to perform within that unity. Father, Son and Holy Spirit. God is God and cannot change.

When the Son of God came to the earth His divinity came with Him but veiled whilst He was among men, because man cannot look upon the holiness of God and live. As soon as He returned to heaven victorious, having conquered sin and death, He was seen once more in His glorious state by the apostle John during his spiritual experience in heaven whilst being punished for his faith on the island of Patmos (Rev. 1; cf. Dan. 7). What an amazing thing to happen. Whilst being punished for his faith by men, God took John into heaven to see His glory and meet again with the risen Messiah; to see sights that no other man was able to see, and experience the wonder of all that was to come that the Lord Jesus promised to those willing to surrender their wills to Him.

What the Bible also makes very clear is that God has never had a beginning and will never have an end. That he exists in limitless space, space that has no end and that God fills that space without it weakening His power and authority in any way. No true and honest book about God that refers to His attributes and person can start without this concept of God being even partially understood and accepted as the foundational principle of what is to be considered. That is reality in its truest form.

So with all the sophistication of the modern research mind, it is the simple God focused mind of the writer of Genesis who was able, with God's inspirational help, to explain how the world and its surrounding cosmos came into existence, leaving the modern mind to work out the technicalities of how it was done minus the understanding of the mind, power and creative skill of its creator. It must be remembered that science sprang from man's investigation into all that God created. Therefore the world of science is not separate from the knowledge of God but intrinsic to and solely dependent upon that knowledge. However, scripture told us about it first long, long ago.

It is essential to remember that man did not create God; God created man in His own image, and God is all powerful. Not one word of scripture was written without God and to argue with that puts the inerrancy and reliability of scripture in doubt (Jn. 1:1 – 3). Think carefully what the Lord Jesus said to the learned men of the day:

> *"'If I testify about myself, my testimony is not true. There is another who testifies on my behalf, and I know that His testimony on my behalf is true. You sent messengers to John, and he bore witness to the truth about Me. Not that I accept such human testimony, but I say these things so that you may be saved."*

Or for you to be so convinced by the revelation of truth through the Holy Spirit that you accept me as your Lord and Saviour.

God can testify to others about Himself because there is no higher authority than He. The Messiah acknowledged the requirement for two or three witnesses, so He would not provide His own testimony and although John gave a clear account of who Jesus was, it was only by inspiration from God that individuals could fully appreciate just who He was.

"I have a testimony greater and more powerful than John's. The works that the Father has given me to complete, the very works that I am doing, give witness to who I Am, and that the Father has sent me. Indeed the Father who sent me has Himself testified on My behalf. You have never heard His voice or seen His form, and you do not have His word abiding in you, because you do not believe Him whom He has sent."

These are telling words because it emphasized the fact that although they knew about God, those who thought they knew all about God in fact had no personal spiritual relationship with, or understanding of, Him (Jn. 3:5 – 8). On the other hand the Lord Jesus expounded the scriptures with authority far greater than any of the religious elite at that time, because He, through the Holy Spirit, was the cause of them being written, but He also consistently did miraculous things to a far greater extent than any of the prophets of old had ever done

"'You search the scriptures because you think that in them you have eternal life; and it is they that testify about Me. Yet you refuse to come to me to have [spiritual] life. I do not accept glory from human beings. But I know that you do not have the love of God within you. I have come in my Father's name, and you do not accept me; if another comes in his own name, you will accept him. How can you believe when you accept glory from one another and do not seek the glory that comes from the one who alone is God? Do not think that I will accuse you before the Father; your accuser is Moses, on whom you have set your hope. If you believed Moses, you would believe me,

*for he wrote about me. But if you do not believe what he wrote, how
will you believe what I say?"'*
(See Jn. 5:31 – 47)

What the Lord Jesus is saying is that if you only listen to men and
study what men have taught and written, then you are not listening
directly to God and all that the Holy Spirit is saying to men and therefore
you will inevitably become spiritually dead (which is why Nicodemus
was told he needed to be born again, but this time of the Spirit – Jn. 3:5
– 8, this is because he was not tuned into God because the spirit within
him was not made alive by the Holy Spirit) and die without meeting
with God the creator and saviour. This is a very serious matter and can
be said of many leaders and preachers in the church today.

How can you believe when you do not focus on God and seek insight
into the God inspired scriptures, which speak of world history from the
very beginning and explain how men can commune with God, if the
spirit within you has not been reborn, made alive by the regenerating
work of the Holy Spirit? The world will one day disappear, the scriptures
tell us as much. But God is eternal, therefore let us focus on God and
use what men find out as useful inputs into the reality of spiritual things
in a physical world, without being distracted from what God wants to
say to us individually.

Now consider what the second verse of Genesis chapter one says:

*The earth was a formless void; and darkness covered the face of the deep,
while a wind from God swept over the face of the waters.*

In my book 'The Origin of Life : God's Relationship With Man in
Genesis' the creation is discussed in detail including an account of it from
the Jewish perspective, so there is no point in duplicating the subject
here. However, the error of Adam in doing something God particularly
forbade him to do must be considered with regard to the creation and
who owns the whole of creation.

The problem with the theory of evolution, and we must remember it is still a theory however compelling the science, is that it starts with the Big Bang and of those who are involved in studying it and all its implications for life on earth many have become so obsessed with it that it has left them with a mental block concerning what was before the Big Bang, even to the point of refusing to even consider it. Therefore ownership of planet earth and all that it contains is left open, an unanswered question, and the matter of sin, which those with a 'religious bent' have found it necessary to consider, is beyond their ability to comprehend, yet the fact that there was something before the Big Bang will not go away and must be considered by all those living on planet earth if they are ever to understand why we are here and what happens to us after we die.

The inventor/creator of a commodity of any sort, or a process, or a piece of music not only owns it and can allow its use by others with the payment of a fee, but rightly provides the rules/instructions on how it is to be used to the best advantage. For it to be used in any other way will defeat the purpose of the design. For instance a public bus or coach cannot be used as a ship, to consider a particularly bizarre example.

For someone that makes something for their own good pleasure, what they make is owned by them, unless they sell it, and it is theirs to decide not only who can use it but how it is used.

The problem of the creation in which we live is that God created it for His good pleasure and, because He has never sold it, which is because there is no one like Him that is able to purchase it and control it, the whole of creation still belongs to Him and he is able to decide on the rules of its use. There is no getting away from this crucial point that all that we see and experience within His creation, even ourselves, all of it belongs in its entirety to God.

As independently minded people, we are not easily given to the idea that someone owns us, and we are right in thinking like that because in creating man God gave us all a freedom to live our lives in the way we desire so that we were not to become automatons but free thinking people, *but* that freedom had to be within the constraints decided by God.

Please remember what God has said:

> For every wild beast of the forest is mine,
> And the cattle on a thousand hills.
> I know all the birds of the air,
> and all the wild beasts in the field belong to me.
> 'If I were hungry, I would not tell you,
> for the world and all that is in it is mine.
> (Ps. 50:10 – 12)

Not only was man made for God's good pleasure, after all He made man in His image for the purpose of God and man communing one with the other, but because God wanted that relationship to become central to the life of man with man's consent, He set the test of the two trees in the centre of the garden into which He had placed man (Gen. 2:8) to see if man was willing to work with Him so that there could be a deep and lasting relationship between Him and mankind to the advantage of both.

Before any reader questions why we are on the one hand given a free will and then told that God has laid down certain conditions for that free will let me explain. In creating man God made the wholesomeness of the life of the individual dependent upon both the physical life, which is sustained by food and exercise of both the body and the mind, and the spiritual life, which can only be sustained through spiritual intercourse with God because His word, whether directed to the whole of mankind, such as the scriptures, or to an individual, feeds our spiritual lives. Only in that way can man be complete in himself. Because God, through His creative powers gave birth to man and is the only one who can sustain him, we have a duty to live within the bounds God set as our supreme designer.

Remember the Lord told Satan that man shall not live on physical bread alone, because such food only satisfies the body, but for his spiritual health man must also feed on spiritual food which is obtained by reading and hearing the words (messages — statutes and promises) of God and from God (Matt. 4:4). Many have heard God speaking to them direct, not only the prophets of old.

Have you noticed how trains have to run on rail tracks, and ships on the sea because that is the way they were designed? God was perfectly satisfied with being self-contained, and self-sustaining. Why He suddenly decided to create the universe and the earth we are not told. However the purpose for Him creating man was for man to be made spiritually compatible with Him so that a relationship could be established between man and God and God could shower His infinite love on man. That is the very reason we were promoted above the animal kingdom and why no animal has eternal life.

What is of particular importance is that all those who have sought after a relationship with God have had their lives transformed and given far more depth of meaning than would otherwise have been the case. Being born again by the Spirit of God (Jn. 3:5, 6) is crucial if we are to be trained by the Spirit for eternal life, which has certainly been my experience. The more intimate I am with God the deeper I want that intimacy to become, because experientially the love of God has been transforming me and will continue to do so until I am refined and made perfect in His sight by the time I am called to leave this mortality and enter immortality to meet with the Saviour (Mal. 3:3; 1 Cor. 15:42 – 58).

God is completely pure and holy and He wants us to be like Him in all our ways and only in that way will we be complete in ourselves. So although we do have a free will, after all we can chose to accept God or reject Him, it is only by not just accepting Him but seeking to become at one with Him that He can lead us into a completely fulfilled life in the Spirit which brings us joy and peace in our inner man. *Behold! I am standing at the door [of your heart], knocking; if anyone hears my voice and opens the door, I will come in to them and eat with them, and them with me (see Rev. 3:20).*

There is another aspect of man that is deceptively important, and that is our inner, God breathed spirit, our inbuilt emotions, which have such an effect on the way we think and act, and an inner need to belong.

At the beginning of all family trees, our ancestral roots, is Adam, the first man, and how he came into being as a man. But before Adam was the eternal God who created him, and He alone is the true source of our life.

In saying that Adam is our ancestral root let me be completely honest and say that I believe in the whole of the Bible, and in studying it I rely on God to interpret it to me through His Holy Spirit as has been explain above. Now some are bound to ask me if I really believe in the account of the creation of Adam and Eve as it is described in Genesis. My answer is, "Yes. Why not, is it not in the Bible?" But you say, "It is in picture language?" "So?" It is not the style of writing that is important, rather it is what is said by whom and to whom that is important, the underlying message that God is giving to us. We have already discussed the fact that, just as God is truth, so is the Bible, because it has been written under the inspiration of God by godly people, must also be consider to be truth (2 Tim. 3:16, 17). As soon as you question the validity of scripture you are doing Satan's work for him and destroying the effectiveness of the only book that is central to, and the foundational document of, the Judeo/ Christian faith.

The whole purpose of the account of the creation of Adam and then Eve is to acknowledge that God made a man and from him a woman and the principle of our life and the way in which men and women interact has consolidated that belief in me; and I do not see how else I can understand the development of man except that we are made by God and for God without changing the wording of the Bible.

Are those who question the authenticity of the account of the creation of Adam saying that humanity appeared in some other way? If so by what means? Certainly such doubt raises the question, 'Where is Satan in all this?' for it is he who spreads doubts in the mind of man as he did in the beginning. This is assuming Satan's reality is not also in question.

When God created the whole cosmos and then lavished His attention on the earth, and in particularly man, He laid down certain rules of engagement that had to be observed for everyone's benefit. Obedience within certain natural freedoms to live as individuals. It is something parents of well balanced children insist on. Unless certain rules are laid down and observed, chaos reigns! Indeed it is evident from history, clearly illustrated by the message of the First Testament, that men without God produce a society that is corrupt and lawless.

Our relationship with God can easily be summed up as being that of a loving and pure God whose only desire is for us to love Him and be obedient to the rules of life He laid down for us, for by living according to His rules we will live a life of purpose, fulfilment and meaning.

The God/Man Relationship

The test God put before the first man and woman was the fruit of two trees in the Garden he had specially prepared for them to live in and where He met with them and conversed with them freely to the enjoyment of both God and man. This was a time of spiritual intimacy and freedom, when God showed Himself to man in the form of a man fully exercising the spirit within man. What one might call a spiritual utopia.

Consider this carefully. Throughout scripture God the Father is portrayed as the one member of the Trinity who is consistently in heaven;

I watched as, thrones were set in place,
and the Ancient of Days was seated;
his clothing was white as snow,
and the hair of his head like pure wool;
his throne was fiery flames,
and its wheels were burning fire.
A fiery stream issued
and flowed out from before Him.
A thousand, thousands ministered to him,
and ten thousand times ten thousand
stood attending him.
The court sat in judgement,
and the books were opened.
(see Dan. 7:9, 10).

The Holy Spirit is the unseen member who is active on the earth and within the hearts and minds of all those who truly love God; He was present at the very beginning before the earth gained its form and outer clothing of vegetation, or came alive with living beings, *"And the Spirit of God hovered over the face of the deep"*, whilst the Son of God is the only one that has appeared to men from the beginning:

> *"… they heard the sound of the Lord God walking in the garden in the cool at evening time, and the man and his wife hid themselves from the presence of the Lord God among the trees of the garden. But the Lord God called to the man, and said to him, 'Where are you?'" (see Gen. 3:8, 9),*

and:

> *"As I watched in the night visions,*
> *I saw one like the Son of Man*
> *coming with the clouds of heaven.*
> *And he came to the Ancient of Days*
> *and was presented before him.*
> *Then to him was given dominion*
> *and glory and a kingdom,*
> *that all peoples, nations, and languages*
> *should serve him.*
> *His dominion is an everlasting dominion*
> *that shall not pass away,*
> *and his kingdom is one*
> *that shall never be destroyed."*
> *(Dan. 7:13, 14)*
> *"My kingdom is not of this world*
> *else my servants would fight to prevent me*
> *from being delivered to the Jews.*

26

My kingdom is not here."
(see Jn. 18:36)

The Son also appeared to Abraham in the valley of Shaveh (the King's Valley) after his defeat of Chedolaomer and the kings who had allied themselves to him:

> *"And King Melchizedek of Salem*
> *brought out bread and wine;*
> *he was priest of God Most High*
> *(in Hebrew El Elyon).*
> *He blessed him and said,*
> *'Blessed be Abram by God Most High,*
> *maker of heaven and earth;*
> *and blessed be God Most High,*
> *who has delivered your enemies into your hand!'"*
> *(Gen 14:18 – 20))*

Long before His birth as a human being in Bethlehem, the Son of God appeared for a second time in the form of a human bring but not in human flesh as He was to be in the future. A further explanation of the relationship of the Son of God with Melchizedek is found later in this book.

Continuing our thoughts on Adam and Eve, there was plenty for them to eat in the whole of the garden. The two trees God caused to grow in the centre of the garden, and notice they were central to their relationship with God their creator, were additional to their plentiful food supply. Of these two trees the man and the woman were free to eat the fruit of one but were forbidden to eat the fruit of the other. The responsibility for obeying that instruction was given to Adam because it was to him that God gave the commandment, *'you shall not eat the fruit of that particular tree'*. Also it was man God created first, and from Adam's rib God created the woman who was to be man's helper, his support. The penalty for disobeying God's command was spiritual death. That means that sin, which is the result of man directly disobeying the command of God, causes spiritual activity between God and man to end and because of that inactivity the spirit within man gradually dies through lack of the life giving spiritual food from God. It is only those who respond to the call of God who receive the life giving spiritual food that brings our spirit back to life.

It was Eve who was deceived by the fallen angel, Satan, into disobeying God's command and to eat of the fruit of the forbidden tree. Adam's sin was in also eating of the fruit even though God had specifically told him not to do so, thereby openly disobeying God and failing the obedience test.

God is pure and holy and in Him is no darkness at all. As soon as Adam sinned by disobeying God the purity of the relationship between God and man was corrupted making it impossible for God to have anymore direct dealings with man as had previously happened in the Garden of Eden.

There is a very good reason for establishing the fact that, according to God, Eve was deceived but Adam sinned. Paul tells the Romans that sin entered the world through one man and through him to all men (Rom. 5:12). It is not only the fact that we have inherited sin that causes us problems, but that inherited sin makes us tend to sin as individuals. Then to the Corinthians Paul writes that as in Adam all die spiritually because of his sin, so in Christ, that is when in repentance and faith we ask God to forgive us and we accept Christ into our lives, we are made alive spiritually through the work of the Holy Spirit.

This whole matter of sin gives further importance to the need for Christ to have come, born of a virgin, and to die on the cross. As in Adam all die — spiritually, so in Christ all will be made alive — spiritually. But Christ also had to rise from the dead, thus defeating the power of death, so that death is not the end for those who believe, just the beginning of a new chapter in their spiritual life (1 Cor. 15:42 – 58). Now in verse 45 Paul speaks of Christ, the last Adam, being a life-giving spirit, because although His human body died, it was transformed into a living spiritual body so that He could become the first fruits of them who have died, being the first to rise from the dead, clearly demonstrating God's power over life and death.

At first to maintain spiritual contact between man and God, God allowed animals to be sacrificed for the sin of man. This instruction was probably delivered by an angel representing God because God cannot look upon sin of any sort. The man and the woman were provided with clothing through the sacrificing of animals, giving them an example of how a much more muted relationship could continue. The lesson must have been learned by that first couple because their son Abel sacrificed a lamb without blemish to God for his sacrifice to have been accepted and receive forgiveness of sin. Sadly Cane sacrificed things that he had produced by the sweat of his brow, not wanting to realise that it was by the shedding of blood sins are forgiven. Such was his pride and arrogance, when his sacrifice was not accepted he rebelled further and cut himself off from God completely (Gen. 4:3 – 12) not realizing that his life not only had a beginning but also an end at which time his spirit would still live but he would have to pay the consequences for his godless actions during his life.

Man did not die physically but spiritually and the first couple came to realise the significance of what they had done when they were ejected from God's presence and their life became hard and uncertain. Although God had already planned the means by which man could receive forgiveness of sin, it was not until the sacrifice of the Son of God and the release of the Holy Spirit into the world that the full rebirth of man's spirit was enabled.

What needs to be learned and understood is why the death of an animal was required when it was a spiritual death man suffered.

Consider what God had done. He had created the heavens and the earth, the sea and the dry land, the fish of the sea, the birds of the air and all the living beings on the land. Man was made the pinnacle of His creative skills and what elevated man above all other living things was the breath God breathed into Adam which gave him spiritual life, enabling man to communicate directly with God. Man has the breath of God in him, is that not amazing? First breathed by God directly into

Adam, it was first passed on to the woman before being passed on to all their offspring.

That life God breathed into man suffered death, by starvation of spiritual contact with God, as the direct result of sin:

> *"… but you shall not eat of the fruit of the tree of the knowledge of good and evil, for in the very day [the very moment] you eat of it [and thereby disobey God and rebel against Him] you shall [most definitely] die"*

and that death did not just apply to man's existence on earth, but it was to be a permanent spiritual death separating man from the Spirit of God even after his physical life on earth had come to an end. Because of the elevation of man above all other creatures on the earth through that 'breath of God', such was the permanence of that separation that man was made virtually totally dead in relation to God except he would continue to live in spiritual form but in a place God had prepared for them that He did not enter. Consider the parable our Lord gave to the people:

> *"There was a rich man dressed in purple and fine linen who feasted sumptuously every day. At his gate lay a poor man named Lazarus, covered with sores, who longed to satisfy his hunger with what fell from the rich man's table; even the dogs would come and lick his sores. Finally the poor man died and was carried away by the angels to be with Abraham.*
>
> *The rich man also died, was buried and his soul went to the place of the dead, where he was being tormented. Looking up he saw Abraham far away with Lazarus by his side. He called out, "Father Abraham, have mercy on me, and send Lazarus to dip the tip of his finger in water and cool my tongue; because I am in agony in these flames." But Abraham said, "Son, remember that during your lifetime you received your good things, and Lazarus in like manner evil things; but now he is comforted here, and you are in agony.*

Besides, between you and us a great chasm has been fixed, so that those who might want to pass from here to you cannot do so, neither can one cross from there to us." He said, "Then, father, I beg you to send him to my father's house, for I have five brothers so that he may warn them, to prevent them coming into this place of torment." Abraham replied, "They have Moses and the prophets; they should listen to them." He said, "No, father Abraham; but if someone is sent to them from the dead, they will repent." Abraham replied, "If they are not willing to listen to Moses and the prophets, neither will they be convinced even if someone rises from the dead.""" (See Lk. 16:19 – 31)

What is the Lord saying to the people through this parable? That there are two places they can choose to enter after they have died. One of joy for the obedient, and another of torment for the disobedient. How much do you value the word of God? Is it essential reading in order to be food for your spirit (Matt. 4:4)? Or is it a book to be argued over and discussed to the point where it becomes irrelevant? Or is it kept on the book shelf and never read; just politely ignored? Yet it is in this life that a person qualifies for that place of rest God has prepared for all those who love Him, and all the information to enable a person to qualify for that joyous life is contained within the word of God.

Consider what the writer to the Hebrews wrote:

> *Therefore, as the Holy Spirit (2 Pet. 1:21) says,*
> *'Today, if you will hear his voice,*
> *do not harden your hearts as in the rebellion,*
> *in the day of testing in the wilderness,*
> *where your ancestors put me to the test,*
> *yet they had seen my works for forty years.*
> *Therefore I was angry with that generation,*
> *and said, "They always go astray in their hearts,*
> *and they have not known my ways."*
> *In my anger I swore,*

"They will not enter my rest." '
(see Heb. 3:7 – 11; cf. Num. 14:22, 23)

When asked by a lawyer which was the greatest commandment in the law the Messiah replied:

You shall love the Lord your God with <u>all</u> your heart, and with <u>all</u> your soul, and with <u>all</u> your mind. This is the greatest and first commandment And a second is like it: You shall love your neighbour as yourself." On these two commandments hang all the law and the prophets." (Matt. 38 – 40)

Notice the commitment must be all consuming *'with <u>all</u> your'*, representing total commitment of the individual to God.

The only means by which man's spiritual life could be reborn and maintained has, with the assistance of the Holy Spirit, always been through feeding off the word of God (Matt. 4:4; Jn. 3:5 – 8), absorbing into their mind and heart the message and instructions it contains and using that information as spiritual food thus enabling him to enter into communion with the creator and loving God.

As a temporary measure God allowed substitutional death, that is the sacrificial spilling of the blood of a substitute offering (taking the place of a man), but the effectiveness of that process was for the one offering the sacrifice to be fully repentant of heart for their sin and sinfulness, and a true faith in God (Neh. 1:5 – 11). The sacrifice was to be a specified substitute animal for a man, apart from set occasions when a lamb was sacrificed for the whole nation of Israel by the high priest.

When permission was given to Noah to eat meat, God identified the blood of the animal as representing the life of the animal (Gen. 9:4), and God forbade the eating of any meat with blood in it, thus requiring all blood to be drained from any meat to be used for human consumption. The critical importance of that symbol of life was finally made clear when the price of salvation and the forgiveness of sin was fully paid by the Messiah on the cross.

Right from the start of human existence God was laying down the principle that the blood was the crucial element in all sacrifices made to God as they were the forerunners of the ultimate sacrifice the Messiah (the Christ, the anointed One) made on Calvary, something that would have been unknown to the Israelites until prophetic announcements of the coming of the Messiah became more prominent.

The blood shed by the sacrificial animals had to be seen as precious because of its relationship to the crucial shedding of the blood of the Messiah which deprived Him of His human life. Satan caused his followers to anticipate the death of the Messiah by their human sacrifices to various gods in pagan ceremonies.

By reading the First Testament of the Bible from Genesis to Malachi, the building blocks of God's ultimate plan of salvation can be identified, along with the increasingly symbolic nature of the annual celebration of Passover when the Israelites were rescued from Egypt, a country and dictatorship that represented the world (see The Tent of the Meeting : Illustrating God's Plan of Salvation which gives a full explanation of God's plan of salvation from Genesis to Revelation).

The True Status of Man

Without the full acceptance of the power and authority of God over the whole of creation, not only the Bible but life itself becomes totally meaningless. How did all that is seen come into being and what is the purpose of man in this life with its continual round of birth, life and death? Why the continual conflicts between individuals and nations which cause so much needless suffering to ordinary folk? Why the diseases and epidemics, the earthquakes and environmental turbulences? Why is it that some have a mind that is focused on doing others harm in order to gain power and financial well being, particularly when so many escape punishment and personal suffering?

With the purchase of an item of equipment comes a set of instructions for the use of that equipment and in some cases its maintenance. Believe it or not the Hebraic/Christian Bible is the instruction book of life on earth for men of which, sadly, so few take much notice. Yet it is that book which provides the curious with all the answers they need, and it does that by explaining who God is and man's relationship with Him as the Holy Spirit gives us understanding.

What is more we are promised an interpreter so that we can understand the deeper meaning of what we read. And who is this interpreter? The Holy Spirit. Consider what our Lord and Saviour, Jesus Christ the Messiah to the Jews said to His disciples, *"But the Advocate or Helper, the Holy Spirit, whom the Father will send in my name, will teach you everything, and remind you of all that I have said to you" (Jn. 14:26)*. Not only was the Holy Spirit provided for the benefit of the disciples on the day of Pentecost enabling them to speak with boldness, but he is available and as powerful today in order for us to understand the Word of God and speak confidently in His name, although it will always be imperfect.

Not only did the Lord Jesus instruct His disciples to *"Go and make disciples of all nations, baptizing them in the name of the Father and of the Son and of the Holy Spirit, teaching them to obey everything I have commanded you"* but it tells us of those who received the baptism of the Holy Spirit, and the source of their special gifts such as speaking in tongues and prophesying.

Please be assured, having received that same baptism myself many years ago, I would not have written this or any other of my books had God not encouraged and inspire me to write, interpreting the scriptures to me and guiding me to various sources that enabled me to understand, in some small way, what God was seeking to say in His word as written down by men. Not magic writing on the wall, as happened at Belshazzar's feast which Daniel interpreted, but men being obedient to the guiding of the Lord and writing as He gave them the words and understanding to record what He wanted mankind to know.

As discussed in the previous chapter, the book of Genesis is the only God given record of how the world came into being and how man became what he is today; after all God Himself was the only person present when He created all things by whatever means He decided, which for scientists is a joy because of the joy of investigating how He went about creating what we see, even though they can merely scratch the surface. It also explains the role of both men and women in their earthly habitat, who before God are treated the same but whose particular tasks in life are in some ways dissimilar yet completely complimentary.

The only way Cain appeared on the earth was for the man (Adam) to have sexual intercourse with the woman (Eve). Believe it or not God created a man and a woman, not two men or two women. And the purpose of God's design was for the seed of the woman to be fertilized by the man so that the woman became pregnant and the body of Cain grew in the woman's womb and was born. It is the woman who is generally the home maker, the man's helpmeet, and the man who is the supplier of food and the provider of shelter. That is the way things are according to God's design. Although in this modern day not only do women need to work, as my wife did, but sometimes are able to earn a better income than the man. Changes have brought about househusbands, one our sons being one before the children went to school.

But that is not the only thing that happened. Something far more momentous and life changing occurred that not only gave purpose to the course of history but emphasized that man was not just another earthly creature, but the apex of God's creation.

Remember how the Bible explains that into Adam's nostrils God breathed His Spirit, which is referred to as the breath of life? Because of that one act of God, Adam was elevated out of being a member of the animal kingdom! In a moment he became a God sensitive, morally upright spiritual being, raising him above all other creatures because, having received that spiritual life, Adam was transformed into a being in God's image, having the characteristics of God, and, having received that greater gift of spiritual life. By that means man became the only created being with the personal independent knowledge, intelligence and understanding that enabled him to communicate directly with God, to enter into intelligent, reasoned conversations with God who is pure Spirit. What other being on earth is like man in intelligence, with decision making and creative abilities that matches man's capabilities?

Therefore how can some believe that we are no more than members of the animal kingdom?

Then, because the woman was created by God using a rib bone from the man, she also received of that same Spirit, becoming a spiritual person in her own right and therefore spiritually aware. It is evident that all the offspring of that first couple have received that breath of God even to this very day, each with the ability to become spiritually aware and able to enter into communion (which means the ability to share intimate thoughts and feelings) and converse directly with God, if, that is, they are willing to accept the reality of God and receive the rejuvenating touch to their spirit only the Holy Spirit can provide.

What fouled up the whole process is sin. It was that act of defiance, first by the deception of Eve by Satan, the first confidence trickster, and then deliberately by Adam, that brought about the enforced separation between God and man, making that intimacy of relationship infinitely more difficult, particularly from man's perspective. To correct this aberration, this major disruption to what had been an intimate and loving relationship between God and man, a solution had to be found. God's love for the man He had created was such that He was determined to provide a solution, a way back to Himself for man, even though it would cost Him dear.

PROPHECY

What is Prophecy

There are two important aspects of prophecy, *forthtelling* and *foretelling*. At its heart, however, is God communicating directly with mankind through chosen individuals. Indeed, it is all about the Spirit of God talking to the God breathed spirit within a man, where it has been rejuvenated by God's Holy Spirit. But this can only happen within those individuals who have recognized their sinfulness and need of salvation, and then through repentance and faith have not only returned to and entered into communion with God, but, like Isaiah, have committed themselves to God in service saying, *"Here am I, send me"*. There had to be a willingness to put themselves at God's disposal for Him to be able to use them.

Consider carefully a statement twice uttered by our Lord Jesus Christ and the context in which it was uttered, *"For many are called, but few are chosen"*. Everything about man's relationship with God has everything to do with the degree of willingness of the individual to engage with God and abandon themselves to His almighty will for their lives. The greater the willingness of a person to abandon themselves to the will and loving care of God, the greater will be God's involvement in their lives.

Forthtelling: this was the foremost task of a prophet because the prophets were primarily spokesmen for God. Abraham was the first significant forthtelling prophet in recording the covenant God made with him. Such was Abraham's strong relationship with God, because of his willingness to leave his home and family and spend his life being guided by God. Added to this was his willingness to sacrifice his true son Isaac at the command of God. It was because of this selfless devotion that God told him about the covenant He was making with him, a covenant that concerned his descendants, who became Israel through Jacob.

The intimacy Abraham had with God was illustrated when three angels of God spoke with him about the birth of his son Isaac before telling him about the destruction of Sodom and Gomorrah, and Abraham's plea for his family living there which caused them to rescue Lot.

Consider three other major prophets, Moses, Isaiah, Jeremiah and Ezekiel. All three spoke as God gave them a message:

Moses	the greatest of all prophets received the word directly from God and initially passed it on to Aaron whom God appointed as his spokesman before Pharaoh, because Moses was to become a god to Pharaoh. Indeed, Aaron's ministry clearly demonstrates his role as that of a spokesman. By the time he became the acknowledge leader of God's people, and Aaron had demonstrated his flawed character in molding the golden calves for the people to worship, Moses began to speak directly to the people, even to the point where the people asked him to hide his face with a veil because of the brightness of his countenance after he had been in the presence of God and had received to himself a portion of God's glory.

Isaiah	who was in the temple when he saw the Lord (Is. 6:1, 9), warns the Israelites in the first chapter that they could not fool God into thinking that they were sincere when presenting their sacrifices and seeking forgiveness of sin because He looked into their hearts and governed their offerings by their attitude towards their sin and towards Him.
Jeremiah	was commissioned when he was still in his mothers womb (Jer. 1:4 – 7), and, when suffering a bout of self-pity, God called him back and appointed him as His mouth (Jer. 15:15 – 20). *"The prophet who has a dream,"* says the Lord, *"Let him tell a dream; And he who has my word, let him speak My word faithfully."* (Jer. 23:28, see 29).
Ezekiel	was commissioned when he was in exile and the Spirit of God entered into him (Eze. 2:1 – 7), and spoke the words of God to his fellow countrymen, many of the nations religious leaders being in denial that it was their departure from covenants of God and their complete disregard to commandments of God that brought about the exile.

Many of the minor prophets start with their commissioning by God, *"The word of the Lord which came …"* or *"The burden which the prophet … saw …"*. Included in their record of God speaking to them is *"Thus speaks the Lord of Hosts, saying: …"*. These were messages direct from God spoken by individuals who were attuned to God speaking to those to whom the messages were addressed.

Today there are many forthtelling prophets, but are we listening to them? Most important of all is the question, "Are the members of church congregations listening to them?" Paul warned the Ephesians about many wolves, who would seek to destroy the church (Acts 20:29 – 31) and that, according to my experience, is happening within the established church right now. John in his first letter warns his flock:

> *"Children, it is the last hour! As you have heard that antichrist is coming, so now many antichrists have come. From this we know that it is the last hour.* They* [false teachers confessing to be Christians who change scripture to suit themselves and lure weak member of the church away from the true Christ] *went out from us, but they did not belong to us; for if they had belonged to us, they would have remained with us. In fact by going out they made it plain that none of them belongs to us.*
>
> *But you have been anointed by the Holy One, and you know all these things. I write to you, not because you do not know the truth, but because you know it, and you know that no lie comes from the truth. Who is the liar but the one who denies that Jesus is the Christ, the Messiah? This is the antichrist, the one who denies the Father and the Son. No one who denies the Son has the Father; everyone who confesses the Son has the Father also. Let what you heard from the beginning abide in you. If what you heard from the beginning abides in you, then you will abide in the Son and in the Father. And this is what he has promised you, eternal life. I write these things to you concerning those who would deceive you. (1 Jn. 2:18 – 26)*

It cannot be emphasized enough that it is the responsibility of every individual believer to reach out to God and become spiritually attuned to Him, with the less mentally able given special help from the Holy Spirit to know within their spirits that they belong to God. Theologians, preachers, teachers and leaders within the earthly church beware that they do not put stumbling blocks in the way of the more vulnerable and non-academic believers for they will be judged far more harshly, and that warning applies to me as much as to anyone else. Do not become a wolf in sheep's clothing, but sensitive to the leading of the Holy Spirit.

Foretelling: is all about God giving man a warning or promise of what is to come.

Abraham was the first significant foretelling prophet in recording what God told him concerning his seed; their 400 years of affliction in a foreign land; that they would leave with great possessions; and that it was to Abraham's descendents that God was giving all the land through which he had journeyed.

Many Biblical prophecies have been fulfilled although there is not enough space here to give examples, the web holds a lot of information (http://www.reasons.org/articles/articles/fulfilled-prophecy-evidence-for-the-reliability-of-the-bible). The reason for this is that God knows the end from the beginning and the beginning from the end, indeed nothing is unknown to Him, so it is obvious that He alone above all gods that are worshipped, or have been worshipped, in the world would be able to tell Divinely ordained prophets exactly what was going to happen:

Remember this and consider,
recall it to mind, you transgressors.
Remember the former things of old;
for I am God, and there is no other;
I am God, and there is no one like me,
declaring the end from the beginning
and from ancient times things
that are not yet done,
saying, 'My counsel shall stand,
and I will fulfil my pleasure',
(Isa. 46:8 – 10)

Moses warned the children of Israel about being faithful to the God who had rescued them from Egypt if they wanted a good life in the promised land. If they went after other gods and neglected their marriage to Him, God would withdraw His protection from them and allow other nations to subdue them (Deut. 30:15 – 20). The book of Judges gives many examples of their suffering through disobedience. Why should it be any different for us?

Prophecy Relating to the Messiah

As the subject matter of this book concerns the true meaning of Easter, it is essential that the focus is on the Messianic prophecies, starting with those in Genesis.

Regarding Satan and Messiah — Consider some of the prophetic announcements contained in the First Testament and particularly the very first in Genesis 3:14 – 15:

> *"The Lord God said to the serpent,*
> *'Because you have done this,*
> *cursed are you among all animals*
> *and among all wild creatures;*
> *upon your belly you shall go,*
> *and dust you shall eat*
> *all the days of your life.*
> *I will put enmity between you*
> *and the woman,*
> *and between your offspring and hers;*
> *he will strike your head,*
> *and you will strike his heel.'"*

"The Lord God said to the serpent ...", the Hebrew word for Serpent is *'nachash'* meaning to hiss, mutter, whisper as do enchanters. Although Satan is not actually named as such in the First Testament, it is clearly he who is described figuratively in Genesis 3, for the method he used to entice Eve to sin was serpent-like.

Notice in particular the last two lines, *"He will strike your head, and you will strike His heel.'* and the fact that God refers to a single person in each case (consider Gal. 3:15 – 18; cf. Gen. 22:18).

He will and ***you will*** : He, that is the one who was to come to pay the price for sin, was to strike Satan's head, which meant He would cause Satan's demise because as Satan's poison is in his head, it was by his speech that he enticed Eve to sin, a bruise on that part is fatal. In the act of crushing Satan's head Satan was to be permitted to bruise merely the heel of the coming Messiah (although He is not referred to as such until much later in the history of the nation of Israel), thereby afflicting the humanity of the Divine Son of God by having Him sent to the cross. Satan had no power whatsoever over the Messiah's Divine status because the Spirit within the body of the man Christ Jesus, Messiah to Israel, was the true born Son of God and eternal, having been responsible for the creation of Satan as the senior angel. (For a full explanation of just who Satan is please refer to my book "The Tent of the Meeting : Illustrating God's Plan of Salvation")

There was a period years ago when many Christian leaders and clergy taught that Christ gave up His Divinity when He came to earth, which is a heresy called 'Adoptionism' which was the belief that Jesus was born as a mere man, who was supremely virtuous and later adopted as "Son of God" by the descent of the Holy Spirit on him at his baptism. But the Prophet John had previously referred to the Messiah as the one who could baptize with the Holy Spirit (Matt. 3:11, 12), and God called the Lord His Son of whom He was well pleased [See list of Christian heresies on the 'Wikepedia' web site. Although this particular heresy was first mooted about 190AD it has been resurrected from time to time]

But God cannot change, for He is the same yesterday and today and forever. So to suggest, as so many did, that the Christ was fully human is a lie for He was both Divine and human. How did the Christ confound the religious elite in His day with His knowledge of the scriptures at 12 years of age if He had not come from above and retained His Divine status as He said He had?

It is by knowing and understanding the prophecies leading up to the Cross, that its importance at the start of a remarkable process designed by God can be more fully understood. Easter is at the pinnacle of the annual Christian celebrations, therefore, to better understand the mechanics of all that happened that weekend makes the moment when salvation for all men became available all the more potent. The joy of the exclamation

"He is risen!" And the response, "He is risen indeed!" proclaims the essence of the meaning and purpose of Easter because it was all that happened then, that we are saved from our sin.

> *For if the blood of bulls and goats, and the sprinkling of the ashes of a heifer on the unclean, sanctifies those who have been defiled so that their flesh is purified, how much more shall the blood of Christ, who through the eternal Spirit offered himself without blemish to God, purify our conscience from dead works to serve the living God! (Heb. 9:13, 14)*

The prophetic utterances relate to the period from the beginning of time, as with Adam and Eve committing the first sinful act, until around 430BC.

"I will put enmity between you and the woman, and between your offspring and hers ... ": it is obvious that the Messiah would be the offspring of Eve (see Gal. 4:4), for He would be born of a virgin, but here God is laying out the fact that there would be spiritual conflict between man and Satan, between those that love God and those that follow and serve Satan and his demonic forces. This is because God is the God of Love whereas Satan encourages hatred and chaos.

Importance of Blood — Another easily missed prophecy concerns the symbolic nature of blood. Adam had been a vegetarian but God allowed Noah and his family to kill animals and eat their flesh with certain very important conditions.

> *Only, you shall not eat flesh with its life, that is, its blood.*
> *For of your own lifeblood I will surely require a reckoning:*
> *from every animal I will require it and from human beings,*
> *each one for the blood of another,*
> *I will require a reckoning for human life.*
> *Whoever sheds the blood of a human,*
> *by a human shall that person's blood be shed;*

for in his own image God made man.
(Gen. 9:4 – 6)

And the importance of blood with regard to the sacrifices offered for sin is clearly laid out in Leviticus 17:11:

For the life of the flesh is in the blood;
and I have given it to you for making
atonement for your lives on the altar;
for life is in the blood
and it is the blood that makes atonement.
(see Lev. 17:11)

God had said to Adam, if you eat of the fruit of the forbidden tree, and thereby rebel against Me, you will surely die. Which is why blood, "*For the life of the flesh is in the blood*", must be shed to satisfy the sentence of death God required of man "*… and it is the blood that makes atonement*". This might seem a rather severe sentence, however, because it was in the flesh that man disobeyed God, and God is so pure that He cannot look upon sin, in order to save the soul and spirit of the man it was necessary to deal with the flesh of man to ensure his eternal spiritual future with God was assured. Therefore no sinner has ever been allowed to approach God except when they approach Him, first with the shed blood of an animal and then by calling on the shed blood of the Messiah, Jesus Christ, in penitence and faith to ask Him for mercy and forgiveness. It is by grace we have been saved, by faith and even our faith is God supplied.

Although God knew that His Son was willing to die in man's stead as the Lamb of God, there can be no getting away from the fact that such an act would incur much suffering, not only because of the spiritual and human opposition He would attract from those who were not servants of His but of Satan, but also from the severity of the torturous death God the Son set Himself; that of crucifixion, the most painful and long suffering death known to man.

Disobedience is sin and it is sin which separates man from God. The salvation God has provided must be initiated by man. First comes the realisation of sin, then comes remorse and the desire for forgiveness, which is called repentance, then the confession of sin and asking for forgiveness. What is particularly precious is the fact that as God calls the sinner to repentance, so it is God who enables the sinner, through His Holy Spirit, to respond. God both calls and enables the true seeker after truth, leading them into the light of the gospel, but only where the sinner's heart is right with Him. Sometimes this enabling could be God positioning one of His servants in the right place at the right time, or even urging the sinner to pick up a Bible for Him to speak through it to the sinner.

Through atonement God bestows forgiveness, but *"according to the law, without the shedding of blood there can be no remission"* (remission - cancellation of a debt, charge or penalty, which is sin) (Heb. 9:22).

It is through the shed blood of Christ that we are saved. That was the currency of the payment God decided was required for our salvation, initially life for life, but for our full conscience cleansing salvation only the sacrifice of a perfect human life would suffice.

From the time of Adam, when we have the example of righteous Abel sacrificing a lamb to God, through to Moses who formalized the sacrificial services in the Tabernacle he made to God's design, blood became the supreme and sacred currency of man's salvation. The prophecy about blood may not be a prophecy such as Isaiah's oft quoted, *"a virgin shall conceive and bear a son"*, but it is a significant prophecy nonetheless.

Christ the Messiah paid for our salvation with His perfect human life blood, and even though He was Divine, because God cannot be anything other than God and Christ Messiah was God incarnate, it demonstrates that He was living in a fully grown human body with all its immediate emotions, which is clearly demonstrated because He did not look forward to the suffering he would experience at the hands of evil men, even though He was prepared to go through with it.

Importance of the Lamb in Sacrifice — The first occasion when the act of sacrifice saved a life was when God, knowing all that was to come, commanded Abraham to sacrifice Isaac, his long promised and only true son of promise (Gal. 4:22, 23). What is particularly relevant to us today is that Abraham, not knowing what was to come, obeyed God's command without question. His faith in God was profound because of his many experiences of serving God. As they were walking towards the site set by God for the sacrifice, Isaac asked his father where the lamb was for the sacrifice, to which his father replied that God would provide it (Gen. 22:3 – 14). And that is exactly what happened for a ram, a male sheep, was caught in a thicket which Abraham used for the sacrifice, foretelling of the man Christ Jesus who would be sacrificed for us on that very spot.

God is referred to in shepherding terms. Moses was a shepherd before being given responsibility for shepherding God's people Israel towards the Promised Land. It is interesting that the Egyptians, who were not followers of God, despised shepherds. In Isaiah there is much reference to mankind as being sheep that have gone astray (Is. 53:6), so it would be unreasonable if the Messiah, who was born into human kind, should not also be referred to in the same terms.

Why the Virgin Birth? — As this has been dealt with in some depth in my book "The Tent of the Meeting" I shall enter only a brief explanation here.

Put simply the instruction that although the fruit of the tree of life could be eaten, the fruit of the tree of the knowledge of good and evil must not be eaten was given to Adam before Eve was created from one of his ribs. Therefore it was Adam who was made responsible for that instruction to be obeyed. Knowing that God had given authority over all the creatures of the earth to man, the senior rebel angel Satan, who wanted to usurp the throne of God, knew he needed to persuade the man to eat the fruit of the forbidden tree in order to steal control of the earth from man, even though that control would be limited by the overwhelming authority of the creator God.

It was obvious that, being the devious character that he is, Satan would target the weakest point which was the woman Eve who had been told about the restriction by her husband Adam. However, her understanding of the restriction depended on the way he had told her. We know that through Satan's strategy Eve was deceived whereas, because he directly disobeyed God's instructions, Adam committed sin by eating of the fruit of the forbidden tree. It is interesting that, it was not Satan who caused Adam to sin, rather it was the woman. This was not to be the last time that a woman caused a man to be swayed. Sarah, the wife of Abraham caused him to lie with her maid Hagar to produce an heir even though God had promised them a true born son.

But it is not just the women who caused problems, because the only reason Bathsheba gave birth to David's successor Solomon was because, after committing adultery with his wife, David had had Uriah the Hittite killed in battle most cruelly. And the only reason Solomon, who was in the line of the Messiah, ascended the throne of his father David was because of the actions of Nathan the prophet. At various times David's other sons tried to take the throne from him because David would not say who would be his successor. However, it is clear that Solomon was God's chosen, for he was the only one of David's sons that did not try to become king through his own efforts.

O the imperfections of humankind!

Because Adam was declared by God to have sinned, all progeny that involves the man inherits his sinfulness. Therefore, for a man to be sinless at birth he had to have been born of a virgin, that is without the involvement of the man's sin corrupted sperm. Also, if the Son of God was not to be considered as just another human being, which would have happened if the man had been involved, it was necessary for God to bring about Mary's pregnancy which resulted in the birth of the Son of God in a miraculous way. Thus was the arrival of the Son of God on earth to become the Son of Man fully orchestrated by God Himself.

Let me explain further because this is a critical factor in the legitimacy of God's salvation.

God is pure and therefore any method of satisfying the death sentence served on man because of his sin has to be irreproachable.

We have already discovered that God provided an imperfect means of covering over man's sin through the sacrifice of a substitute in the form of a lamb or other appointed animal, which had to be perfect in form, just as a farmer selects the best animals from which to breed.

The question that needs to be asked is this, "What is the point of merely covering a man's sin rather than washing it away so completely that even the conscience of the repentant sinner was cleansed thus removing all the stain of sin completely away?" Surely such a cleansing would not only unite the sinner with his God all the more closely, but also bring about a permanency to the cleansing. Of course for such a cleansing to be provided a perfect, a sinless man had to be sacrificed in lieu of the lamb, of which the aborted sacrifice of Isaac by Abraham was a foretaste; after all it was man who received the conviction of sin with its sentence of death, therefore a man had to die as a substitute for mankind, as the high priest Caiaphas so rightly stated (Jn. 11:50). It was all in God's plan that at the right time in human history according to God's judgement, the righteous Son of God came to the earth by way of Mary to reveal more about God His Father and suffer and die for mankind.

Thus the pure Spirit that was the Divine Son of God made the transition from pure Spirit to be clothed in human flesh by entering the body of a baby in the womb of a woman. So the Holy Spirit using His creative skills caused Mary to become pregnant with the embryo of a boy child into which the Spirit of the Son of God entered in order for the baby Jesus to be born. Surely it is because only God and Mary were involved that the baby was born uncontaminated by sin. However bizarre this may seem it is worth thinking through the mechanics of it very carefully. This is my years as a technical author showing itself.

The miracle is not only that the eternal Spirit that is the Son of God entered into the womb of the young virgin Mary, who was engaged to be married, and in that culture marriage would have taken place, but that He was born into the world with a human body and then patiently waited as the body developed and grew to the point where His appointed time of ministry came. The Spirit that was the Son of God within the body of a child was the same as that which lived before the world began.

That illustrates the incredible power and ability of God.

A normal baby must develop and spend much time learning to gain knowledge and understanding, but because the Spirit of the Son of God was in the child, the knowledge He had when He entered the embryo did not diminish, which shows just how patient the Son of God was over the 30 odd years of His time waiting for His ministry to begin.

Again these thoughts might seem bizarre, but the point has already been discussed above that God cannot change and therefore the Spirit that was in the body of the Son of Man was the unchanged Son of God with the same power and authority He had before the creation, therefore, the time the Son was in the body of the growing child had to be the same as that in the body of the Messiah when discussing scripture at the age of twelve in the temple and during His years of ministry. God cannot change! He is always the same God from eternity to eternity. The same yesterday and today and forever. Can we reasonably say that the developing human brain restricted Him?

We can conjecture that during that time of being in the growing body enabled Him to experience life as a human being and understand first hand all the learning necessary for ordinary people as they grew up into adult life, and the trials and temptations all humans experience (Heb. 4:14 – 16).

It also allowed Him to establish communication and communion with His Father through the work of the Holy Spirit so that during the time of His ministry and life on the earth the trinity was in full working order for nothing is impossible to God, nor can God be anything other than the same God who existed from before the creation.

Moses was told that he could not look upon God's face, yet members of the Messiah's family will have seen Him more than most, and Mary would have had the Messiah within her womb. What the body of the Messiah did was to attenuate the glory of God so that ordinary people could look upon Him and not die.

Why crucifixion? — Why was Christ murdered by being crucified? Because God laid out the conditions of His death in Deuteronomy:

"If a man has committed a sin punishable by death
and is executed, and you hang him on a tree,
his corpse must not remain all night upon the tree;
you shall bury him that same day,
So that you do not defile the land that the Lord your God
is giving you as an inheritance,
for anyone hung on a tree is under God's curse"
(Deut. 21:22, 23).

"Since it was the day of Preparation,
the Jews did not want the bodies left on the cross
during the Sabbath, especially because
that Sabbath was a day of great solemnity.
The Jews asked Pilate to have the legs
of the crucified men broken (to hasten death)
and the bodies removed"
(Jn. 19:31).

Our Lord Jesus Christ was made a curse for us:

Christ redeemed us from the curse of the law
by becoming a curse for us, for it is written,
'Cursed is everyone who hangs on a tree'
(Gal. 3:13)

And what was the prophecy given to Abraham but that everyone would be blessed through his willing obedience to the call and guidance of God:

"… in order that in Christ Jesus
the blessing of Abraham
might come to the Gentiles,
so that we might receive the promise
of the Spirit through faith."

(Gal. 3:14; cf. Gen. 12:1 – 3; 15:6)

These prophecies are essential to the fuller understanding of what happened during that first Easter.

There is much that could be included in this chapter regarding the various prophecies about the coming of the Messiah, but to include them all would require a separate book, therefore I have included a list of most of the Messianic prophecies in the appendix at the end of the book for you to study (see Appendix A).

The principle aim here is to point out just how important it is to understand the significance of studying the Messianic prophecies in order to properly understand the sacrifice our Lord and Saviour made at Easter and the victory He achieved over death through His resurrection. **Timing of Messiah's arrival** — In a later chapter we will read of a Rabbi Cohn DD who was challenged by the constant reciting of one of the twelve articles of the Jewish creed, *"I believe with a perfect faith in the coming of the Messiah and, though He tarry, yet will I wait daily for His coming."* Yet there was every reason to believe that He should have already come. Here is a good example of the Holy Spirit guiding the thoughts of a seeker after the truth leading him to discover the truth in the word of God that is hidden from those who believe themselves to be wise.

Studying Daniel 9 from verse 24, Rabbi Cohn received from God a moment of inspiration that, as far as he was concerned, proved the Messiah should already have arrived:

When he read the ninth chapter (of Daniel), light began to dawn upon him. He had struck a mine of hitherto concealed truth, covered up by the commentaries of the revered doctors of the law. From the twenty-fourth verse of the chapter before him he deduced without difficulty that the coming of the Messiah should have taken place 490 years after Daniel received from the divine messenger the prophecy of the Seventy Weeks. Rabbi Cohn, accustomed to the intricate and often veiled polemical treatises of the Talmud (collection of ancient texts written by men), now found himself strangely captivated by the clear and soul-satisfying declarations of the Word of God, and it was not long before he began to question in his mind the reliability of the Talmud, seeing that in matters so vital it differed from the Holy Scriptures. (Obtained from www.shalom.org.uk/rabbis/cohn.htm)

So what does Daniel tell us that identifies the time of the Messiah's coming?

Israel had been self-governing in spite of those times when God sought to teach her a lesson by allowing the nation to be subjected to others, but it was always on their own land. This situation changed when the priests were worshipping gods within the temple sanctuary, having turned away from the true worship of God. This is illustrated in Ezekiel chapter 8 when the elders of Judah came to see the prophet and God gave him a vision of the accursed abominations that had been perpetrated in secrecy within the Temple inner courts, which were controlled by the priests. To demonstrate just how far the priests had moved from the knowledge of God, they had come to believe that God could not see them. God gave Ezekiel a vision of priests standing with their backs to the temple of the Lord facing towards the East worshipping the sun (Eze. 8:15 - 16), such was the priests contempt for God in spite of all the teaching of scripture.

Because of such gross sin perpetrated by those who were responsible for leading the people to God and being God's intermediaries to the people, the Jews were removed from their land and exiled to Babylon, which according to Jeremiah was to last for 70 years. At the time of the exile, free First Testament theocracy, where the priests ruled in the name of God, came to an abrupt end, never to be reinstated. It is said that the Jews, especially the priests, had become so corrupt and abhorrent to God that the need for a change became imperative. It would seem, therefore, that God withdrew Himself from direct contact with the nation because no prophetic utterances were received for the next of 400 years.

Just as the furniture in the Holy of Holies disappeared when the temple was destroyed and was not to replicated because the word of God was, according to both Jeremiah and Ezekiel, to be in men's hearts, so the whole structure of the nation was to be no longer focused on the priesthood but on God himself. In this way God was preparing the nation as a whole, and individual citizens in particular, to focus their individual attention upon God, because the Messiah was coming to introduce the need for every individual to be personally responsible for their own salvation. As the Messiah said to the Samaritan woman at the well, *"The time is coming, indeed now is, when the true worshippers will worship the Father in spirit and in truth."* That is the God given breath of spiritual life within the individual had to be exercised in worshipping God directly.

The seventy weeks mentioned in the prophecy was to start at the beginning of the exile and end on the commissioning of the rebuilding of Jerusalem and the temple, which was started by Nehemiah and Joshua the High Priest and Zerubbabel the governor of Jerusalem and encouraged by Habakkuk and Zechariah.

It was God's plan that the Messiah should be born when the nation was ruled by Rome and the religious leaders of the Jews were powerless. They tried to compensate for their lack of power by interpreting the law for a fee, but it was necessary for a Gentile to initiated His crucifixion, a Gentile form of execution, so that all should be done according to prophecy.

It was the considerable area around the Mediterranean sea controlled by Rome that allowed free travel throughout that area, including England, so that the message of salvation could be quickly spread to the then known world. The message would also have gone along the trade routes to the East. But it was a message that was not generally accepted by the Jews scattered throughout the Roman Empire leading to the persecution and eventual death of Paul. But such opposition never ended.

Going back to the story of Rabbi Cohen:

In his euphoric state Cohn tried to share what he had found with a fellow rabbi who had been particularly kind and helpful to him, but this man's response was far from what Cohn had expected.

"The Messiah whom you say you found is none other than the Jesus of the Gentiles. And as for this book," he said, tearing the

New Testament from Cohn's hands, *"a learned rabbi like you should not even handle, much less read this vile production of the apostates. It is the cause of all our sufferings."* And with these words he threw the book to the floor and trampled upon it with his feet.

"You search the scriptures," the Messiah said to the Jewish leaders, *"for in them you think you have eternal life; and it is these that testify of Me"* (Jn. 5:39).

Jeremiah said that God was near in the peoples mouths, but far from their minds (Jer. 12:2c), and consider what the God said to Ezekiel, *"So they come to you as people do, they sit before you as My people hearing your words but not doing them"* (Eze. 33:31).

Sadly it seems none of the scribes or Pharisees, chief priests or leaders of the Jews had the Spirit of God within them that they should read and properly understand what the Hebrew scriptures were telling them about the arrival of the Messiah, or what He should be like, as we shall discover in the next chapter. Certainly that unbelief has followed the Jews down through the centuries as is seen by the reaction of the Rabbi above to the moment of Leonard Cohn's realisation that the Messiah had indeed arrived in the form of Jesus of Nazareth, as witnessed by His Jewish disciples.

The curiosity of the academics called to the presence of King Herod, when the wise men asked where the Messiah was to be born, was not aroused by the request for information about where the Messiah should be born. The Jews surrounding their Messiah and trying to trick Him with their questions, did not do their research to find out facts about His life such as where He had been born, nor learn from His considerable ability to use the scriptures to confound them.

As Rabbi Cohn realized, with the truth recorded in detail in the Second Testament by three of the disciples and Luke, *"… I could at least see that the Messiah's name was Yeshua, that He was born in Bethlehem of Judah, that He had lived in Jerusalem and communicated with my people, and that He came just at the time predicted in the prophecy of Daniel. My joy was boundless."* This was the Spirit of God speaking to Rabbi Cohen's spirit and bringing it alive; no wonder his joy was boundless, he had experienced his epiphany moment. I had the incredible privilege of leading Rabbi Aaron to experience his epiphany moment.

It is no wonder the leaders of the Jews at the time did not see the truth about the Lord Jesus Christ, Yeshua of Nazareth.

ISAIAH 53

This chapter of Isaiah has proved to be the greatest stumbling block to Jewish scholars of theology because it refers to the coming of a suffering servant and what they wanted was a mighty warrior to lead them out of bondage; yet the biggest problem the Children of Israel had was being in bondage to sin, which is rebellion against the very God that chose them to be His very own people. This is not just a matter of errant physical activity but more a spiritual one because it matters how the individual lives their life in relation to our Spiritual God. For those that do not know God there is the problem of not having any understanding of what sin is or what God thinks about it.

For the Israelites the continual need for the slaughter of animals had become routine and long since stopped being particularly meaningful to the ordinary person, indeed not only Isaiah (chapter 1) but Malachi (chapter 1) too challenged the people and the priests to be honest with God about the state of their heart and their relationship with Him when offering sacrifices and, from the prospective of the Priests, the quality of the sacrificial animals being offered. God cannot be fooled.

From the point of view of the individual, it was not the actual sacrificing of the animal for their sin offering that was important, rather the fact of whether or not they really were repenting of their sin and concerned about their sinful state. From the aspect of the priests, were they mindful of the importance of offering only the best quality animals to God, or was their concept of God such that they believed any animal would do?

Isaiah called on the people to:

> *Wash yourselves; make yourselves clean;*
> *get your sins out of my sight;*
> *cease from your evil ways,*
> *Learn to do good;*
> *seek justice,*
> *rescue the oppressed,*
> *defend the orphan,*
> *plead for the widow.*
> *(Is. 1:16, 17)*

Their lives were corrupt, from within their heart, their innermost being, and that did not change by offering sacrifices. They were not in a right relationship with God because they did not have the right mindset and attitude towards Him.

Malachi's prophecy was directed at the priests who God saw were corrupt in their hearts towards Him just like the sons of Eli and Samuel. The priesthood had not changed although it was probable that there were within the priesthood those who did have respect for Him.

> *A son honours his father, and servants respect their master.*
> *If then I am a father, and a master*
> *where is the honour and respect I deserve?*
> *You have shown contempt for my name*
> *But you say, 'How have we not honoured you or shown you disrespect?*
> *By offering defiled sacrifices on my altar.*
> *But you say, 'How have we offered defiled sacrifices?*
> *By offering blind, disease ridden animals*
> *that have been rejected by the owner.*
> *Try presenting gifts like that to your governor;*

And see how pleased he is with you? says the Lord of hosts.
Go ahead implore God to be merciful to you.
Why should He show you any mercy at all?
O that someone among you would shut the temple doors,
so that those worthless sacrifices could not be offered!
I have no pleasure in you, says the Lord of hosts,
and I will not accept an offering from your hands.
(Mal. 1:6 – 10)

This is very serous stuff. Their whole response to God was itself sinful, with regard to both the people and the priests. And so it continued for centuries so that it was very strange when the Jews told Jesus that they had never been in bondage to anyone, when sin was endemic because of the lack of any spiritual contact with God and the country was occupied by Rome.

It was time for change because by God offering His Son as the perfect and eternal Passover sacrifice for sin, man was removed from the whole process of forgiveness. Suddenly sinners had to approach God Himself to receive the forgiveness of sins, and because God always looks into the heart of man He knows those that are truly repentant.

Jesus told the religious leaders that they searched the scriptures because in them they believed they had eternal life, indeed they were intensely proud that God had given those scriptures, including all the laws and statutes of God, specifically to their nation. Yet however much they searched those scriptures they did not find the glaring references to the coming of the Christ who was standing directly in front of them because, without understanding the spiritual nature of God and their need for the influence of the Holy Spirit in their lives, the true meaning of those scriptures was hidden from them. Had they known God, and able to understand all that the Holy Spirit inspired prophets of old had written, they would have realized that He was that suffering servant.

As it was it was not up to them to decide what sort of Messiah they wanted. Rather they were sent the type of Messiah God knew they needed, and He was to be one who would not only save His people from their sins but the sins of the rest of humanity too.

Within their physical world and often very limited spiritual understanding of the scriptures, the majority of the Jews were not really close to or inspired by God as were the prophets such as Isaiah, Jeremiah and Ezekiel or finally John the Baptizer. Ezekiel received a message from God in which He told the prophet the people had the eyes to see and the ears to hear, indeed in the scriptures they had all they needed to relate to God, but they chose not to see or to hear all that God had to reveal to them. Moses was asked to cover his face after he had been with God because his face shone with the radiated light of God which the people found disturbing, most probably because they realized that Moses and the God with whom he had just met must have been extremely pure and the shining of his face, even though diminishing, made them feel inferior. It was just too much for them. Consider what Paul wrote to the Corinthians (2 Cor. 3:12 – 17):

> *Therefore, since we have such confidence in this new way,*
> *we act with great boldness,*
> *unlike Moses, who put a veil over his face*
> *to prevent the people of Israel from seeing fading glory*
> *that was being set aside.*
> *But the minds of the people were hardened.*
> *Indeed, to this very day, when they hear the reading of the old covenant,*
> *that same veil remains,*
> *since only in Christ can it be set aside.*
> *Indeed, to this very day whenever Moses is read,*
> *a veil prevents their mind understanding the truth.*
> *It is only by believing in Christ that the veil is removed.*
> *Now the Lord is the Spirit,*
> *and where the Spirit of the Lord is, there is freedom.*

What was the new way in which we can have such confidence? Is it not the forgiveness of sins and the baptism of the Holy Spirit so that we are no longer under the law but under grace? Each and every believer becomes a temple of the Holy Spirit, no longer separated from God by the priests or having to sacrifice an animal at the temple. When Moses had been with God his face shone with reflected glory, just as the moon reflects the light of the sun at night. The people did not want to see the brightness of his face, something that should have encouraged the people because it demonstrated that with God only brighter things could be expected. Sadly they did not want that direct reference to the brightness of their God so by putting a veil over his face the people were being prevented from fully understanding the greatness of their God above the every day.

So why does believing in Christ the Messiah bring us freedom? Because our commitment to Christ means that there is no impediment to becoming intimate with God. We no longer learn the Bible by rote. Rather by committing ourselves to Christ we are able to receive the baptism of the Holy Spirit meaning Christ is in us through the work of that same Holy Spirit. It is the truth that by allowing the Holy Spirit to work in our hearts He is not only able to activate the cleansing of the blood to cleanse us from all sin, but also by bringing alive the spirit that is within us we have direct communications with God who is able to inspire us and provide us with wisdom and knowledge and understanding as the first few chapters of Proverbs so eloquently teaches us (see my book The Path of Wisdom which deals with the first four chapters of Proverbs).

There is much in scripture about the remnant, that is those Hebrews who focused their minds and hearts on the living God when all those around them were full of disbelief or self-imposed ignorance. Remember Caleb and Joshua were the only two of the twelve that spied out the Promise Land that were convinced God was able to ensure they succeeded in establishing themselves in the land of Canaan.

Isaiah's first statement in chapter 53 is understandable:

Who has believed our message?
And to whom has the Lord revealed His mighty arm [power]?

The nation had been rebellious from the start. Abraham's descendents cried out to be rescued from the hell they were experiencing as slaves to a despotic Pharaoh. So God sent Moses to rescue them with powerful demonstrations of His mighty power. Ten plagues demonstrated conclusively the inability of the priests of the various gods worshipped by the Egyptians to stand up against the God who had created all things and had total power over all things on the earth, particularly the power over life and death, hence the death of all the non-God focused non-Hebrew first born.

Sadly throughout the wilderness wanderings most of the people found it difficult to understand and conceive a God they could not see except for the pillar of cloud during the day and pillar of fire at night. Isaiah makes the statement:

To whom has the Lord revealed His mighty arm?

Was it not to the Children of Israel in Egypt having been enslaved for 400 years? Sadly it seems during their journey to the Promised Land they were unable to have any conceptual understanding of the spiritual nature of their God and His power over His creation, because so many of them focused on the 'here and now', their immediate surroundings and problems.

The fact that God had rescued them from Egypt where they suffered extreme hardship seemed to have been forgotten and all they could remember was their access to food and water in Egypt, but at what cost to themselves? Time had conveniently allowed them to forget the whips of the taskmasters and the heavy workload and backbreaking loads they had to carry in the heat of the noonday sun. Then they cried out to God in desperation, yet now as freed slaves in difficult situations they wanted to return to the hell of slavery. How short is the human memory? (Ps. 78:40 – 58)

Their lack of belief led them to find it difficult if not impossible to trust their God. Bitter waters, no food, no water. Each and every incident brought a reaction from those who doubted the most and were the most vociferous, with the majority who were unable to understand just who their God was, almost mindlessly joining in the protest so that on many occasions Moses was at his wits end to know what to do, calling out to God to rescue him.

That lack of belief and understanding of their spiritual God continued throughout their history. Time and again God recued them and fought battles for them without them recognizing in the long term how mighty and loving was their God. Isaiah, whose spiritual sensitivity allowed him to have a vision of God in the temple high and lifted up, was given this ministry by God when he spontaneously responded to God's call, *"Whom can we send and who will go for us?"*, replying *"Here am I send me."* But Isaiah found, as had the prophets before him and those after him, that through lack of belief the people refused to believe the message he had received from God resulting in his cry:

Who has believed our message?

The problem of unbelief is that it does not matter how much God reveals His power, far too many will forget it or ignore after a while and particularly in times of difficulty, which is the whole point of the parable of the sower and the seed (Matt. 13:1 – 43). How many of the people who escaped Egypt were prepared to remember the demonstration of God's power over the Egyptian ruler when faced with bitter waters, the look of which was so tempting to thirsty people, but useless for quenching their thirst? How intensive and overwhelmingly powerful the sense of their desperation at that time?

They seemed to have no concept of the fact that if God was all-powerful in Egypt to free them from the tyranny of the Pharaoh, surely He could solve the problem before them now. All they had to do was to ask Him, "so brothers and sister let us get down on our knees and pray to our God who has so recently recued us and ask Him to tell us how to purify the waters to make them drinkable." That is exactly what Moses did. No, they had no time for that. They desperately wanted a drink but the waters were undrinkable therefore it is time to complain. How often is this the case today for so called believers?

But let us put those two questions together:

Who has believed our message?
And to whom has the Lord revealed His mighty arm [power]?

Or perhaps to help us understand them more fully let us reverse them and modify the language:

Of those to whom the Lord has revealed His mighty arm [power],
Who has believed our message?

The history of the people was one of following God for a time and then deserting Him before crying out to Him again to rescue them from foreign armies that were oppressing them. Prophet after prophet had been sent by God to His people and all had been rejected, abused and even murdered. Sadly the people were not prepared to listen because they had their own agenda. As such were the priests and zealots, like Judas Iscariot at the time of Jesus, who were looking for a warrior Messiah to lead them in battle against the Roman occupiers mindless of their need to get right with God.

The whole purpose of the blood sacrifices in the temple were to cleanse them of outbreaks of that rebellious nature known to us all as sin, a three letter word poignant with a powerful message of rebellion causing separation between man and God. Until sin was dealt with permanently rather than relying on the continual sacrificing of animals, the coming together of God and man was impossible. The altar of sacrifice was the first item of temple furniture the repentant sinner met in their journey to meet with God (see my book The Tent of the Meeting).

For he [my servant] grew up before God like a tender shoot,

It is obviously important not to read more into scripture than is definitely there, but here is a clear statement that God's promised servant, the Messiah would grow up, in other words He started as a babe in the womb of a virgin (Isa. 7:14), and was born and then grew up to be a man in a humble home and this was prophesied nearly 700 years before Christ was born.

and like a root out of dry ground;

Now this statement is interesting because the spiritual ground when Christ was born was dry; desert dry. The sheer weight of opposition He experienced demonstrated just how desperately spiritually ignorant were the Jewish people, and particularly the religious leaders, hence the meeting Nicodemus had with the Lord, and the fact that he had no knowledge of the spiritual whatsoever. Born again? How can a person be born a second time? The physical was all they seemed to know which is why they could not see God because they were of the flesh with a spirit within them that was dead for lack of true spiritual food from God, whereas He, the Messiah, even though He had clothed Himself with a physical tent, was Spiritual. He was a full member of the Trinity.

In fact the ground was so spiritually dry the ordinary people soaked up all that Jesus taught them because at last here was a man who did not prevaricate like the religious lawyers and Pharisees who in answering a question hedged their bets because they did not fully understand the scriptural text.

In his appearance there was no beauty or sense of majesty,
there was nothing about him
that we should particularly desire him.

Jesus experienced the life of an ordinary Jewish boy as He grew up and looked just like an ordinary Jew, because He was born into a human body that was under the law of God. It was made in the likeness of sinful flesh just like all His human brethren, with the only exception being that He, the Spirit within the body, was not born in sin. Whilst on earth Christ magnified the law making it honourable, clearly and easily demonstrating that without sin life could be lived within the law of God. What the law did, as Paul so eloquently put it, was to show up the hereditary and personal sin within fallen man. The law was the plumb line that showed up all the defects. It was only by living a life in the <u>likeness</u> of sinful flesh that the Messiah could legitimately bear all the sins of the people on the cross. An innocent man killed for the sake of my sinful state and yours.

When he started His ministry He did not stand out from the crowd because He did not come to the earth to enhance the Godhead, which had already over the history of man shown its sovereignty and overwhelming power and authority, also its love and mercy. Christ Jesus came to give the chosen people a message from the Father and to provide that once and for all sacrifice that would bring man and God together in joyful unity.

He was despised and rejected;
a man of suffering and acquainted with deepest grief;
embarrassed we turned out backs on Him.
He was despised, and we did not care.

The opposition experienced by the Lord Jesus Christ was understandable because the religious class could not align the scriptures with this man who did not fit into any of the various moulds of men of the time. They assumed He was the son of Joseph and Mary, for God had kept the actual date of the planned arrival of His Son on the earth a secret until His birth. The authorities were totally unaware of the method God used for His son to come to the earth and the place of His birth, even though the prophets had provided much of this information through prophetic utterances. However, the cattle stall was the last place the authorities would have guessed for the arrival of the Son of the Living God. No grand palace, no servants, no interference from men, just their awesome, almighty and eternal God arriving on planet earth in the simplest and most inconspicuous, self-deprecating way possible to demonstrate His humility and grace. After all He Himself declared to

His disciples more than once that He had come to serve not to be served.

Surely there was no better way of demonstrating that Jesus Christ, Son of God, Son of Man had not come to enhance or prove the sovereignty of God, but to come as a servant, therefore if He had come to serve, all those called to serve Him must do the same. As the Lord told His disciples whoever desires to be great among you must be the servant of all.

Without carefully studying the scripture with the guidance of the Holy Spirit no one would have any idea of where He had come from or where He was born or any of the other events in the young child's life post dedication in the temple eight days after His birth. God had chosen to do things quietly His way, which means that if we want to understand what God is all about we must spend time with God in prayer with minds open to the leading of the Holy Spirit in private. Preconceived ideas are an impediment.

At His human birth God drew despised Gentiles (wise men) and despised shepherds to His Son now born in flesh, of whose testimony no one took any notice. So the Jewish religious leaders had no idea of His heritage. The fact that it was all in the scriptures they so assiduously studied if only they had the time and tenacity and willingness through prayer to find all the references and join them together, but the availability of that God focused process seemed to have escaped them.

Full of pomposity and pride the religious leaders (Pharisees, Sadducees, priests and high priest) thought they knew all there was to know about their scriptures and, believing that this man was not of the scholarly class, the religious elite, they assumed Him to be unlearned, in fact they were made particularly angry when He seemed to know more about the scriptures than they did. He even took them to task about their interpretation of those scriptures, something that did not normally happen and because it was done in public when they challenged Him they were made to look stupid, seriously hurting their pride.

Because of their lack of understanding concerning the spiritual nature of God, it was not possible for them to be in-tune with God through the Spirit of God, therefore it was no wonder they were so far from the truth, always asking for a sign when only the sign of Jonah would be given, and even this they could not understand. The three days Jonah spent in the belly of the fish was a prophetic sign that the Christ would be three days in the tomb, which also confirmed the validity of the account of that prophet. They just did not believe He was the Christ, the long promised Messiah.

Surely he has taken upon himself our infirmities
and carried our diseases;

When the first man was created and placed in the Garden of Eden there were no diseases. It was that first man's rebellion against God's instruction that not only brought hardship but introduced ailments of many types. What the couple did not realize was that far from being an honest advisor, Satan was the author of chaos and turmoil, of mental disorder and the breaking up of all God had so lovingly designed into the human persona.

What we must realize is that with God there is no disease, indeed he has total control over all diseases, which is why He was able to heal the sick and mentally deranged and cast out demons. Sadly, when we reject God we open ourselves up to diseases and infirmities, which in Satan's hands abound.

Throughout their lives the Jewish people were given two choices. Be obedient to the will of God by obeying His Laws and the covenant God made with His people and He would bless them with a good life here on the earth with the prospect of a life with God for eternity, or be rebellious and suffer the withdrawal of His protection and desire to bless them, and an eternity in that place where God is never present, and as God is the one and only source of love it is not a place anyone would willingly want to go.

Consider the fact that it was not just Satan who opposed the creator God, but he took with him a host of angels, who in their rebellious state tried to oppose God, thereby causing mayhem amongst those they were able to influence, which was all those who had turned their backs on

God, Cain being the first to do so.

When the Lord Jesus Christ came to the earth it was to take on those diseases, for it was He who healed the sick and exorcized demonic powers that had enslaved their victims.

yet we considered His sufferings were punishment from God caused by His own wrong doing,

Indeed our first thought when someone is suffering some malady or other is "what have they done to deserve that?" (consider John 9). The taunts by His persecutors and accusers, "You who said you are going to destroy the temple and rebuild it in three days, if you are the Son of God save yourself and come down from the cross', how sad that they did not understand! But what would have gone through their minds when not all that much later the temple itself was made redundant with the tearing of the curtain and then its ultimate destruction by the Roman's. How many will have thought back to this time when the name of Jesus was being worshipped and glorified, and the number of His followers grew and grew and miracles were performed that had not be performed prior to His ministry. We are unlikely to ever know.

What the Messiah suffered with all the opposition and public murmurings against Him were from sinners and haters of God, so many unwittingly so, such as the likes of Nicodemus before his conversion and Saul before he became Paul. The Pharisees thought they were pure by obeying all the rules, but as Paul was brought to recognized all his efforts to obey the law were of no avail and it was only the Messiah dying on the cross that cleansed him from all sin, which is why he promoted the cross of Christ, the central theme of which is that it is the only way for man to receive the forgiveness of sins.

Writing to the Galatians Paul said, *"For those who depend on works according to the law to make them right with God are under a curse for as the scripture says cursed is everyone who does not continue in all things written in the book of the law to do them",* whereas, *"Christ has redeemed us from the curse of the law, having become for us a curse by being hung on a tree".* Then again to the Corinthians, *"For the message of the cross is foolishness to those who are perishing, but to us who are being saved it is the power of God.*

> *But he was wounded because of our rebellion,*
> *crushed for our sins;*
> *all the punishment he received made us whole,*
> *through the scourging He received we are healed.*

Just think about this matter for a moment. This is central to the whole gospel message received by a prophet of God in Israel a good 700 years before the arrival of the Messiah. The intensity of God's hatred of sin, the rebellion of man, which so effectively and completely destroyed His loving design for man on the earth, was displayed by the severity of the treatment metered out to God's own Son, surely it must have broken the Father's heart to have His Son go through such cruel and degrading suffering. The trials, the whipping with barbed whips making His back like a ploughed field, the sleep deprivation and then the ignominy of having to carry the cross to which He would be nailed and suffer for six hours watched by a mostly hostile crowd whipped up by the religious leaders Satan had so effectively enraged. This pure and sinless man became sin for us. Do you the reader take this as seriously as you should? Do you appreciate the severity of His suffering for us, and be in no doubt His physical suffering was intense both spiritual and physical.

It was not because he had sinned, but because of our sin that He went through all that murderous suffering. This was man at his cruelest, with all that Satan stimulated anger being directed at the Son of God, the Jewish Messiah promised throughout the history of the people of Israel. Sadly the people who were there shouting abuse at God's Son who had come to save them from being rejected by God had no idea that in rejecting the message they had been given over three and one half years allowed the enemy of man to possess them, a fact that the people of today also do not realize.

It was because of the rebellious Israelites that He suffered, that is true, but the whole of mankind was contaminated with sin and therefore Christ Jesus suffered and died for all mankind, not just Israel - *But he was wounded because of **our** rebellion, crushed for **our** sins.* By being purged, Christ, the only man to ever have lived a sinless life, was making us whole and healing us because He was taking over all of our rebellious nature on our behalf because only one born pure could do so. Man dying for the whole of mankind.

By the time Christ had set off on the road to Calvary He was not in a good state. This is what Isaiah wrote in Chapter 52:13 – 15.

> *See, my servant shall prosper;*
> *he shall be highly exalted and lifted up,*

What we have to remember is that when He came to the earth the Messiah continually said that He was about His Father's business which meant that as the bronze serpent was lifted up for the healing of the nation in the wilderness, so must the Son of Man be lifted up in order for Him to draw all mankind to Himself. He knew when He finally set His face towards Jerusalem for that last time exactly what would happen to Him. That is why He sweated great drops of blood in the garden of Gethsemane, knowing the horror of what He was about to endure. Not just the torture, which was bad enough, but also the humiliation of standing before the leaders of His chosen people to be insulted and humiliated by them. As He carried the cross to the place of execution:

> *Many were astonished at him*
> *his face being marred beyond human semblance,*
> *and his appearance seemed barely human.*

But He also knew that after He had endured the trial and crucifixion His human body would come to life again but not as a physical but a spiritual body, the first fruits of those who would arise from the dead, as all believers will do one day, and He would return to His Father in heaven, that place beyond the creation. But first the horror of the cross.

Just to consider this whole bizarre unfolding drama, even though it is so familiar, is truly startling. Here we have the Son of the Living God who was Himself a member of the triune Godhead whose sovereign will was to create all that is seen and unseen for no other reason than He decided to do it. He had seen man become totally rebellious because of a senior angel, who wanted to be God, tempting His created man.

Knowing all that was going to happen He still went through with the creation and put in place a means of rescuing man (see my book The Tent of the Meeting) that would be fulfilled with the Son coming to earth to suffer horrendously, shedding His own blood in the process so that those who believed on Him would have eternal life.

The whole concept is bizarre but that is what has happened. Standing before the Sanhedrin was their long awaited Messiah. Impossible. God standing before men as a man being treated like a criminal, and all because of God's intense love for man? But he knew about the future marriage of the true church of born again, Holy Spirit filled believers, with the Lamb who died and rose again. All true believers in this life enter into a Jewish style engagement with God that is legally binding, waiting for the return of the Christ after he has prepared a place for us His bride. O so symbolic!

No wonder Isaiah was led to write:

> *So he shall startle many nations;*
> *kings shall stand speechless before him;*
> *for they shall see what had not been told them,*
> *and understand what they had not been told.*

Going back to chapter 53 we read:

> *All we like sheep have gone astray;*

we have left God's prescribed path to go our own way,
yet the Lord has laid on him
the iniquity of us all.

This in essence encapsulates the love of God. The people were to sacrifice an animal, to gain temporary forgiveness for a sin committed in ignorance, a covering over of their sin. In this case, however, because it involved the whole of mankind past, present and future, only a perfect man could be the sacrificial victim. What is important to remember is that the sacrificial animal could not answer back. What could the Son say? After all in total ignorance they were putting God on trial? But for the sake of mankind He had allowed Himself to be put in that position. At any time He could have called on a vast angelic host to rescue Him, but He just stood there saying nothing <u>in His defense</u>; indeed He had no defense because he was taking on the sins of the world and had to die.

He was oppressed, treated cruelly,
yet he did not utter a word;
like a lamb he was led to the slaughter,
and like a sheep before its shearers is silent,
so he did not open his mouth.

At no time did He utter a word in His defense because he had come to die, so the Lord Jesus took all the illegality and humiliation of the trials. What finally caused the first trial to result in a conviction was when the Lord was challenged by the high priest and in reply said to the Sanhedrin, *"From now on you will see the Son of Man seated on the right hand of power with God."* which the unbelieving religious leaders present considered blasphemy. A mere man claiming to be God was to them blasphemy.

But the main trial before the leaders of the Jews and then the subsidiary trials before Herod and Pilate were completely without any legitimacy, what is now termed kangaroo courts. They were a farce, a means to an end enabling the Jewish the authorities to have Him crucified.

By a perversion of justice he was taken away.

Don't forget Isaiah was writing this about 700 years before the events he was talking about.

No one was concerned he would die without descendents
His life cut short in mid life,
For he was struck down for the transgression of his people.

What was significant was that He, who had done no wrong, only healed the sick and set others free from demonic control and taught the people the truth of God without any deceit found in his mouth, was crucified between two felons who had been rightly sentenced, and then hurriedly taken down from the cross without ceremony and bundled into the new tomb of a rich man

Buried like a criminal
and buried in a tomb with the rich,

When we read the book of revelation it is clear that all this was planned before the beginning of the world. The scroll sealed with God's seven seals was what God intended to do all along.

Yet it was the will of the Lord to crush him with pain.
When his life is made an offering for sin,

Sin had to be dealt with to satisfy the purity of God, for He cannot look upon sin, it is abhorrent to Him, which is why the Lord cried out, *"My God, My God, why have you forsaken Me?"* knowing full well that His Father had to look away from Him as he took upon Himself the sin of the world, but it demonstrated the stress the Lord was under as He went through with the plan to provide us with salvation because it was the only time from eternity that the Son was separated from the Father. Imagine that.

There is a great sense of loss and sadness when a wife or husband dies after tens of years together or when a parent dies. But the unity of the Trinity is beyond our comprehension and had lasted from eternity. Suddenly the Son was separated from the Father for three hours, O what trauma was that.

John the baptizer pointed the Lord out as *"the Lamb of God who takes away the sin of the world" (Jn. 1:29).* And Paul writing to the Corinthians said, *"For He (the Father) made Him (the Son) who knew no sin to be sin for us, that we might become the righteousness of God" (2 Cor. 5:21).* This is why He came to the earth. To die for the sin of mankind as a once for all sacrifice. No longer was there the requirement to offer an animal sacrifice in the temple in Jerusalem for the Lamb of God had come to take away our sin by dying in our stead, a once for all sacrifice because He had come in the body of a man to represent mankind.

> *he shall have many offspring, and enjoy a long life;*
> *and the Lord's plan shall prosper in His hands.*

In Hebrew we read:

> *Christ came as high priest of the good things to come,*
> *Entering the greater and perfect tabernacle in heaven*
> *[the original of which Moses was told*
> *to make an exact copy on earth],*
> *he entered once for all into the Holy Place*
> *of the heavenly tabernacle,*
> *not with the blood of goats and calves,*
> *but with his own blood,*
> *by which he obtained eternal redemption.*

> *For this reason he is the mediator of a new covenant,*

so that those who are called may receive
the promised eternal inheritance,
because a death has occurred that redeems them
from the transgressions under the first covenant.

Thus we have:

.. a great high priest who has passed through the heavens,
Jesus, the Son of God, let us hold fast to our confession of faith.
For we do not have a high priest
who is unable to sympathize with our weaknesses,
but one who was in every respect tested as we are, yet without sin.
Let us therefore approach the throne of grace with boldness,
so that we may receive mercy
and find grace to help in time of need.

Consider the multitude of true believers in the Lord Jesus Christ both Jews and Gentiles who have been saved to the uttermost, their lives transformed from despair to joy. So it is true *he shall have many offspring, and enjoy a long life; the Lord's plan shall prosper in His hands* for these prophecies have come true, praise His name.

When he sees all that has been accomplished through his suffering
he will be satisfied.
And through that experience, my righteous one
Will enable many to be made righteous
For he will take upon himself all their sins.

We have the victory because of the sacrifice of the one who was to come, for He came and gained the victory over spiritual death caused by the sin of Adam. This was accomplished by Him dying as a man and then for His human body to rise, not as a human body, but as a spiritual body, the first fruits from the dead.

All those Jewish leaders who witnessed the execution of the Son of God believed that they had removed from their midst an irritant, one who claimed to be the Messiah but was an imposter. What was completely hidden from them was that far from being a disaster, a terrible defeat, what he had accomplished was the greatest victory the earth had ever known and will ever know!

What the haters of their Messiah did not realize was that the Spirit that was the Son of God could not die. His body did but the essential Spirit of the Son of God lived on because we are told that His Spirit left His human body and was then reunited with His physical body when it had been transformed into a spiritual body. This was beyond the understanding of those who wanted to rid themselves of Him, but He was so much alive that He appeared to Saul of Tarsus through whom the basic theology of the new spiritual church of the living Christ was established and will continue until the return of the Messiah. The battle against all the forces of Satan had been won, therefore Satan and the power of sin can never have the hold over those who accept Christ as Saviour it once did.

Therefore I will give him the honours due to a victorious soldier,

John, the disciple whom Jesus loved, had an experience whilst on the island of Patmos. He bodily, or in his spirit, was taken up to heaven and saw the Son of God in heaven in glorious attire, and then as a Lamb as though it had been slain taking the scroll that had been covered both sides with the plans of the creator before time began ready to open the seven seals.

and he shall divide the spoil with the strong;

What does it mean *and he shall divide the spoil with the strong?* What is the spoil? Surely it is the ability all believers have, that is victory over Satan and his demonic forces and a passport into God's resting place

As Paul wrote to the Corinthians:

The sting of death is sin,
and the power of sin is the law.
But thanks be to God,
who gives us the victory
through our Lord Jesus Christ.

And Isaiah takes up the theme:

because he poured himself out even to death,
and was numbered with the transgressors;
yet he bore the sin of many,
and made intercession for the transgressors.

In Hebrews we read:

Christ came as high priest of the good things to come,
Entering the greater and perfect tabernacle in heaven
[the original of which Moses was told
to make an exact copy on earth],
he entered once for all into the Holy Place
of the heavenly tabernacle,
not with the blood of goats and calves,
but with his own blood,
by which he obtained eternal redemption.

Thus we have:

.. a great high priest who has passed through the heavens,
Jesus, the Son of God, let us hold fast to our confession of faith.
For we do not have a high priest
who is unable to sympathize with our weaknesses,
but one who was in every respect tested as we are, yet without sin.
Let us therefore let us approach the throne of grace with boldness,
so that we may receive mercy

and find grace to help in time of need.

This is the victor's spoil, we who have been saved and elevated to the body of the saved, who are part of the spiritual building that is the church rescued from Satan's power!

THE VIRGIN BIRTH

Fully God Became Fully Man

We have been discussing prophecy and in particular the prophecy concerning the Messiah who was to come initially to be the eternal sacrifice for sin by being crucified on the cross at Calvary, outside the city wall of Jerusalem where God had focused His presence. The whole purpose of His coming was ultimately to die an ignominious death, taking on the sins of the whole world to satisfy the death penalty earned by the first man when he rebelled against the command of God not to eat the fruit of the tree of the knowledge of good and evil. God Himself, therefore, became the substitute sacrifice for the sin of all mankind.

What is of great importance, yet is more often than not completely missed from the conscious understanding of the Easter message, is its foundation at the time of the birth of the nation of Israel in Egypt.

Although the plagues God brought upon the nation of Egypt as signalled by Moses because of the rebellion of Pharaoh, ruler of Egypt against God's desire for His people to be freed from slavery, affected the whole nation, there was yet one more plague that would directly affect the Pharaoh and be so devastating that he would not just grant the release of the children of Israel, but urge them to go.

The children of Israel must first be prepared so that they did not suffer the same disaster that would engulf the whole of Egypt. As each family unit needed to be a minimum of ten members, according to the Jewish historian Josephus, small families were to join together.

On the tenth day of the month each family unit was to take a year old lamb that was without blemish (see Malachi 1:6 – 8) and keep it separated from the flock until the fourteenth day when, in the evening (between the time the sun started to go down and sunset – corresponding to our 1500 hrs – 3 p.m.), it was to be killed and its blood painted on the door posts and the lintel of the house (or tent) in which they lived as a sign for the angel of death to pass over that dwelling. This was the very first Passover which protected the firstborn of Israel.

It is interesting that Malachi foretells the arrival of John the Baptizer, and introduces the time of the final Passover celebration:

"Behold, I am sending my messenger to prepare the way before me, and then Lord whom you seek will suddenly come to his temple." (Mal. 3:1)

This came to pass starting with the priest Zachariah who had an amazing experience in the Holy Place, which was not a big room, as he was doing his duty burning incense when an angel appeared to him. What was particularly remarkable is that his section of priests were on scheduled duty that week and he had been chosen by lot to serve in the Holy Place this particular day and he and his wife Elizabeth were childless. That was God in action. Whatever the chances of this happening ordinarily is of no consequence but this was obviously God at work at the right time. However, having been promised by the angel Gabriel that his wife would become pregnant with a boy child, because he found it difficult to believe that his wife, who was well passed child bearing age, could conceive, he became dumb (Lk. 1:1 – 25). This became general knowledge because when he came out of the Holy Place he could not speak and therefore the people assumed he had had a vision.

For Elizabeth to suddenly become pregnant in her advanced years was another sign that something special was happening and that after the child's birth he was named John, not Zachariah as was the custom and Zachariah the priest regained his voice.

The same angel then appeared to Mary, an unmarried virgin, who was told that she too would become pregnant. It must have been a real problem for Joseph that his intended became pregnant for he naturally assumed that she had gone with a man when engagement for Jews was a legally binding arrangement and only divorce could stop the wedding going ahead.

This matter is very interesting because the bride of Christ is the spiritual church on earth, but the marriage does not take place until His second coming, therefore we who are believers as part of the church are engaged to be spiritually married to the Lord Jesus. But this arrangement is obviously not a physical arrangement, as between humans, but a spiritual one. Marriage is a serious affair. It is the giving of oneself to another with whom you want to be in an intimate relationship *'for as long as you both shall live', and our life after death is eternal.*

When a believer accepts Christ as their Lord and Saviour they are entering into a pre-marriage type covenant relationship with God, a commitment to be obedient to and serve God with all their heart, mind, soul and strength and exclude all other spiritual alliances, until the whole spiritual church (which is spiritual Israel) marries (is spiritually united with) the risen Christ at the great banquet. This is why there are a number of parables about weddings in the Second Testament.

Water baptism is symbolic in that the new believer dies to self and rises to Christ. The whole matter is that serious. It is all about total commitment.

Joseph, being a man of principle thought of divorcing Mary quietly until God told him that the child was His creation and for him to marry Mary so that she became his wife and the child would be born into a legitimate family, but Joseph was to have no sexual relationship with Mary to prevent the sinlessness of the child being contaminated.

Notice too that both John and Jesus were first born sons, in other words Elizabeth and Mary were pure for the birth of their sons John and Jesus (Yeshua in Hebrew), except John was born from a union of man and woman. This was particularly important in the case of Mary, who had never known a man, so that she was pure for the birth of the Son of God when He became Son of Man.

What is more the nature of His birth was prophetic of the manner of His death.

First He was wrapped in swaddling bands which Mary would have worn in case she died on the journey so that had that happened she would have been buried in clean linen. Linen was also a sign of royalty, so that the baby Jesus was acknowledged as being a king from the start. After the death of His human body He was wrapped in linen, as his mother would have been had she died on the journey to Bethlehem.

Second He was laid in a manger which could have been a hollowed out lump of stone, in a stable which would have been a cave. At His death He was laid in a recessed area on the floor of a hollowed out cave.

Thirdly He was visited by shepherds that looked after the sheep used for sacrifice who were alerted to His birth on a dark night, at a time which was a dark time for the nation.

In Luke 2:12, we read *And this will be the sign to you: You will find a Babe wrapped in swaddling cloths, lying in a manger*. The sign was not only about His birth, but that he was a sacrifice and the manner of His burial.

Let us further consider the remarkable birth process of this baby. The birth of every baby heralds the birth of a new person (Body — Soul — Spirit). But Mary was told that the child born to her would be called the Son of God, therefore the child would not be a 'normal' child in the accepted sense. Furthermore the Messiah, the promised anointed one, who was to be born of the virgin Mary, was not a new person for we are told that the Spirit within the body was not only present before the world came into being, but part of the triune God who created the world and all that surrounds it,

"In the beginning was the Word ...
He was in the beginning with God ...
without Him nothing was made
that was made ... "
(see Jn. 1:1 – 5).

So how do we link this knowledge with the birth of a baby boy born to a virgin chosen of God? Simply by accepting that, through the miraculous and creative work of God, the Spirit that was the Son of God at the time of the creation somehow came down to earth and fitted into the embryo of a baby boy developing in the womb of the virgin.

It is essential that we do not confuse the spiritual with the physical. The Messiah as the Son of God is an integral part of God and a Spirit being. Therefore He needed a human body to be born as a man on earth. The scripture tells us that, *"... a body You have prepared for Me ... " (Heb. 10:5 – 7)* The Spirit that is the Son of God had to enter the body that was prepared for Him in Mary, who was told by the Angel that she would be delivered of a son even though she was a virgin (Lk. 1:26 – 38) by the power of God.

There is no other way to understand the transfer of the Spirit that was the Son of God in the heavenly realm into the body of a child on earth so that He could become the Son of Man, for there is no doubt that He became a true human being, and accepted as such by everyone He met, even though He retained His divinity, which was demonstrated by the power he had over nature as well as the infinite knowledge of the scriptures and the authority of His speech and teaching (Matt. 7:29).

Thus instead of:
Human Body   Soul   Human Spirit

for the 'normal' baby, in the case of the Messiah we have:

Human Body   Soul   Eternal Divine Spirit,
also called the Son of God

Charles Wesley put it this way in one of his hymns:

Our God contracted to a span
incomprehensibly made man.

It is possible for us to understand the soul of man, but the soul of the Messiah is a mystery, for even His body did not rot in the grave (Gen. 3:19) but in rising again His earthly body, that His generation saw and touched, became the first fruits of all those who believe. That is, when He rose His body was transformed into a spiritual body, the first man to take on incorruption. (1 Cor. 15:35 – 57) Even though He had an earthly body yet He was born of God and was wholly spiritual, never carnal.

When the soul was originally created in man it was under the authority of the spirit that God had breathed into man. Man became a living being before God and able to communicate and relate to Him because the spirit took charge of the soul, which ensured the man showed the attributes of God in whose image he was made. Unfortunately, after man had sinned and the spirit in man had become dead because it was no longer able to communicate with and therefore relate to the Spirit of God, except in special circumstances, as a result the soul started to take orders from the body and became earthly or 'carnal', which means to be sensual, fleshly (Ro. 7:14).

All flesh has a soul. The original meaning of the word for soul 'psuche' is given in the Greek lexicon as "animal life". As far as fallen man is concerned, it is the person we are before our regeneration when God the Holy Spirit causes the rebirth of our spirit (Jn. 3:3, 6). The whole process of a repentant sinner being saved and going on to enter into a spiritual life depends on the inner change that retrains the soul to come under the authority of the spirit not the body. (Ro. 8:9) That is, we change from a life focused on the flesh to that focused on the spirit. But this is dependent on a realisation within the saved person of the importance of the new life he has been given through the Spirit of God that was made available through the sacrifice of the Lord Jesus Christ (Heb. 8:14; Ro. 8:14). This requires him to leave his old earthly-focused life and pursue a spiritual life focused on God that will lead him into a spiritual union with God that is able to get deeper and more spiritually aware if the person is willing to leave their interest and desire for the things of the earth to focus his attention on the things that will involve him in the things of God through his relationship with the Spirit of God. (Ro. 8:6 – 8, 10, 11)

Without this willingness of the individual to allow God, through an inner refocusing of the purpose and direction of his life, to bring about that all important transforming inner change (Ro. 8:12 – 13) then their regeneration into a renewed spiritual being will not progress for they will retain a life which has an earthly or carnal focus. (Ro. 8:14 – 16) This will either mean that person is accepted into heaven by the skin of their teeth, or will miss out on the spiritual future with God that they could and should enjoy (Ro. 8:17 - 30). (Watchman Nee in his book "The Spiritual Man" considers this matter in depth; it is a valuable resource for the believer who wants to gain a greater understanding of how we can grow ever closer to God.)

Thus the Messiah, who was fully divine, being the true born son of God the Father (begotten not made), became fully human through the reproductive services of Mary without His eternal spiritual nature being compromised. The body the Messiah received from Mary had been initiated in her by the unique and eternal creative power of the Holy Spirit (how the third person of the Trinity did this is beyond our understanding, but so is the creation of all that we see around us and all that is hidden from our sight). Even the miracles performed by the Messiah are beyond our understanding.

To provide a more complete understanding of this miraculous event we need to consider other scriptures that will hopefully make things clearer. Consider this abridged extract from 'Appendix A' of my work 'God Rescues His People : Birth of Nation According to Exodus'

> *"Sacrifices and offering You did not desire,*
> *But a body You have prepared for Me.*
> *In burnt offerings and sacrifices for sin*
> *You had no pleasure.*
> *Then I said, 'Behold, I have come -*
> *In the volume of the book [the First Testament]*
> *it is written of Me -*
> *To do Your will O God.'"*
> *(Heb. 10:5-7; Ps. 40:6-8)*

Verse 5 of Hebrews 10 is not a direct quote from Psalm 40 for the line

> *'My ears you have opened'*

which was achieved through persistent effort, has been changed to,

> *'but a body you have prepared for Me'*

which was necessary for the statement,

> *'behold I have come'*

to become a reality, for it tells of the coming of the Messiah in human form.

This is the obedience of the One who is written about in the volume (the First Testment). But why should we accept this interpretation of the verse in the Psalms? Because of the reality of the Messiah who lived on this earth and gave witness to the fact that the Father had sent Him saying, *"… And the Father Himself who sent Me has testified of Me …"*. *(Jn. 5:37)*.

With the Jewish leaders wanting desperately to kill Him because He broke the Sabbath rules, many of which they had created and imposed on the people themselves, and proclaimed that God was His Father, the Messiah told them clearly that they were unwilling to accept Him because they did not have the God they purported to worship abiding in their lives; they were in effect spiritually dead. The fact that they searched the scriptures diligently was pointless, because they were spiritually dead and therefore unwilling to seek after the true spiritual knowledge of God and thereby understand that those scriptures spoke of Him. (Jn. 5:39)

The Son, who existed before the world began, came that He might impart spiritual life to those who were willing to believe (Matt. 4:4) because He was Spirit and therefore spoke of the truth that existed in the beginning because He was there at the beginning. The Messiah was speaking from first-hand knowledge when He said that, *"It is the Spirit who gives Life; the flesh profits nothing ... " (Jn.6:63)* for God gave the spirit, that is life, to man when He breathed into his nostrils the *'breath of life'* (that is the spirit) which man then totally ignored because he allowed his body through his eyes to lead him into sin; therefore it is the flesh that carries in it the sentence of death through sin and it is the flesh that is sentenced to death for it is totally corrupt.

The physical death of the sinless Son of God has release the soul and spirit of man to be released from spiritual death through the process of being totally committed the God and by welcoming the Holy Spirit into their hearts which re-establishes spiritual communications between the individual and the eternal God. It is worth repeating that, *"It is the Spirit who gives Life; the flesh profits nothing ... " (Jn.6:63).*

It is the body of the Messiah that people saw that made Him the Son of Man and therefore suitable for sacrifice and it was His body that was killed, murdered on the cross, held there by His obedience to the commands of His Father and the love of His Father for the chosen race; but it was the spirit of the Son of God that rose triumphant, undefeated, taking with it the transformed body of the Son of Man when He ascended back to His Father, so that nothing was left behind. The body might have died but the spirit that was the Son of God (Lk. 1:35) did not die but went into hell to preach to the spirits there (1 Pet. 3:18 – 22; cf Jn. 5:25) and then ascended to where He had been before, accepted by His Father because of the marks on the hands of His physical body, and his ankles and side where the soldier's spear pierced it that He had received from men during the crucifixion.

There must be no doubt in anyone's mind that the Messiah, the anointed of God, suffered the full force of the physical agony incurred by the stripes and barbarism of the crucifixion whilst hanging there on the cross until He gave up His own spirit and the body died. The suffering was real and altogether what any one of us would suffer in a similar experience with the additional fact that spiritually He was separated from His Father because the Father could not look upon Him as He carried the burden of our sin. Such suffering is beyond our imagination or comprehension.

The cleansing we receive because of the blood He shed does nothing for the filth of the flesh, for flesh and blood cannot inherit the Kingdom of God which is spiritual, but it transforms the spirit within us which is made alive to the Messiah because of the work of the Holy Spirit (Jn. 6:63), giving us a clear conscience (Heb. 9:14, 15). The time will then come when we will put off the corruption of this body and put on the incorruption of the body that we will receive (1 Cor. 15:42 – 58).

As we shall see as we study the pictorial message of the tabernacle Moses produced at God's command, and the references to God's plan of salvation throughout the scriptures, there is within it the prospect of the coming of a Messiah who would save from their sins not only those of God's people Israel who were and are willing to believe in Him, but all who would trust in Him for salvation, and then rise again in glory.

The sin offerings and sacrifices were offered according to the law, but were not always offered with the right attitude of heart for them to be genuine (Is. 1; Mal. 1). The visitation of the Messiah was according to the Love of God and was completely genuine.

According to prophetic utterances the Messiah was born into the world to do the Father's will and demonstrate, for us all to see, what God has always meant by willing obedience. We know from the writings in the Second Testament that the Messiah throughout His life did not sin, but was fully committed to doing the will of God His Father (Matt. 3:17; 17:5; Jn. 12:28). Therefore being without sin from the beginning, being born through the Virgin Mary without any contamination from the sin of Adam, and being able to live a life without sin, the Messiah was able to take on the sin of the world and die in the place of man at the time of, and in the place of the Passover Lamb.

The body provided by Mary was the instrument God used to provide the perfect sacrifice for sin. It was the spirit of the Son of God who wore that body through obedience to His Father, assisted by the Holy Spirit , and carried through to completion God's plan of salvation.

TWO MESSIAHS?

The Hebrew scriptures contain prophecies about the Messiah in two completely different ways. In one case it is all about suffering and in the other He is triumphant. What the rabbis could not agree on was whether there was to be one or two Messiah's. This is possibly because they would not have been able to understand that the person Moses spoke about was to be none other than the Son of the Living God (Yahweh), in fact some still did not accept that although God was truly One God, there were three members of God: Father, Son and Holy Spirit. The paradox is that He has to be referred to as God, singular. God is one, which He is but in a unique form as we shall see later (see Appendix C).

Within their physical world and often limited spiritual understanding of the scriptures, the majority of the Hebrews were not really close to or inspired by God as were the prophets such as Isaiah and Ezekiel. This was made clear when Moses was asked to cover his face after he had been with God because of the reflected glory which shone; indeed there is much in scripture about the remnant, that is those Hebrews who focused their minds and hearts on the living God when all those around them were full of disbelief or self-imposed ignorance.

There were some, Judas Iscariot being one, who desired, from their own perspective, that the Messiah should be a warrior king who would drive the Romans, which were the occupying forces at the time, from the land and for the nation to be able to be free to govern itself again. Yet in the context of the scriptures that was not the purpose of His visit, nor was it the basis of their problem. Their lack of freedom and ability to self-govern finally came to a head because of the anti-God activities of the people led by the priests and Pharisees, the controlling factor being the unwillingness of the religious leaders to recognize their sinfulness and their desperate need of true salvation.

During their exile in Babylon when the elders of Judah visited Ezekiel, God showed him in a vision (Eze. 8) the depths of evil depravity to which the priests had descended causing the nation to fall to Nebuchadnezzar. Transporting him in a vision to the temple in Jerusalem, God said to Ezekiel, *'lift up your eyes now in the direction of the north.'* In doing so he saw, north of the altar gate, in the entrance, an image of jealousy (possibly of Astarte, the Syrian Venus worshipped with licentious rites and erected by Manasseh as a rival to Jehovah).

Again God said to Ezekiel, *'do you see what they are doing, the great abominations that the house of Israel are committing here, to drive me far from my sanctuary? Yet you will see still greater abominations'* (v6). In other scenes Ezekiel witnessed priests in a secret chamber worshipping wicked abominations and abominable beasts painted on the walls (vs. 7 – 12) and then other priests with their backs towards the temple worshipping the sun in the East (vs. 15 – 16).

What these scenes demonstrated was just how out of touch with God and how poor an understanding the priests had of God. Worshipping in a hidden chamber in the temple complex they thought God could not see them. Yet the scriptures speak of the majesty and mighty power of God (Isa. 46). David wrote of the all seeing nature of God (Ps. 139:1 – 13), and many other scriptures that were recorded for the priests to study. This is such an important point that affects each one of us right now:

O Lord, you have searched me and know my heart
And everything about me.
You know when I sit down and when I rise up;

you discern my thoughts from far away.
You see clearly the path I take and my lying down,
and are acquainted with all my ways.
Even before a word is on my tongue,
O Lord, you know it completely.

Where can I go from your spirit?
Or where can I flee from your presence?
If I ascend to heaven, you are there;
if I make my bed in hell, you are there.
If I take the wings of the morning
and settle at the farthest limits of the sea,
even there your hand shall lead me,
and your right hand shall hold me fast.
If I say, 'Surely the darkness shall cover me,
even the night shall be light about me,
for the darkness is not dark to you;
the night is as bright as the day,
for darkness is as light to you.

For it was you who formed my inward parts;
you knit me together in my mother's womb.

Surely this Psalm alone should have alerted the religious leaders of all generations to the fact that nothing whatsoever is hidden from God!

The heinous activities of the priests in the temple in Jerusalem were now coming to light. Ezekiel was telling the leaders that had come to consult with him that God knew all about their crimes against Him and it was their activities that had caused God to condemn them, allowing the nation to be conquered and sent into exile for 70 years.

As priests of Almighty God, the God of Israel, their whole purpose in life was to direct the people's attention to their God in penitence and to encourage their faith in Him and observe the first commandment which was to love their God with *all* their heart, soul, mind and strength.

Instead of total commitment, God saw priests dedicated to His service totally ignoring Him and worshipping forbidden things, believing God was powerless and could not see them.

If the centre of the worship of almighty God was totally corrupted by the priests responsible for directing worship, what possibility was there for the honest and pure worship by the general population of the God who had love them and blessed them to the extent that He had over their history? It must grieve our God that the same is happening in Gentile churches throughout the world today.

Just as the time came for God to punish the Canaanites for descending into such depravity that God could stand no more by sending His people in to take over the land from them, so first Israel and then Judah were to have their freedom curtailed and the final process started for the Messiah to come to the earth to provide full and free salvation, not for the Jews only but for all mankind.

Following the new start from the time of their release from exile, and a new, albeit far less glorious, temple being erected on the foundations of the glorious temple of Solomon that the priests had previously abused, the nation had to wait four hundred and ninety years for the appearance of John the baptizer, the last of the First Testament prophets and messenger announcing the arrival of the Messiah as the suffering servant. During that 490 years there was no word from God, no prophetic announcements.

The chequered history of the Jewish nation, oscillating as it did between faithfulness and faithlessness, did nothing to focus their attention on the fact that out of all the nations on the earth they were the nation chosen by the creator God to be His special people, which was a considerable privilege if they did but realized it. Nor did they fully appreciate the spiritual and almighty nature of God or mankind's intrinsic sinfulness and their need for a way of salvation only He could offer. This beggars the obvious question, "Would we have acted any differently had we been alive at that time?" It is easy to criticize, but how sure are we of our faith, and how close are we to almighty God?

Another unfortunate aspect was that the nation had become so insular and inward looking that they could not understand that the salvation God was offering to them was for the whole of mankind because all men were created in His image, not just Hebrews, and all men are in need of His salvation *"for all have sinned and fallen short of the glory of God." (Rom. 3:23).* What they did not comprehend is that they did not choose God rather God chose them, therefore their special position before God was not a right but a blessing and responsibility to be His missionary people to the world.

In the "Service of the Synagogue – Passover" these things are repeated:

> *"Blessed are you, O Lord our God, King of the Universe, who has chosen us from all peoples, and has given us your Law. Blessed are you, O Lord, giver of the Law."*

and

> *"Blessed are you, O Lord our God, King of the Universe who has planted everlasting life in our midst. Blessed are you, O Lord, giver of the Law."*

In Acts 11 we read of the opposition from those of the circumcision to Peter eating with the Gentile Cornelius and how he had to relate to them the whole account of God leading him from Joppa to go with the messengers Cornelius had sent him. In Acts 10:44 – 46 we are told that those of the circumcision who had come to believe in the Messiah were astonished when the Holy Spirit fell upon all the uncircumcised causing them to speak in tongues magnifying God. Sadly they had come to believe that eternal life was for their nation alone, yet why should they believe that they could receive eternal life whilst the rest of mankind went to hell?

Suddenly the Jewish believers in Messiah were having to come to terms with the fact that the salvation God had offered them was not theirs alone but for the whole world! Indeed the salvation they had been taught belonged to God, therefore it was His to give to whom he chose and was not theirs by right. They had not realized that through the example of the temple and its sacrificial services God was offering salvation to the whole of mankind, after all the outer court was open to Gentiles, which was why He told them to welcome strangers into their midst.

What the Messiah achieved on that Friday, the 14th day of Nissan, went far beyond what the nation had been used to when offering animal sacrifices in the temple:

> *For this reason He [the Messiah, the Christ, the Son of the Living God] is the mediator of a new covenant, by means of death, so that those who are called may receive the promised eternal inheritance, because only through death is redemption from sin possible under the first covenant. Where a will is involved, the death of the one who made it must be established. For a will takes effect only at death, since it is not in force as long as the one who made it is alive. For this reason not even the first covenant was inaugurated without blood. When Moses announced every commandment to all the people in accordance with the law, he took the blood of calves and goats, with water and scarlet wool and hyssop, and sprinkled both the scroll itself and all the people, saying, 'This is the blood of the covenant that God has ordained for you.' And in the same way he sprinkled with the blood both the tent and all the vessels used for worship. Indeed, under the law almost everything is purified with blood, and without the shedding of blood there is no forgiveness of sins.*
>
> *Thus it was necessary for the [temple and all it contained which were] copies of the heavenly things to be purified with these,*
> *but the heavenly things themselves need better sacrifices.*
>
> *Christ did not enter a sanctuary made by human hands, a mere copy of the true one, but he entered into heaven itself, now to appear in the presence of God on our behalf. Nor was it necessary to offer*

himself again and again, as the high priest entered the Holy Place year after year with the blood of another; for then he would have had to suffer again and again since the foundation of the world. But as it is, he has appeared once for all at the end of the age to remove sin by the sacrifice of himself.

And just as it is appointed for mortals to die once, and after that the judgement, so Christ, having been offered once to bear the sins of many, will appear a second time, not to deal with sin, but to save those who are eagerly waiting for him. (Heb. 9:15 – 28)

The whole of mankind, in the bodies of Adam and Eve, was condemned to spiritual death, cut off from God because of Adam's disobedience which was accounted for as sin, and the result of sin is spiritual death. To enable man to receive forgiveness and keep his relationship with God alive, God provided the substitute animal sacrifice, and that sacrifice-for-sin was crucial to man's relationship with God.

Abel offered the first recorded perfect sacrifice of a lamb and his sacrifice was accepted by God, whereas Cain offered what was imperfect, because it was the product of his own labour. Scripture is very clear on this matter, *"without the shedding of blood there can be no forgiveness of sins" (Heb. 10:22)*, therefore Cain's sacrifice was rejected causing him to remain in his sinful state. His refusal to obey God's instructions caused him to remain separated from God; after all it was man who sinned by breaking the creator God's rules, for which there was a prescribed penalty and a means of receiving forgiveness. What we must remember is that both the penalty and the means of receiving forgiveness belong to God who is the person against whom man sinned.

The question that needs to be asked is, "If the forgiveness of sin is so crucial to man's active personal relationship with God, why then did the Jews want a warrior king to come?" Sin had first to be dealt with once and for all before the status of the Jews before the nations of the world could be dealt with. Yes they had been chosen, but chosen for a particular task that they had failed to properly perform as God had desired because of their doubts and rebellions and unfaithfulness. They had got their priorities all wrong and it could be asked if the church has not fallen by the wayside for the same reasons. It is so easy to criticize from the sidelines, but we need to closely examine our own thoughts, motives and attitudes towards God and others. "Are we perfect?" I know I am not!

The priority, therefore, was to first end the continual slaughter of animals and for this a man had to die because the death penalty was against man himself. But as all men are born in sin, there was no one who could die for mankind. This is the reason God had to supply the once-for-all sacrifice, a man who would replace the ever changing human high priest, to become a high priest in spiritual places and someone who could be with God the Father eternally.

The promised Messiah who came was appointed by God the Father as the eternal spiritual high priest, just as Aaron was appointed thousands of years earlier as the first of many human high priests. The difference is that the Messiah, instead of offering animal sacrifices, gave of His own body to be the once-for-all living sacrifice, because He was:

- God incarnate and therefore eternal and pure

- provided with a human body uncontaminated by sin (provided by a virgin and the creative power of the Holy Spirit).

- able, through being God and aided by the Holy Spirit, to live a sinless life.

- able to serve as God the Father's appointed representative of the Godhead, and be the perfect human sacrifice require by God's judgement, that is the death sentence imposed by God on man because of sin, yet, because he is spiritually eternal, be able to overcome death, which is eternal separation from God, by rising again, something no other man could achieve. He also had the authority to speak directly to His chosen people the words of

God His Father. The teaching He has provided enables us to know and serve the Lord God of Israel far more intimately.

- able to die in the place of man in His position as Son of Man and as the Passover Lamb of God and as the eternal High Priest appointed by God, in place of the purely human and frail high priesthood.

- able to rise again from the dead. Don't forget that the Spirit of the Son of God entered a human body. What died on the cross? It was the body made from the dust of the earth (1 Pet. 3:18, 19), the Divine Spirit within the body, which cannot be destroyed, was still living, and it was that Divine Spirit that preached to the spirits in prison whilst His human body was in the tomb; those who had disobeyed God long ago whilst Noah was building the ark. Yet it was the Holy Spirit that caused the body of the Messiah to be brought back to life again, not as a body of flesh but as a spiritual body (1 Cor. 15:44); the first to be so raised to life thus He is the first fruits of those who will be called up to heaven by God.

- able to ascend to heaven to return victorious to His Father from whence He had come.

Unless the spiritual element of salvation is understood, there is no possible way that anyone can even begin to understand the Easter message.

What point is there, as the Jews wanted, seeking for a man to bring earthly freedom through physical conflict, when man has a limited life span and even the earth itself will not last forever? History has proved territory on the earth has changed hands many times over throughout the history of man, therefore any territory gained can easily be lost by a later generation. Consider what Moses taught the people about the need for obedience (Deut. 30:15 – 20). This is such an important point that it is worth reading the choice Moses put before the people there in the wilderness

> *Today I have set before you the choice between prosperity and disaster, between life and death. If you obey the commandments of the Lord your God that I am commanding you today, by loving the Lord your God, walking in his ways, and observing his commandments, decrees, and ordinances, then you shall live and become numerous, and the Lord your God will bless you in the land to which you are going to possess.*
>
> *But if your heart turns away and you refuse listen [to God or be mindful of all his laws], being drawn away from God to bow down to other gods and serve them, I warn you now that you shall perish; you shall not enjoy a long and prosperous life in the land that you are crossing the Jordan to enter and possess.*
>
> *I call heaven and earth to witness against you today that I have set before you life and death, blessings and curses. Choose to love the Lord your God, obey him, and hold fast to him so that you and your descendants may live a joyous, long and prosperous life in the land that the Lord swore to give to your ancestors, to Abraham, to Isaac, and to Jacob.*

Providing the people lived their lives according to the commandments of God and worshipped Him as their God and held firm to Him, they were free to live their lives as they thought best. Why worship gods that were human design weird creatures when they could love and worship the living God and enjoy His blessings and be prosperous and happy. It was because they did not do that that they found themselves under the yoke of others. The choice for them as it is with us is to choose either life or death (v. 19).

Yet spiritually awakened man attuned to God enjoys His power and protection and an eternal future that is not anchored to the earth.

For Satan reigns in the hearts of all those without God, and Satan, who has never created anything, brings to his followers, whether conscious followers or not, conflict and chaos, as we have seen from the endless human conflicts around the world over the centuries, and still experience them today.

The whole matter of man's earthly situation is bound up in his relationship with the creator God and God's requirement for justice. Without the forgiveness of sin no man has a future, other than eternal spiritual death. Therefore the continuing and essential purpose of Easter and the death of the Lamb of God is to provide that way of eternal salvation that will allow the repentant sinner to get back into a relationship with God securing his eternal future.

The matter of sin had to be dealt with once and for all, which required a suffering servant to come first. Only when sin had been finally and decisively dealt with could the same Messiah make His triumphal appearance. The fact that the eternal God incarnate came and was triumphant in dealing with sin, thus demonstrating His great power, gives us confidence that His coming again in glory to rule over the earth will be far more significant. Indeed it will be glorious!

Having surrounded themselves with books, written by men, on how to interpret their scriptures, the learnéd men of each generation of Israelites could not possibly have had the conceptual capacity to understand the Messiah's power over life, or how, as a Spirit, He was able to inhabit a human body produced by a virgin, live a pure life and then die yet live again, because it was not until He came and demonstrated His power to the people and leave a record via the disciples that such things were possible; because it was all so new to them.

We must therefore give credit to those who first believed in the Messiah because of who they believed He was, especially the disciples (Jn. 1:44 – 51). For consider what the Lord said about eating His flesh and drinking His blood? With the guidance of the Holy Spirit we are more able to understand that what He meant was that His flesh and blood represented all that He was, the Word made flesh, therefore by eating and drinking of the Word we will live spiritually more effective lives. Our lives in communion with the living Christ can be likened to the Israelites in the wilderness because that was their training school in preparation for their time in the promised land. It is how determined we are to not only live in loving obedience to the Lord, but how committed we are to also serve Him. Sadly during the wilderness years and at the time of the disciples many stopped believing in Him because it went against all that they had grown up to believe.

We who study the scriptures have a distinct advantage over those who have gone before because of all the good teaching that is available and better understanding of the scriptures, although even believers today find it all a very difficult concept to understand. Also there is much errant liberal teaching in the churches that is adding to their confusion.

The appearance of a Messiah was expected to be just an ordinary individual, born in the normal way to a father and mother, yet become specially anointed like Moses, even though they had never collectively entertained previous prophets with much enthusiasm (Matt. 23:29 – 36).

However, the life and work of the Messiah could only be achieved by God Himself appearing as a man because of the way in which He was able to have complete power over His life, over the natural elements and over sickness and disease and, most significantly, know the scriptures in the way He did, because He had caused them to be written.

As we read and study the life of the Messiah it becomes clear that this is the only way the perfection that is God could come to earth in the form of man to be our substitute to pay the price of sin, because even though the body He assumed died, His eternal Spirit did not and therefore victory over death was assured. It was not merely a case of a man dying that brought about eternal salvation, rather it was His ability to die and then rise again in the same body that had been changed by God into a spiritual body, that gave victory over sin and death.

The Son of God as the Messiah had to come as a man, experience all the problems, temptations and limitations of men, preach with greater power and insight into the things of God than any human scholar, allow His physical body to be killed and then, because the Spirit within the body can never die because God cannot die, for the body to rise again, not as a physical body, but as a spiritual body having been transformed whilst in the tomb, prove to His closest friends that He really was alive and then ascend to be with His Father (1 Cor. 15:42 – 45), having commissioned His disciples to preach and baptize in His name those who receive their message as the Holy Spirit enabled them.

It was only by the Messiah being God that death could not hold Him because He, along with the Holy Spirit, who was with Him continually, had complete power over both life and death, and He was able to return from where He had come and sometime in the future, at the time the Father decides, to return to the earth, not to suffer again but to be triumphant over all created life.

Much of the transcript of events as recorded in the early chapters of John's gospel speaks of the spiritual nature of the Messiah. Therefore let us carefully consider two old testament passages that will shed light on this matter.

Suffering Servant Messiah

Isaiah 53 — *Who has believed our report? And to whom has the arm of the Lord been revealed? (v1)*

Like many of the other prophets, Isaiah was not taken seriously (Matt. 23 esp. vvs. 27 – 39; cf. Ps. 118:26a; Zech. 12:10). *"Who has believed our report?"* cries the prophet.

The Hebrew scriptures make clear that throughout the life of the nation of Israel only a remnant believed God and were willing to be obedient to His word. *"And to whom has the arm of the Lord been revealed?"*, with the word *arm* meaning power, it was as though the prophet was propelled to the time of Messiah's appearance and was deeply moved and saddened by how few really believed in Him. Paul, taking up Isaiah's message, writes to the Romans:

> *"But not all have obeyed the good news of the gospel;*
> *for Isaiah says, 'Lord, who has believed our message?'*
> *So faith comes from what is heard,*

and what is heard comes through the word of Christ."
(Rom. 10:16, 17 —consider the whole of Rom. 10).

The Jewish leaders did not believe in the Messiah, mostly because they did not receive the scriptures in spirit and in truth, yet Anna and Simeon recognized Him even when He was a baby because the Holy Spirit was in them. We have already considered the manner of the birth of John the Baptizer and Jesus and the prophecies recorded in the First Testament telling the manner of their coming and the fact that the first would proclaim the appearance of the second. The ministry of John was very public and the manner of his preaching regarding the need to be baptized and renewed in their relationship to God was clear enough had the leaders of the Jews taken the trouble of searching the scriptures in a way that allowed the Spirit of God to lead them in their search. John the baptizer was clearly His forerunner and herald, even quoting the word of Isaiah in reply to their questions:

"I am the voice of one crying out in the wilderness,
"Make straight the way of the Lord""
(Is. 40:3; Matt. 3:3; John 1:23).

However, many of the ordinary people did believed in Him, not being burdened with the truth obscuring teaching of the ancients, and were baptized unto repentance, having been told about the One coming after him who would baptize not with water but with the Holy Spirit. Malachi announced John's arrival thus

See, I am sending my messenger
to prepare the way before me,
and the Lord whom you seek
will suddenly come to his temple.
The messenger of the covenant
in whom you delight—indeed,

he is coming, says the Lord of hosts.
(Mal. 3:1)

However, in the very next statement he warned the people that the Lord's arrival would introduce a time of testing:

But who can endure the day of his coming,
and who can stand when he appears?
(Mal. 3:2)

Those sent by the Pharisees questioned John about his ministry and he told them that he was the voice of one crying out in the wilderness to make straight the way of the Lord. Yet they pestered him for more clarification, clarification that they could find in their scriptures. One of the problems today is that there are so many books written on scripture that there is a danger of believing what is written by men rather than that which is written on instruction from God.

They asked him, 'Why then are you baptizing if you are neither the Messiah, nor Elijah, nor the prophet?' John answered them, 'I baptize with water but here among you stands one whom you do not know, the one who is coming after me and will soon begin His ministry; I am not worthy as a slave to untie the thong of his sandal.'
This took place in Bethany across the Jordan where John was baptizing.
The next day he saw Jesus coming towards him and declared, 'Look there is the Lamb of God who takes away the sin of the world! This is he of whom I said, "After me comes a man who ranks ahead of me because he existed long before me." I did not know him; but God sent me to with water in order that he might be revealed to Israel.'
And John testified, 'I saw the Spirit descending from heaven like a dove, and it remained on him. I did not know him, but the one who sent me to baptize with water said to me, "He on whom you see the Spirit descend and remain is the one who baptizes with

the Holy Spirit." And I have seen and have testified that this is the Son of God.'
(Jn. 1:25 – 34)

For those well versed in the scriptures what John told them should have resonated with them, but although they confessed to searching the scriptures it was a mechanical affair so that they understood what they wanted to understand or were told. Those sent from the Pharisees were so obviously deplorably deficient in their knowledge of scripture that they went away empty.

At the beginning of all my books there is the recommendation that everything they contain must be check with scripture. There are no direct quotes in any of the books for although reference books and others by known Christian authors are read, time for meditation and the study of the word of God always prefaces anything written, therefore as I write I am plugged into the Spirit of God, although because of sin nothing I write can possibly be declared totally accurate because I am a sinner saved by grace, which is why the reader is urged seek the guidance of God's Holy Spirit.

All the signs were there. Seeing John and listening to what he was teaching them confirmed the scriptural prophecies to those who studied the scriptures and were open to God, as Anna and Simeon were, yet the Jewish religious leaders were not properly searching the scriptures under the guidance of the Holy Spirit to honestly try to understand what was happening. It was as though they were ignoring all the information they had available and were taking things at face value from a purely human view point. How many theologians and clergy, preachers and teachers today are merely repeating the mistakes of those sent by the Pharisees to speak to John?

We have the benefit of the scriptures, both First and Second Testaments, but are we truly studying them to be sure of what we believe? The wise men believed as did the shepherds; the disciples also believed, and of Nathaniel the Messiah said, *"Behold an Israelite indeed, in whom there is no guile (dishonest or of devious behaviour)"* and when Nathaniel asked the Lord how He knew him, the Lord replied, *"Before Philip called you, when you were under the fig tree I saw you"*, which impelled Nathaniel to declare Him as both the Son of God and King of Israel.

"Who has believed our report?", cried Isaiah to those who are truly God focused and have believing hearts, for it is to them that God speaks, even in these last days.

Isaiah 53 describes perfectly the human life of the Messiah. By comparing this chapter directly with the account in the Second Testament of the life of suffering of the Messiah, the similarity is striking.

Consider the case of another Rabbi, who, when reading the Hebrew scriptures with a Gentile pastor objected to reading the 53rd chapter of Isaiah, which was specifically given to the Jewish people for their enlightenment. This is Satan in action, depriving the people of instruction and knowledge written on God's authority by men inspired by the Holy Spirit.

> In the course of their reading they came to the fifty-third chapter of the book of the prophet Isaiah. Many Jewish people are afraid of this chapter because Christians say it describes the manner and meaning of the Messiah's sufferings, death, and resurrection, and Rabbi Gurland therefore asked Pastor Faltin not to read it. Pastor Faltin said: "I shall pray that God may give you courage to be willing to know His saving truth." From that time the rabbi could not help thinking about that remarkable chapter, and felt it was cowardly to be afraid to know what truth God had revealed in it.
>
> The following week Rabbi Gurland expressed his willingness to read the fifty-third chapter with Pastor Faltin. First of all Pastor Faltin read to him the story of Christ's sufferings as contained in the New Testament. After that they read Isaiah fifty-

three, which was written more than 700 years
before Jesus was born. Rabbi Gurland admitted
that the chapter was a perfect picture of what Jesus
had suffered and acquired for us at Calvary and
he eventually desired to confess the Lord Jesus
Christ in baptism. After instruction in the faith
the 33-year-old Gurland and his wife were to be
baptised.

The excitement and indignation of the Jewish
population was great when they heard that Rabbi
Gurland was to be baptised in Pastor Faltin's
church, and confess publicly his faith in Jesus.
Many Jews were so enraged that they wrote to
him that his baptism would be a disgrace and a
calamity to the Jews. They told him that a number
of Jews had sworn that if he dared to go through
with it, they would kill him in the church after
his baptism. Pastor Faltin asked the rabbi whether
he would not prefer to be baptised quietly in the
manse. "No," he answered, "Jesus the Messiah is
a living, mighty Saviour. He can protect me; but
even if He does not, I am willing to suffer and die
for Him."

When the day of the Rabbi's baptism arrived,
the Jews were greatly excited and the church was
overcrowded with both Christians and Jews. The
service went on quietly. The minister preached
about the Messiah who came to seek and to save
that which was lost. Before the baptism, Gurland
gave a short address, in which he stated how he
received the heavenly light through reading the
fifty-third chapter of Isaiah, and that he believed
Jesus of Nazareth to be the promised Messiah and
Saviour.

During the act of baptism and the rest of the service everything was quiet. Jesus had once calmed the raging sea, now He had pacified raging hearts. After the service an elderly lady told Gurland that for eighteen years she had prayed to God and pleaded with Him to save his soul.

The misinformation put out by the members of the Sanhedrin and Chief Priests after the death and resurrection of the Messiah to the Jews has had a devastating effect on the message Jesus Christ had come to give His own chosen people. But it opened up the way for that same message to transform the lives of millions of Gentiles. However we are warned that the time of the Gentiles will come to an end and then countless Jews will come to know the truth.

(An extract from my book Seeing Into The Future : Understanding the Revelation of John)

Prophecy Identifying Two Messiahs

Consider Isaiah 61:

The spirit of the Lord God is upon me,
because the Lord has anointed me;
to bring good news to the poor,
to heal the broken-hearted,
to proclaim liberty to the captives,
and release to the prisoners;
to proclaim the acceptable year of the Lord,
(Is. 61:1, 2a)

The Suffering Servant Messiah — This is what the Messiah had come to do during His life's ministry for 3.5 years. He brought good news to the poor, particularly in spiritual terms, to heal the sorrowing, to proclaim liberty to those bound in sin and release to those blinded by the darkness of errant doctrine then being taught by many teachers who were totally ignorant of the truth of God as revealed in the scriptures.

The people had become shepherd-less and no word had been received from God through a prophet for over 400 years. God chose this time to come down personally to teach the people the true word of God, a message He had received directly from the Father, and then to pay the full price of sin by giving His body to the smiters, who were those totally ignorant of who God is as ordered by those who should have known God personally.

What is so important to remember is that the Messiah knew all that would happen to Him from the start, which is why He was able to warn the disciples about His future traumatic death, tell Pilate that no human power had authority over Him, *"You could have no power over Me unless it had been given to you from above"*, and tell His judges about His return to His Father, *"Hereafter the Son of Man will sit on the right hand of the power of God"*.

When He spoke to the people, and particularly the disciples, it was God Himself in human form speaking directly to them. He who had been sanctified in Mary's womb:

> *"The angel said to her, 'The Holy Spirit will come upon you,*
> *and the power of the Most High will overshadow you;*
> *therefore the child within you will be holy;*
> *he will be called Son of God."*
> *(Lk. 1:35)*

which continued into manhood:

> *The child grew and became strong, filled with wisdom;*
> *and the favour of God was upon him."*
> *(Lk. 2:40)*
> *And Jesus increased in wisdom and in years,*
> *and in favour with both God and men.*
> *(Lk. 2:52)*

110

The most important factor in the life of the Messiah is that He did not do His work alone, *"The Spirit of the Lord is upon Me ..."* (v1), which was confirmed by the dove coming down from heaven during His baptism by John and the Lord's announcement in the synagogue, *"Today this scripture is fulfilled in your hearing"* (Lk. 1:35, 4:16 – 21; Jn. 1:32; 3:34; consider Ps. 45:6, 7).

If our Lord Messiah was inspired and directed by the Holy Spirit (Jn. 3:34 – 36), how much more do we need to rely on that same Holy Spirit?

Luke did his research and wrote down *an orderly account* of all he had discovered from the very first so that the recipient of his labours, the *most excellent Theophilus*, would know the certainty of those things in which he had been instructed (Lk. 1:1 – 4). Luke took the time and trouble to find out and then write his findings down in an orderly fashion for the instruction of another. This was something to which the energies of the religious leaders should have been directed.

Luke tells us:

> *"When he came to Nazareth, where he had been brought up, he went to the synagogue on the Sabbath day, as was his custom. He stood up to read, and the scroll of the prophet Isaiah was given to him. He unrolled the scroll and found the place where it was written: 'The Spirit of the Lord is upon me, because he has anointed me to bring good news to the poor. He has sent me to proclaim release to the captives and recovery of sight to the blind, to let the oppressed go free, to proclaim the year of the Lord's favour.' And he rolled up the scroll, gave it back to the attendant, and sat down. The eyes of all in the synagogue were fixed on him. Then he began to say to them, 'Today this scripture has been fulfilled in your hearing.'"(Lk. 4:16 – 21)*

The Messiah put the book down at this point because *"the acceptable year of the Lord"* had started with His arrival and would end at *"the day of vengeance of our God"* which would apply at His second coming when His final victory over evil and Satan would be accomplished.

Consider now the final line of the reading the Messiah had used in that reading in the synagogue, *"To proclaim the acceptable year of the Lord"*, but what was the acceptable year of the Lord? It was the 50th year, the year of Jubilee, during which year liberty was proclaimed to the captives (Lev. 25:8 – 10). It is here identified as a space of time during which God is pleased to accept all those willing to fully repent of their sins and turn to Him for forgiveness.

In this case it is not confined to a year, for we are given the time we are alive on the earth to respond to this open invitation from God. However it is also true that many are called but few are chosen because only a few will repent and live in full surrender to God in accordance with God's criteria for salvation. As at the time of the Messiah, many believed according to their own ideas of the faith. Remember Cain? How he would not offer the proper sacrifice for sin? So it was with the Jewish leadership that stoned Stephen and spread lies about the resurrection.

We must not allow ourselves to become complacent because at a time of God the Father's choosing the Messiah will come again in glory. Also Paul speaks about the time of the Gentiles coming to an end, *"I want you to understand this mystery:"* says Paul to the Romans, *"a hardening of their heart towards the gospel has come upon some of Israel, until the full number of the Gentiles has been saved."* Or to put it another way, there will come a time when God will cause the eyes of unbelieving Jews to be opened to the fact that the Jesus of Nazareth really was their long promised Messiah; at which time the focus will move from the Gentiles to the rescue of Israel.

The Victorious Messiah — Consider what Paul wrote to the Thessalonians who, by enduring persecution and tribulations with patience, were demonstrating the depth of their faith in Christ Jesus: and through that endurance were promised rest with Paul and all other true believers,

> *"…when the Lord Jesus is revealed from heaven*
> *with his mighty angels in flaming fire*
> *inflicting vengeance on those who do not know God*
> *and on those who do not obey the gospel of our Lord Jesus.*

These will suffer the punishment of eternal destruction,
separated from the presence of the Lord
and from the glory of his power
when He comes in that day, to be glorified in His saints"
(2 Thess. 1:7 – 10a)

The coming of the victorious Messiah is awaited by believing Jews and Gentiles alike, a coming that cannot be missed because of the spectacular way He is due to come, with trumpet sounds and an angelic host, not quietly at night before shepherds, but from out of the sky so that all the world will be able to see Him come.

PASSOVER

A boy child was born to a devout Levitical couple enslaved by the Egyptians. Although the edict from the Pharaoh was that all such children had to be murdered, this couple delighted in their newborn son and wanted to give him hope. The account of how Moses was saved and 'adopted' by the daughter of Pharaoh in defiance of her father's edict and brought up in the royal household as his people suffered, demonstrates the power of God over human authority. The story goes that he killed an Egyptian and had to flee the country and during his exile was trained by God as he tended his father-in-law's sheep until he was 80 years of age when he was called by God to serve Him.

That time in the loneliness and wildness of the wilderness, with just sheep for company, took its toll on his confident authority when amongst people, so when God commissioned him to lead His people Israel, Moses was none too keen on the idea and gave many excuses. Finally God won through and Moses went on his way back to Egypt and we know the increasing boldness with which he confronted the Pharaoh, initially using his brother Aaron as his spokesman.

The First Passover

Finally the moment came when God told him that the time was near when the Pharaoh would release them and in preparation God gave

Moses specific instructions for the first Passover.

In my book 'The Tent of the Meeting' I wrote this:

> The people were given strict and detailed instructions regarding the first Passover sacrifice with clear knowledge, since it was such a momentous event, that it was to be remembered by an annual celebration year after year in perpetuity. It was also made very clear that this first sacrifice of a lamb was to protect their first-born from the work of the angel of death whom God would send throughout the land and would finally lead to their release from captivity and oppression. Previously God had targeted the plagues at the Egyptian areas of the land thus protecting the Israelites. This time it was their task to protect themselves by acting in obedience to God's instructions.

- The time they were in was to be to them the first month of the Israelite religious year.

- Annually on the 10th day of this month each family was to obtain a lamb that was to be consumed three days later in the evening with nothing of the animal left over. Small families that could not consume a lamb in one sitting were to join with another family, or other families, and share a lamb; larger families would need more than one lamb.

- The lamb, of the sheep or the goats, was to be of one year old and a male (as for a burnt offering) without blemish, free from any defect (Malachi 1:6-8). The emphasis was that the lamb was symbolically innocent and free from sin.

- As the Israeli day was counted from 1800 hours to 1800 hours, the lamb for the Passover sacrifice was to be obtained on the 10th day but sacrificed on the 14th day which was three days later (10/11 [selection]-11/12 [day one]-12/13[day two]- 13/14[day three].

- The lamb was to be killed by the head of the household at dusk, between three and five, and the blood painted on the lintel and doorposts of the houses in which the people ate the meal. It was called the Pascal or Passover lamb because at the sight of its blood the angel of death would pass over that house leaving the first-born alive. It is this saving of the first-born that led to the instruction that all first-born must be dedicated to God, the first-born children being bought back with an offering before God, just as Isaac was.

- The lamb was to be roasted, not boiled, because fire represented purification and sacrifice. It had to be completely consumed (Jn. 6:53 – 58), anything that was left had to be fully consumed by fire with nothing left over for scavenging animals or birds. It was also to be symbolic of Messiah's death, for the Cross represented the consuming fire of sacrifice. Jesus was totally consumed on it because of His death. Not a bone of the Pascal Lamb was to be broken for not a bone in the Messiah's body was broken, whereas the bones of the criminals crucified with Him were (Jn 19:31-37).

By eating the Passover Lamb the people were taking unto themselves the salvation of God, there being no time to drain the carcass of all its blood. By eating the 'flesh' and 'blood' of the Messiah, His listeners were likewise taking into themselves who He was and the teaching He was giving to them. He was the living Word and Perfect Man who had come directly from God. He, although many did not realise it at the time, was central to their future life with God as the sacrifice for sin on the altar. By accepting Him fully into their lives, as with their intake of food and drink, they were assured of salvation and were free to enjoy personal communion with God as a priest.

There are, however, two parts to the problem of sin; our intrinsic sinful nature, which causes us to set our hearts against God, and our personal sinful acts in which we personally rebel against God. From the first we must be delivered, and this is done by the blood of the Messiah not cleansing our hearts but cleansing our conscience from dead works, that is works made dead by the sinful nature within us. With regard to the second, the blood is for our atonement, or at-one-ment with God, and is for God to see. Our spirits cannot become regenerated within us except we open our hearts to God in such a way that He is able to deal with both types of sin.

This Passover sacrifice was a sin offering for the first-born of the Israelite nation and had to be repeated year on year. Christ's sacrifice, on the other hand, is a once only, never to be repeated sacrifice providing the repentant sinner with full cleansing even to their conscience. As the first born of Mary His sacrifice was, and is, for all those who believe and accept that they are sinners in need of a saviour and who want to be freed from the penalty of death, whether Jew or Gentile. The relationship between the sacrificing of the Passover lamb and the sacrificing of Christ on the cross is that they happened at exactly the same time in God's calendar of feasts the Jews were to follow, fulfilling John the baptizer's claim that Jesus was the Lamb of God; but the blood He shed on the cross was an all-sufficient sacrifice for the cleansing of all the sins of those who would confess their sins and seek God for cleansing. None are turned away. Salvation is available to all.

- Bitter herbs were to be eaten representing the bitterness of the Egyptian bondage.

- The people had to eat the first Passover meal fully dressed, with shoes on ready to start their journey at a moment's notice, which is why the celebration of the Passover is with the participants fully dressed.

As Moses and Aaron began to instruct the congregation of the children of Israel the two men became God's ambassadors to both Pharaoh and Israel. This change in their role signalled the end of one relationship and the beginning of a new one that would last until Moses' death.

By setting this festival as the first festival to be celebrated at the start of each religious year, God was identifying the Passover experience:

- as the birth pangs of a new nation; a time when He, by His mighty power, separated them from the world (represented by Egypt) and its oppression in the form of sin (slavery). Israel would utter the cry of freedom on their release but the Egyptians would utter the cry of despair. The Passover was the culmination of years of hardship and grinding oppression. This was God in action; and for those who have come to faith through acceptance of the Son of Man, Jesus Christ, it is just as important to them symbolically as it is to the physical seed of those who finally left Egypt.

- with death as the basis of their freedom from the world and the cleansing of personal sin. The blood on the doorpost and lintel was only made available through the death of a lamb without blemish that died in place of the first-born. As they journeyed through the wilderness the people were required to continually sacrifice a lamb for an atonement of their personal sin; that was to restore their at-one-ment with God. This sacrifice for sin was to be repeated year after year until Christ's death on the cross, which represents the moment of our freedom from the spiritual oppression of the world. His is the once for all sacrifice that does not need to be repeated; for as we accept Jesus as our Passover sacrifice the Father sees the blood in relation to our sins and the angel of death (that is the second death) passes over us.

- as the gateway to the path that led to the Promised Land. All those who accept Jesus Christ as Lord, whether Jew or Gentile, become members of the redeemed, the remnant of Israel enter through the gateway that leads to a new life in Christ and the way to the New Jerusalem. We no longer look, as those who were released from Egypt did, to the land of Canaan but to the New Jerusalem that our Messiah, our saviour the Lord Jesus Christ is preparing for us (Jn. 14:1 – 11; Rev. 21:9-11).

- as the beginning of a nation that accepted Him as their King and God. All those who left Egypt were to celebrate this festival once a year without fail. But only those men who had been circumcised, and therefore identified as belonging to God, could take part. Slaves and servants were to be circumcised and guests who wanted to join in the celebrations also had to voluntarily be circumcised. This celebration was only for those who were born into the nation of Israel and had been circumcised by believing parents or who wanted to be part of this worshipping nation.

Israel was not just a nation but also a religion, for it had been chosen by, and was to believe in Elohim Adonai, the God of Abraham, Isaac and Jacob from whom they had descended. (Abraham is the father of all believers whether or not they are his physical descendents.)

No other nation on earth can claim such a heritage; that is, to have been chosen by the creator of all things seen and unseen. For them to be a discipleship nation to the world is unique. Their whole way of life was to be bound up with the worship and service of God. And of all those not born an Israelite who have come into the faith in this same God, God expects nothing less. We should not live like those in Egypt who are of the world and slaves to it, but unto Him who has called us just as Abraham did.

The sacrificing of the Passover Lamb was the most significant event in the history of the people of Israel! For the first time the symbol of a lamb without blemish, without spot, being sacrificed specifically for the salvation of individuals was introduced as a required sin offering before God. Previously it had been the patriarchs who had offered such sacrifices of worship to God; now it was incumbent on all members of the nation of Israel to offer such sacrifices, the Passover lamb being the first occasion.

The full procedure for the sacrificing of the Passover Lamb is laid out in the book of Exodus (see my book "God Rescues His People : Birth of a Nation According to Exodus") and had to be strictly obeyed.

By daubing the blood from the sacrifice on the outside of the lintel and door posts and the people closing the door and eating the sacrifice within so that nothing was left, they were telling God that they were believers, although events during their travels in the wilderness suggested that the belief of some was somewhat suspect.

The act of sacrificing and eating the sacrifice described what was to happen in the future when the promised Messiah would give totally of Himself, an all-consuming sacrifice, for He died with nothing left of His human life. But it also allowed God to bring death to all those families who did not believe in Him and were therefore of the household of Satan, with whom He was doing battle. Rich and poor, slave and free, all suffered if they were not of the people of Israel or those who had come to believe with them and had joined their company.

There are some other important conditions God laid out regarding the sacrifice of His Son before it was realized that it was the Messiah, the Son of God who is identified by all the prophecies. The full sacrifice of killing and roasting was to be carried out in one place and none of its bones were to be broken (Ex. 12:45; Ps. 34:20; Jn. 19:31 – 36).

The Annual Passover Celebration

The importance of the annual Passover celebration cannot be over emphasized, representing as it does the beginning of the nation's new life of freedom from the slavery from Egypt, and a completely new relationship with God that would be sealed at a meeting with Him on Mount Sinai at Pentecost, though not in the same year. The nation and the national 'religion' were the same, because their whole life and future were bound up in their relationship with the living, creator God who had called them out of slavery and into a new life with Him who became their God and King.

What was just as important as the people's observance of the necessary celebrations, such as Passover and Pentecost, and rituals including the sacrificial services introduced by Moses in the Tabernacle, was their faith in God, that is an ongoing living belief in the reality, authority and power of God, which was the one element of faith that could change their concept and acceptance of the rule of God in their personal lives and the life of the nation.

That first Passover meal was held at night. It was a hurried meal at which the people had to be fully clothed and ready to move out at a moments notice, and it saved the nations firstborn. With the blood of the sacrificed lamb painted around the door of the homes of the chosen nation, it was the firstborn of the Egyptian families and the first born of all other nations represented in the country, both free and slave, that died that night, including the firstborn of the Pharaoh.

The Haggadah — The whole purpose of the celebration was to pass on in a special form to subsequent generations what happened on the original night of Passover, a celebration based on the single Biblical injunction:

> *"You shall tell your son on that day,*
> *"It is because of what the Lord did for me*
> *when I came out of Egypt.""*
> *(Ex. 13:8)*

Tell in Hebrew is *hagged*, and *haggadah* means 'telling'. Put simply, this ancient ritual is the recounting of the story of the original Passover meal that initiated the nation's exodus from Egypt to the assembled household at the time of the Passover celebrations. literally in response to God's instructions to Moses that were recorded in scripture.

The Seder — As the lifestyle of subsequent generations of the Children of Israel changed, once they had settled into the promised land, so their remembrance of the night of Passover, which was celebrated religiously on the same night every year, gradually developed. The 'Seder' or 'Order of Service for the Night of Passover' continued to develop over the centuries to what it is today. It can only be celebrated by those men who have been circumcised.

The first Passover happened at night (important to read Exodus 12 and 13) so that it was during the night that the Israelites were ordered to leave Egypt, having consumed the sacrificial lamb fully clothed, the blood of the lamb having saved their firstborn from death.

> *"This day shall be a day of remembrance for you.*
> *You shall celebrate it as a festival to the Lord;*
> *throughout your generations you shall*
> *observe it as a perpetual ordinance."*
> *(Ex. 12:14)*

The Order of the Service — using a modern version of the service it is interesting how the Lord made subtle changes to introduce the central feature of the communion service we have today. What follows is a brief resumé of the service, but it is worth getting a copy of 'The Messianic Passover Haggadah' published by the Lederer Messianic Publishers of Baltimore, USA, and looking on web sites such as www.jewishfederation. org for more detailed instructions.

The Seder Plate consists of : six small bowls containing roasted hard boiled egg, parsley, lamb shank bone, chopped apples & nuts (the *kharoset*), horseradish root, bitter herbs surrounding a larger bowl of salt water.

Listed are the main points of the Passover service:

Lighting candles	Ps. 27:1	The candle is lit by a woman; the Redeemer, as the light of the world was born of a woman
Four cups of wine	Ex. 6:1	God's promise to Moses was to remove them from the yoke of the Egyptians, free them from slavery, redeem them with an outstretched arm and make them His own people becoming their God. Not just redemption, but a new relationship
Cup of Sanctification	Ex. 6:6	Recited blessing holding cup of wine in right hand: Blessed are You, Lord our God, King of the Universe, who creates the fruit of the vine. This was a cup the Lord could drink as He dedicated Himself to the service of His Father.

Washing of hands	Ps. 24:3, 4	The washing of hands before a meal is as important today as then; handling food that is to be eaten with contaminated hands could result in illness. The heart also must be clean because God can see in the celebrant's heart how real is their faith.
Parsley	Ex. 2:23	Passover is celebrated in the spring when new life appears. Parsley symbolizes the humble origins of the Jewish nation and spring. Parsley is dipped in salt water to remind the celebrant of the pain, suffering and tears during the years of slavery in Egypt
Telling the story of Passover	Ex. 1:8	Ignorant of the good deeds of Joseph, a Pharaoh arose in Egypt who enslaved the children of Israel, making their lives harsh through servitude and humiliation. The means by which God rescued the people is the basis of the Passover commemoration.

Three matzah	Ex. 12:34	Called by rabbis as unity — considered by some as unity of the three patriarchs Abraham, Isaac and Jacob; by others the unity of worship priests, Levites and people, but for those who know Jesus as the Messiah it represents the unique unity of the godhead of Father, Son and Holy Spirit.
		The middle matzah is broken. One half is returned to the pile, the other is wrapped in a napkin and called the afikomen which means either 'the dessert' or 'the coming one' which, being wrapped in a white cloth, can represent the Messiah's body as it was wrapped for burial because He was the Lamb of God sacrificed just as the Passover lamb was sacrificed.
		It is possible that this unleavened loaf of bread was used by the Messiah to represent 'My body broken for you; do this in remembrance of Me
The Four Questions	Ex. 12:26	1. On all other nights we eat either bread or matzah. On this night why only matzah?
		2. On all other nights we eat herbs and vegetables of all kinds. On this night why only bitter herbs?
		3. On all other nights we do not dip our vegetables even once. On this night why do we dip them twice?
		4. On all other nights there is no restriction on how we eat our meals. On this night why do we eat in a reclining position?

The Answers	Ex. 12:24	We were slaves to Pharaoh in Egypt, when God brought us out with a strong hand and an outstretched arm. If God had not brought our ancestors out of Egypt, we and our children and our children's children would still be subjugated to Pharaoh in Egypt. 1. As the children of Israel fled from Egypt there was no time for the dough to rise. Instead the heat of the sun baked it flat 2. Bitter herbs represent the suffering of the children of Israel during their time of slavery (Ex. 1:12 – 14). In eating the maror (horseradish root) it will cause tears to be shed in compassion for those ancestors who suffered in Egypt

		3. The children of Israel toiled to build, with bricks of straw and clay, cities to hold Pharaoh's treasures. This is remembered using a dark-coloured paste made from chopped apples & nuts. Having already dipped the parsley into the salt water, we now dip the bitter herbs into the sweet Kharoset (or Charoset), which reminds us even bitter situations can be sweetened by the hope we have in God. 4. The Passover was not a routine meal in the day of the family. It was a special meal held at night, as commended by God where the dibers ate fully clothed, ready to leave hurriedly on a long journey with no time for niceties. By reclining fully clothed with shoes or sandals on their feet the people could respond quickly to the call to leave their homes and start their exodus from Egypt.
Cup of Plagues	Ex. 6:6	Moses returned to Egypt once the threat of arrest had gone, to lead God's people before Pharaoh. To bring the Pharaoh to the point of releasing His people God sent 10 plagues, nine natural disasters and one against the people themselves including Pharaoh himself.

		God knew that for Pharaoh to lose his first born son, the pride of his life, at night when he was not in all his gold refinery or surrounded by his officials, his natural obstinacy would be at its lowest ebb and he would capitulate and release His people. A full cup is symbolic of joy, and at this time we are full of joy concerning God's mighty deliverance of our forebears, and therefore of us. The cup is not drunk at this time but a little finger is dipped into it for each of the ten plagues and the wine allowed to drip thus reducing the fullness of the cup and therefore our joy in remembrance of that turbulent time.
Passover Lamb	Ex. 12:13	The essential elements of the Passover are the: • Unleavened bread • Bitter herb • Passover lamb It was the sign of the blood of the male Passover Lamb that saved the firstborn of Israel from death when God passed over the land, and prompted the Pharaoh to release the people from slavery. It had to be roasted – representing complete death; not a bone was to be broken - the final Passover Lamb would not have any bones broken (because He had complete control over the death of His body); blood and water flowed from His side to prove His body had died; the blood is eternally effective in cleansing even the conscience of the repentant sinner through the power of the Spirit of God

		Since the destruction of the Temple in Jerusalem a lamb has not been sacrificed, so it is represented by the lamb's shank bone. The purpose of the temple was superseded when God appointed the Messiah as the eternal High Priest, and every believer became a temple of the Holy Spirit (1 Cor. 6:19, 20)
Afikomen	Is. 53:8	The broken half of the middle Matzah is brought to the table.
Cup of Redemption	Ex. 6:6	It is possible it was this cup that the Messiah used as the first 'cup of the new covenant in My blood which is shed for you'. Just as the blood of the sacrificed lamb saved the firstborn of Israel from death, so the blood of the Messiah can save the repentant sinner from eternal death.
Fourth Cup		This cup is filled for the prophet Elijah who it was believed was to come again. John the Baptizer was asked if he was Elijah returned – although he had the spirit of Elijah, he was not Elijah returned (Jn. 1:21).
Cup of Praise	Ex. 6:7	See Ps. 136 esp. 1 – 16, 26

PASSOVER / COMMUNION

God made the Passover central to His plan of eternal salvation where the sacrifice of the lamb is the essential feature. It is worth considering the four cups of wine that were to be drunk during the service to explain the message that it contains. Consider Exodus 6:6 - 8

1. *Therefore say to the Israelites, "I am the Lord, and I will:*

2. *free you from the burdens of the Egyptians*

3. *deliver you from slavery to them.*

4. *redeem you with an outstretched arm with mighty acts of judgement.*

5. *take you as my people, and be your God.*

6. *You shall know that I am the Lord your God, who has freed you from the burdens of the Egyptians. I will bring you into the land that I swore to give to Abraham, Isaac, and Jacob and give it to you for a possession. I am the Lord." ' (Ex. 6:6 – 8).*

The Four Cups of Wine

In the account of the Exodus God gave the children of Israel four prophetic promises. Confined within the borders of Egypt and oppressed by a tyrannical Pharaoh, seemingly without any hope of escape as a nation, God promised that He would (Ex. 6:6, 7):

1. Take them out from under the burdens placed upon them.

2. Rescue them from the bondage of Egypt.

3. Redeem them with an outstretched arm.

4. Make them His people so that He would be their God, which happened on Mount Sinai proving to Moses that He was able to achieve all that he promised (Ex. 3:12) and sealing His covenant with Abraham concerning his offspring. Moses made it very clear that the only way the relationship between God and His chosen people would work was if they were willing to submit to Him as their leader and ruler (Deut. 30:11 – 20).

In the course of the Passover Seder four cups of wine are drunk that correspond to those four promises. However it is interesting that God led the Israelites out of Egypt to fulfil His promise to Abraham to give the land he had travelled across to his descendents.

The timing was critical because it came when the sins of the Canaanites had reached levels beyond that which God was willing to tolerate. The additional blessing, therefore, was to bring them to the land he had sworn to give to the patriarchs Abraham, Isaac and Jacob (Ex. 6:8), because God knew how low the Canaanites would stoop in their godless lives and His desired to fill that area with a people dedicated to Himself.

There is a corresponding fifth cup of wine called the cup of Elijah, which is filled at a later stage of the Seder but not drunk. It is believed that the arrival of Elijah will herald the final and ultimate redemption. The possible reason for this is that Moses promised that there would come a prophet like himself from amongst them they must listen to (Deut. 18:15 – 22).

As Elijah was taken up to heaven without dying first, it is thought he would return as that prophet even though that is not what God had promised.

> *The Lord your God will raise up for you a Prophet like me from your midst, from among your brethren; take heed to what He says.* (Deut. 18:15).

It is interesting that John was asked if he was the Elijah or the prophet Moses had spoken about,

> *"This is the testimony of John when the Jews sent priests and Levites from Jerusalem to ask him, 'Who are you?' He confessed and did not deny it, but confessed, 'I am not the Messiah.'*
> *And they asked him, 'What then? Are you Elijah?'*
> *He said, 'I am not.'*
> *'Are you the prophet?'*
> *He answered, 'No.'*
> *Then they asked him, 'Who are you? Let us have an answer for those who sent us. What do you say about yourself?'*
> *He said,*
> *'I am the voice of one crying out in the wilderness,*
> *"Make straight the way of the Lord" ',*
> *as the prophet Isaiah said."*
> *(Jn. 1:19 – 23)*

John was confessing to the fact that he was the forerunner of the Messiah, the promised One spoken about by Moses, that is the meaning of John's announcement and reference to Isaiah. This is important because it demonstrates the attitude of the more hard-line leaders of the Jews at that time regarding the interpretation of their scriptures which, although they studied all of them in detail, they could not interpret them because they were not spiritually attuned to their God. This is the reason all but a few Jews still observe the original pre-Messianic Passover Seder, who still look forward to the final and culminating level of redemption. It is clear with the enquiry by Nicodemus directly to the Messiah that not all the spiritual leaders were totally insensitive to the leading of God, however the preponderance of the dominant and unbending chief priests and other religious leaders became the cheer leaders at the Lord's trial before Pilate calling for Him to be crucified.

This final cup is something to which they look forward because they believe it transcends all human efforts, raising them up to new heights of spiritual relationship with their God. Sadly they are looking forward to something that has already happened because their Messiah has come in the form of Jesus the Nazarene whom we Christians, both Jew and Gentile, worship.

The fifth cup cannot be drunk in isolation. Those who cannot bring themselves to believe the Messiah has come can only approach the threshold of this originally Divinely perfect world, through active realization of the first four expressions of redemption whilst awaiting the appearance of Elijah, who they believe to be the herald of the final and ultimate redemption. John the baptizer, although not Elijah, was the last of the First Testament prophets and he had the 'spirit of Elijah'.

The Last Passover

What is so incredible about the Lord Jesus Christ is that He knew from the start how He was to suffer and die at the hands of evil men and kept giving His disciples hints about what was to happen. After all He is the Word and that word was given to the prophets over the years before His arrival on the earth. He carried that burden from the beginning, but as the time drew near it will have inevitably been foremost on His mind.

Consider the moment when Peter, under the influence of the Holy Spirit declared Christ's divinity only to follow it with his own thinking:

> *From that time on, Jesus began to show his disciples that he*
> *must go to Jerusalem and suffer many things at the hands*
> *of the elders and chief priests and scribes, and be killed, and*
> *on the third day be raised. And Peter took him aside and*

began to rebuke him, saying, 'God forbid it, Lord! This shall not happen to you.'
But He turned and said to Peter, 'Get behind me, Satan! You are a stumbling-block to me; for you are not mindful of the things of God but on the things of men.'
Then Jesus told his disciples, 'If anyone desires to become my follower, let them deny themselves and take up their cross and follow me. For those who want to save their life will lose it, and those who lose their life for my sake will find it. For what will it profit a man if he gain the whole world but forfeit his soul? Or what will he give in return for his soul? (Matt. 16:21 – 26)

The meaning of soul is the character of the person which identifies them as an unique individual. It is not just the physical, particularly the facial, features by which we are identified, but by what we do and the way we behave, and in this we are not alone for animals have traits by which we can identify them as individual. Man's uniqueness is because of the spirit of God that is within them.

The Preparation — The seeds of the Lord's death were sown immediately before the disciples ate the final Passover meal. Satan had wanted Christ the Messiah dead and worked through many of the leaders of the Jews to bring it about but was restrained by God from achieving that goal until His appointed time. Many thwarted assassination attempts were made on the Lord's life.

Now, however, the time had come for His death and the biblical text reveals that Satan entered Judas Iscariot who met with the chief priests and scribes who wanted Him dead but did not know how they were going to accomplish it for fear of the people. Now Judas was giving them an answer to their problem by offering to betray Him in a way that would allow them to arrest Him without much fuss.

The authorities may have been rejoicing that at last they had the Messiah in their sights and would be able to silence Him once and for all, not realizing that the God they purported to worship was giving Him into their hands for the purpose of allowing the supreme sacrifice for sin to be offered at exactly the right moment according to prophecy. They were, in fact, carrying out God's plan, doing His will to achieve salvation not just for their nation but for the whole of mankind.

> *Then came the day of Unleavened Bread, on which the Passover lamb had to be sacrificed. So the Lord sent Peter and John, saying, 'Go and prepare the Passover meal for us that we may eat it.' They asked him, 'Where do you want us to prepare it?'*
> *'When you have entered the city, a man carrying a jar of water will meet you; follow him into the house he enters and say to the owner of the house, "The teacher asks you, 'Where is the guest room, where I may eat the Passover with my disciples?'" He will show you a large furnished room upstairs. Make preparations for us there.'*
> *So they went and found everything as he had told them; and they prepared the Passover meal. (Lk. 22:7 – 13)*

It had all been organized. God had done all the initial preparation and now it was up to the chosen disciples to do the rest. To the unwitting disciples this may have been the last Passover meal they were to eat with their Teacher and Lord, but it was also the first communion service administered not by a priest but by the perfect sacrifice Himself.

> *When the hour came, he took his place at the table, and the apostles with him. He said to them, 'I have eagerly desired to eat this Passover with you before I suffer; for I tell you, I will no longer eat of it until it is fulfilled in the kingdom of God.' (Lk. 22:14 – 16)*

The fulfillment and the coming of the Kingdom of God would be very soon coming, when the veil of the temple was torn in two from top to bottom, thereby decommissioning the Temple as God's dwelling amongst men. According to what the Lord said to the woman at the well

136

in Samaria, every true believer would become a temple of the Holy Spirit (Jn. 4:21 – 24; 1 Cor. 3:16, 17; 6:19, 20).

This was to be His final meal with the disciples and His eagerness will have had much to do with the final moments of His time on earth and the imminent establishment of a new relationship with God that was to be made available to all those who would believed in Him. No longer the formality of the temple, dependent as it was on the ministry of men. With the release of the Holy Spirit into the world (Jn. 16:7, 13) to glorify His name and make His sacrifice known, opening up the possibility of personal relationships that would be entered into with Him by individuals of every tribe and tongue around the world. This was to be the result of His sacrifice. Unbeknown to the authorities, the kingdom of heaven would suddenly burst upon the earth and the news of it spread around the world, initially driven by the persecution of the disciples and those who believed in Christ as the Messiah, aided by the power of the Holy Spirit.

The Last Becomes the First — The Messiah officiated at the last Passover which was required by God after the Israelites left Egypt to remind them about all that He had done for them when He rescued them from Egypt. Within that *Haggadah* (the telling) and the *Seder* (the service surrounding it) the Messiah used bread and possibly the third cup of wine, the cup of *Redemption* (although no information is given in the Biblical text), to introduced the first communion service of the New Covenant of grace.

The previous act of remembrance was all about remembering the time when God freed the new nation of Israel from Egypt, which was ruled by an autocratic and demonic Pharaoh, where they had been enslaved for 400 years. The new act of remembrance, is all about remembering the time when God provided the means whereby the whole of mankind can be freed from a World, dominated by Satan and in which they are enslaved by sin, thus separating them from spiritual union with Him, giving them access to the new Kingdom of God.

The difference between the old and the new act of remembrance was where previously the lamb was an animal, for this first Passover /

Communion, that is celebrated in remembrance today, the Lamb to be sacrificed was the One leading that last Passover meal. By using the unleavened bread and the cup of redemption of the Seder, the Lord was using the prophetic example of that first act of salvation, where a chosen physical nation was saved from physical and spiritual enslavement, to symbolically illustrate the new salvation which was all about believing individuals being saved from their spiritual enslavement to Satan and the world he dominates. It was salvation from both the strangle hold of the domination of earthly things and sin, which is rebellion against God, that the Messiah was introducing, and making available to all those who through repentance of sin gave witness to a true and abiding faith in Him .

The first Passover was all about being saved from the angel of death who was to cause the death of all the first born both from amongst man and beast through the blood of an blemished lamb painted on the outside of the lintel and door posts to the house. Passover meant that the angel of death would pass over any house with the blood as a sign on the outside around the entrance.

The second Passover was all about being saved from eternal spiritual death through the shed blood of the eternal Lamb of God. Blood that the Father would see on the head, hands and side of His Son and forget the sins of all those for whom the Son is their advocate (1 Jn. 2:1; see Heb. 4:14 – 16). All those who through repentance and faith have not just believed in the Servant Messiah, the Christ, the anointed One, but have submitted and committed themselves completely to His service. Those who, having been born again through the work of the Holy Spirit, have become spiritually alive to God and have had their consciences cleansed from deliberate evil thoughts and works.

The sin offering He was to offer was not just for the first born of Israel, but for all mankind; a sacrifice on the cross that was to release believers in the God of Israel from slavery to the world and sin and give them a new vision and purpose, with the Saviour being the Way, the Truth and the Life:

Then he took a cup, and after giving thanks he said, 'Take this and divide it among yourselves; for I tell you that from now on I will not drink of the fruit of the vine until the kingdom of God comes.'

Then he took a loaf of unleavened bread, and when he had given thanks, he broke it and gave it to them, saying, 'This is my body, which is given for you. Do this in remembrance of me.'

And he did the same with the cup after supper, saying, 'This cup is the new covenant in my blood, which is poured out for you.
(Lk. 22:17 – 20)

Because He was the Passover Lamb that would be sacrificed within a few hours after this Passover meal, He could not drink that cup of wine because it represented His blood that provided redemption from sin. We are no longer under the law but under grace (Eph. 2:1 -10).

Here we have first the bread of His body and then possibly the third cup of the Haggadah, although the record in Luke does not give any details and the current Seder could well differ slightly to that followed by the Lord in that rather special intimate meal. It would be convenient if the cup of redemption was offered to the disciples in the very first communion service but we cannot be sure.

All we can be certain of is that the Lord Jesus Christ gave bread to His disciples, which was symbolic of His body that was to be given for all of us. Then he instructed them to drink the cup for it was to be symbolic of the new covenant that was to be sealed in His blood when it was shed for us not many hours hence. His request to *"Do this in remembrance of me"* is still valid because it takes us back to the reason why we are saved to the uttermost

It was an intimate meal between the Lord the giver of life and those He had chosen to be taught spiritual truths, the leading religious academics of the day could not understand, in readiness for their future role as the leaders of the new born church whose founder He was.

SPIRITUAL BATTLE

Whether any of the people at the time realized it or not, things were going according to God's plan. Many failed attempts were made to silence God the Son, the Jewish authorities being constrained by their fear of the people and the powerful influence of God's Holy Spirit. But Satan was working behind the scenes through individuals and through the more dominant leaders to entrap and finally silence the Son of God.

The works of Satan

It was Satan who introduced the scourge of sin through deception. Since that time of Satan's personal intervention, he has trained many individuals to do his work for him, allowing him to remain in the back ground; unidentified. Indeed Satan has perfected the trick of having everyone pointing the finger to others saying they are Satan whilst being able to work unrecognized through many people, organizations and national leaders.

This what I wrote in my book, 'The Tent of the Meeting' about this fallen angel:

> God trusted man and gave him authority over all the living things of the earth (Gen. 1:26). At some time, however, in the spiritual sphere of God's creation

a rebellion occurred. An archangel referred to as Lucifer, called "Son of the Morning", who was probably the most senior and greatest angel God created, decided he wanted take God's place and be God. He is described as being the *"seal of perfection, full of wisdom and perfect in beauty"* (Eze. 28:12). Such was his radiance that he was said to have been covered in precious stones and gold, his musical prowess was with timbrels and pipes; this had been prepared in him on the day he was created. He was appointed the guardian angel for the world as it was at the beginning. He is said to have been perfect in all his ways, with unrestricted access to God Himself, and he wielded great power over God's angelic host (Eze. 28:12 – 19). Such was his power and authority that when the archangel Michael disputed with this same angel (the Devil and Satan) over the body of Moses, Michael did not have the authority to accuse him directly but called on a higher authority saying, *"The Lord rebuke you!"*. Although the passage in Ezekiel 28 concerns the King of Tyre, the reference to Eden, the Garden of God, gives the true identity away for it was this angel, Lucifer, who appeared to Eve as an angel of light to convince her that to eat of the forbidden tree was good and not really against God's instruction to Adam.

But how did this remarkable cherub, so blessed by God, end up by being brought so low? The text tells us that his heart was lifted up because of his beauty. It is worth recording here that in the context of scripture the heart is considered to be the centre of a person's will and intellect. Not satisfied with the gifts of looks and music and the position of power he held in God's kingdom, (which he received from God when he was created and did not have to earn it for himself), he wanted more and turned his wisdom to corrupting ways for the sake of his splendour. It must be emphasized that all that he had was not his by right; it had been given to him when he was created. It is essential for each one of us not to allow ourselves to be puffed up before God, particularly if we have an outstanding skill or talent for we have received it as a gift from God for the good of all men.

Confused teaching

Rabbi Aaron admitted to me that at one time he would look at a Hebraic scripture text and 'know' what it meant. His search for understanding was triggered when his brother Derek, who had taken the criminal path, became a Christian whilst in prison. After his release he came under my instruction and finally blossomed as a believer in the Lord Jesus. The books Derek had me write on scripture were copied to Aaron who was increasingly curious to learn more about why Derek had become a Christian. Some years and many experiences later he finally experienced his own moment of epiphany (which means a sudden and great revelation or understanding). It was the moment he finally met with Jesus Christ, the man from Galilee and his Messiah. In a moment his life was truly transformed, indeed he told me that I had changed his life, although it was not me but the Lord's doing. Aaron had that essential personal and intimate spiritual meeting with the Spirit of God.

From that moment every time he read scripture he would discover new truths. That was because he had been baptized in the Holy Spirit and the Spirit Himself was revealing new things to him. To have been used of God to bring a rabbi to that point was a truly awesome experience.

This is an extract from my book on Revelation, "Seeing Into the Future : Understanding the Revelation of John":

How has Satan been able to put forward confusing teaching? By getting eminent scholars to write learned papers that are then studied in detail in conjunction with and carrying as much weight as the Holy Bible. Take the case of Rabbi Leonard Cohn D.D. who was concerned that year in, year out he along with fellow Jews would recite one of the twelve articles of the Jewish creed,

"I believe with a perfect faith in the coming of the Messiah and, though He tarry, yet will I wait daily for His coming."

For thousands of years that prayer has been prayed, but according to Talmudic reckoning the Messiah should have long since come. So this rabbi, in fear and trembling because the teaching of 'the Rabbis' (who said it first is probably not known) says, *"Cursed are the bones of him who calculates the time of the end"*, started to study the word of God part one and reached the book of Daniel.

When he read the ninth chapter (of Daniel), light began to dawn upon him. He had struck a mine of hitherto concealed truth, covered up by the commentaries of the revered doctors of the law. From the twenty-fourth verse of the chapter before him he deduced without difficulty that the coming of the Messiah should have taken place 400 years after Daniel received from the divine messenger the prophecy of the Seventy Weeks.

The scholar, accustomed to the intricate and often veiled polemical treatises of the Talmud, now found himself strangely captivated by the clear and soul-satisfying declarations of the Word of God, and it was not long before he began to question in his mind the reliability of the Talmud, seeing that in matters so vital it differed from the Holy Scriptures.

(From www.shalom.org.uk/rabbis/cohn.htm)

When Rabbi Cohn was given a copy of the New Testament, which he read with alacrity, he quickly realized that it contained information regarding the Messiah that he had been seeking over many tortuous years but the information had been denied him because of the teaching of others. This is what Satan does, and it only requires one person, a respected teacher, to introduce a thought or an instruction that is unthinkingly repeated by his friends and students, as in this case, for it to deprive others of important knowledge and understanding concerning God and His message of salvation.

In his euphoric state Cohn tried to share what he had found with a fellow rabbi who had been particularly kind and helpful to him; but this man's response was far from what Cohn had expected.

"The Messiah whom you say you found is none other than the Jesus of the Gentiles. And as for this book," he said, tearing the New Testament from Cohn's hands, "a learned rabbi like you should not even handle, much less read this vile production of the apostates. It is the cause of all our sufferings." And with these words he threw the book to the floor and trampled upon it with his feet. (Is. 8:11 – 15; Ps. 118:22; Rom. 9:30 – 33)

But Jesus was born a Jew:

"… I could at least see that the Messiah's name was Yeshua, that He was born in Bethlehem of Judah, that He had lived in Jerusalem and communicated with my people, and that He came just at the time predicted in the prophecy of Daniel. My joy was boundless."

God was speaking directly to the heart of this seeking rabbi who obtained the message of truth by faith and not the works of the law. God was able to reveal the truth because his heart had become fallow ground, ready to receive the seed that is the Word of God.

Unfortunately, the senior Rabbi who objected to what Rabbi Cohn had discovered was so chained to the teaching of men he had received over the years, and his heart so hardened by years of trying to attain righteousness by his own efforts developing within him a hardness of heart that prevented him deviating from that teaching through independent personal investigation as Rabbi Cohn had been challenged to do; thus the message of the Messiah became a rock of offence, a stumbling block.

This man was satisfied in his being a Jew no matter how much he suffered because of it. But Rabbi Cohn, in searching for the truth because of a sense of emptiness in his spirit, became receptive to a word from God. The senior man accepted what others had said about the New Covenant as revealed in the Second Testament even though it deprived him of the truth. Rabbi Cohn was not satisfied until he had met with God in Christ and it transformed his life, just as it had the life of Nicodemus. (see http://www.shalom.org.uk/Rabbis/rabbis. htm)

Does this not speak of the potential for such mistaken teaching within the colleges teaching the Christian faith? What is so interesting in the case of the two rabbis mentioned above is how diverse the acceptance of what he was told by the one is contrasted with the active seeking mind of the other that was not prepared to take the easy way of acceptance but was curious that what had been repeated year after year did not seem to make sense. Leonard Cohen had a curiosity of mind that allowed the Holy Spirit to break into his thoughts and lead him to the truth of the Messiah which the obstinate and unreceptive mind of the other prevented.

One minister told me that he lost his faith at a church college. How many teachers/lecturers have experienced the power of God in their lives and received the baptism in the Holy Spirit that Rabbi Cohen and Aaron and many other Jews have received, enhancing their spiritual knowledge of the word of God. It would seem not all of them, for those who taught that minister at a church college had destroyed the faith of some of their students instead of making it stronger, which clearly suggests their knowledge of God was wanting.

Consider carefully the reaction of the religious leadership at the time of the coming of the Lord.

The travel time of the wise men was long, taking many months or possibly even years because of the slow pace of travel at that time, but they were certainly not Jews., Therefore God notified non-Jews first about the coming birth, knowing they would respond to his sign. The three men would not have journeyed alone but would have had a retinue of servants and some security personnel with them especially as they carried treasure for the Lord.

When they finally arrived in Jerusalem, according to the etiquette of the day, especially with quite a large company with armed guards, they called on the king to inform him of their arrival in his kingdom and the reason for their visit. In asking the king where the new king was born they, in complete ignorance, caused consternation because the king would not have appreciated the birth of one who might usurp his hard won position.

The king called the scribes and religious academics along with the leaders such as the high priest. The question he asked is interesting, *"Where is the Messiah to be born?"* According to the thinking of the time the Messiah was expected anytime soon, yet apart from them stating that He was to be born in Bethlehem (Matt. 2:1 – 8), there seems to have been no further investigation on their part as to why the wise men were so sure that their Messiah had arrived, in fact there seems to have been complete disconnect amongst the religious leaders, with not one spark of curiosity. Of course we are not told what the king told the chief priest and scribes, but one would have anticipated that their interest would have been aroused merely by the question.

The king found out how long they had been travelling, determining from them when the star had appeared. Then as we know the wise men not only met with the Son of God but gave Him their gifts and then were told by God to go home without telling the king where in Bethlehem they had seen Him.

When the king realized the visitors had not returned to give him the information he requested of them, he had soldiers go to Bethlehem to kill all male children of two years and under, an act that was prophesied by the prophet Jeremiah (Jer. 31:15; Matt. 2:18).

Thus says the Lord:
A cry of anguish is heard in Ramah,
Mourning and unrestrained weeping.
Rachel is weeping for her children;
and refuses to be comforted
for her children, are no more.

Rachel, the beloved wife of Jacob, was the symbolic mother of the northern tribes, named Israel, who were the first to go into captivity after being conquered by the Assyrians. In Jeremiah Rachel is said to be weeping for the exiles at the deportation staging post of Ramah where she was buried. It was Rachel, who hung onto her father's gods rather than accept Jacob's God as did Leah, which resulted in her being barren and therefore crying out to be fertile. Sadly she died when giving birth to her second son Benjamin whose safety was so important when Jacob's sons went to Egypt to buy grain when Joseph was viceroy. This verse about the death of children is repeated in Matthew's gospel when Herod murdered many sons in order to try and protect his throne, which was not under threat from the Messiah. This illustrates the human tragedy of war and the callous disregard of ordinary people by those in power.

How can we account for the time of His arrival? Jesus had been born whilst Mary and Joseph were registering for the census and we can assume they would have done that the day after they had arrived in Bethlehem. Eight days after He was born our Jesus was presented to the Lord (His Father) at the temple in Jerusalem, according to the laws of Moses, where He was seen by Simeon and Anna. (Lk. 2:21 – 38). Although Luke then says that Mary and Joseph returned to Nazareth, not only did the wise men visit the new born child, but so did the shepherds and then they were told by God to escape to Egypt, which had to be before their return to Nazareth. We are told elsewhere they did return to their home upon their return from Egypt.

To travel from Bethlehem to Jerusalem at that time took a day, especially with a new born child. It is unlikely the family would have returned to Bethlehem. What we do know is that the wise men saw the star and followed it not knowing where it would lead them. According to custom they met with the king and then continued to Bethlehem and saw the child. As has already been established God can only be God and although the Spirit that is the Son of God fitted into the body of a new born and physically restricted baby, He was still God.

Having experienced that meeting with the King of kings and Lord of lords and received that warning from God, it is unlikely the wise men would have stayed any longer than a night before returning home. How long it was before Herod realized they had not reported back is unknown.

Consider the possible sequence of events: Mary and Joseph travel to Bethlehem from Nazareth to register, while they were there the Lord became man, He was visited by the three wise man and the shepherds, on the eighth day he was taken to Jerusalem to be presented to His Father at the temple and was met by Simeon and Anna. As the stable at Bethlehem was merely a place for them to stay for the census and for the birth, it is unlikely they returned to Bethlehem from Jerusalem, because it was a dangerous place for the new born and defenseless Son of God, hence God's warning to Joseph about Herod. It is more than likely they went to Egypt from Jerusalem which was more southerly than Nazareth and with Herod on the rampage it was also a case of getting the child to safety quickly and to accord with scriptural prophecy, *"Out of Egypt I called My Son"* (Num. 24:8; Hos. 11:1; Matt. 2:15).

So why did Herod include children of two and under? He realized he did not know if the child had been born when the star first appeared, in which case the child might have been around two years old, which also gives us a clue as to how far the wise men had travelled although preparation for the journey would have also taken them some time, neither did he know where the child's parents normally lived, merely assuming they lived in Bethlehem. All he knew for certain was that the child was <u>to be born</u> in Bethlehem.

What we can say is that this was Satan trying to get rid of God in human flesh, just as through the Pharaoh he tried to kill off the Hebrew nation of Israel by ordering all the male babies to be killed at birth. Yet God caused Moses to be cared for in the house of the very one Satan was using to crush His people.

It is interesting that the religious leaders did not appear to make any objections to the slaughter of children because they were unaware of any births of note in that city, such was the low key arrival of the eternal Son of God, who, on His arrival, was worshipped by foreigners and lowly shepherds.

No wonder the scribes and Pharisees and religious leaders of the Jews did not take to Him during His ministry, for they wrongly assumed He had been born in Nazareth, a Gentile city.

The Betrayer

Students in primary school cannot possibly handle what the students in junior school are taught, or those in the junior school what is taught in senior school. We all have to start somewhere and then progress to gain knowledge and experience of a subject. The importance is not to stay in primary or junior or senior school but to constantly grow in knowledge and experience which leads to maturity.

Consider what the writer to the Hebrews wrote regarding progressing in the faith. First of all is teaching about the example given to us by the Lord Jesus Christ:

So also Christ did not exalt himself to become a high priest,
but was appointed by the one who said to him,

'You are my Son,
today I have begotten you';

as he says also in another place,
'You are a priest for ever,
according to the order of Melchizedek.'

 In the days of his flesh, he had offered up prayers and
supplications, with loud cries and tears, to the one who was
able to save him from death, and he was heard because of
his reverent submission.
 So, although he was a Son, he learned obedience
through what he suffered; and having been made perfect,
he became the source of eternal salvation for all who obey
him, having been designated by God a high priest according
to the order of Melchizedek².

The writer to the Hebrews had to take his readers to task because
they were not consolidating their knowledge and growing in spiritual
terms because they were not listening and taking what they were being
taught to heart and using it in their daily lives.

 About this matter we have much more to say that is hard
to explain, since you have become dull in understanding,
not willing to learn what you are being taught. For though
by this time you ought to be teachers, you need someone to
teach you again the basic elements of the oracles of God.
 You need milk, not solid food; for everyone who lives
on milk, being still an infant, is unskilled in the word of
righteousness. But solid food is for the mature, for those
whose faculties have been trained by practice to distinguish
good from evil.
 (Heb. 5:5 – 14)

---

2 Some of the information above, such as 'You are a priest forever, according to
the order of Melchizedek', is college stuff, (a more detailed explanation of this appointment
of the Lord as "high priest according to the order of Melchizedek" (Gen. 15:18 - 20) can
be found in "The Origin of Life" chapter three).

This is a condemnation indeed directed at those who refused to grow in their spiritual life; the danger of this attitude is that such believers can easily be led into error. Some do not come to believe in the Lord Jesus until later in life. But whenever a person experiences that epiphany moment that is the time when they need to start learning about spiritual things and growing in the faith so that they can then gain sufficient knowledge to pass on their faith to others. Every believer must seek after God to be able to commune with God otherwise they are dependent on others feeding them with milk that could so easily be contaminated and they would not know it.

An unmarried docker became a believer but had little education. His minister got an exercise book and put in some columns on the first page and wrote in headings. Name, Date and Date. The man was told to write in the names of six people he would like to bring to the Lord and the date he started to pray for them to receive Christ and then record the date that they accepted Christ. As those listed came to know the Lord he was to add more names. When the man died many years later a great pile of exercise books were found in the wardrobe in his home. He served God in his own way and according to his abilities quietly, without fuss and fanfare.

I am not very bright. My qualifications are of little consequence. In fact I used to complain to the Lord about my poor education until one day He broke into my thoughts and said, "Don't you think I can train you in My school?" My complaints stopped immediately. However, I am not a trained or qualified theologian, except what I have been taught by God.

For a believer to be in tune with God, prayer is essential. After conversion and spiritual rebirth, must come a commitment to serve God no matter what lies ahead, along with a strong desire to commune with God — commune means to share ones most intimate thoughts and feelings with someone else. Such things are essential ingredients for all true believers if they are to be able to follow the Lord Jesus Christ and to serve Him faithfully.

Once made spiritually alive, unless the believer seeks to enter into an intimate relationship with God through the office of the Holy Spirit, then there is little point in being born again and makes suspect any claim that they are Christians.

We cannot avoid making mistakes from time to time. However, if we are in tune with God, He can cause even our mistake to become useful in His service, even if they are only good for teaching us lessons of the need to be fully attuned to God and not allowing our own thoughts and ideas to control our actions.

In spite of all the teaching he received directly from his Messiah, the mind of Judas Iscariot was so warped and focused on earthly things (he could not keep his hands out of the bag of money for instance) that his thinking and ideas of the Father's plan for the work of his Master bore no relationship to all that God Himself had planned. Even Peter was called to task when he protested at the possible killing of his Master, but when he was immediately rebuked by the Lord he fell silent being sensitive enough to feel the full force of the rebuke.

Judas was completely different to the other disciples, more used to scheming to get his own rebellious way than listening to God and learning His way of doing things and allowing himself to be transformed. It is believed that he wanted to force the Messiah to become the warrior leader to remove the Romans from the land, but unwittingly he could never succeed in that task because that was not what the Lord was about; rather He was about the salvation of souls. It was when the Lord allowed Himself to be arrested that Judas returned the money and went and hung himself.

Serving God is not about being controlled. God uses the talents of individuals and gives responsibility to those He knows are capable of doing His work in a similar manner to the way the Father gave responsibility to our Lord to do His work on earth.

Because of Judas' insistence of trying to force the Messiah into doing what he wanted Him to do, Satan became actively involved, using Judas' secretive way of scheming for his own ends. To force the issue and get the Messiah to become a warrior King, Judas was willing to betray Him to the authorities. But Judas had got it all wrong.

If we are to come to understand the mind of God in all matters relating to the future, in however small a way, it can only be achieved through the prayerful study of His word and the surrendering of ourselves to His service and not impose our own thoughts and ideas on His plan for us or for the world. The Bible is full of examples of individuals who committed their lives to God and were led by Him to do His work. We must follow their example.

Leaders of the Jews

All men have sinned, so why are we shocked to hear about the failure and corruption of others?

There is a saying, 'Power corrupts; absolute power corrupts absolutely.' Throughout the life of the Lord Jesus Christ there were proud men who were convinced that they knew God. The spiritual leaders of the Jews considered themselves expert at interpreting the word and laws of God, yet one of their number met secretly with the Messiah one night because, experiencing a sense of ignorance, he wanted to understand what was happening. Realizing that this man Yeshua (Joshua, Jesus) was completely different to anyone he had known before he became determined to meet with Him. It was at that meeting the difference between the flesh and spirit within man was clearly explained. Into the created flesh of man God breathed His Spirit, elevating him above the animal kingdom. Flesh naturally gives birth to flesh, and Spirit to spirit (Jn. 3:3 – 12; cf. Gen. 2:7).

To those who studied the Law the Messiah said, *"You search the scriptures, for in them you think you have eternal life."* But it is not the searching that is important, rather the desire of the mind to discover truth as has been pointed out above. The scriptures are clearly spiritual, like the watermark in good quality paper. Did the Lord not say to Satan, *"Man shall not live by bread alone, but by every word that proceeds from the mouth of God"*? The scriptures were, and are, spiritual food from God providing the one interpreting the scriptures to us is the Holy Spirit.

Because they had divorced their studies of the scriptures from God, had not sought God out to receive His interpretation of them, as Aaron the high priest was required to do from the start and Moses did very effectively, they did not realise that, *"these are they which testify of Me and My coming."* Rather they relied on the writings of the ancients in the Talmud, not all of whom were true to God, as Rabbi Cohn realized when he noted that in some respects what had been written differed from the Holy Scriptures.

Consider for a moment the case of the prophet Micaiah. When the kings of Israel and Judah came together to do battle against Ramoth Gilead, Jehoshaphat king of Judah asked Ahab the king of Israel to seek the word of the Lord before going into battle. So about four hundred prophets were brought together to prophecy and all told the kings that the Lord would deliver the town into their hands.

Not satisfied with what they said, the king of Judah asked if there was still not a prophet in Israel. The king of Israel told him that there was one other prophet whom he hated because he did not prophecy good concerning him.

When Micaiah was called he was told to follow the lead of the other prophets when speaking to the king, which he initially did until reprimanded by the king of Israel to tell the truth, which was that they would loose the battle.

Micaiah was then challenged by one of the four hundred 'prophets'. A man named Zedekiah struck Micaiah on the cheek asking him which way the spirit from the Lord had gone from him to Micaiah. In response Micaiah told him, *"On the day you go into an inner chamber to hide."* As it happened, on the day of the battle an archer drew his bow and shot an arrow into the air which miraculously found and fatally wounded Ahab the king of Israel by getting through the joints of his armour.

One faithful prophet of God against four hundred liars and deceivers. Read the full account in 1 Kings. 22:1 – 38.

Is it any wonder then that such spiritually dead religious leaders should still be in influential positions at the time of our Lord? When the wise men arrived at Herod's palace, the king called the Jewish religious leaders to ask where the Messiah was to be born. There are two particularly interesting points about that meeting: firstly as has already been mentioned none of the religious leaders had their curiosity aroused when asked that question, yet it was generally agreed that the Messiah was to arrive anytime soon. Secondly, in spite of the fact that it was God who was sending the Messiah, and God was all powerful, the king still thought that he could kill the messenger from God thereby securing his position as king when that was not the reason for His coming. Although we cannot know how many in the leadership were secret believers, this gives us some idea of just how far part of the religious and civil leadership of Israel were from any true knowledge of God.

THREE TRIALS

Historical facts

As an introduction to this chapter it is worth spending time looking into the great disaster that affected Israel (both the northern tribes and Judah) when they were taken into exile by the Assyrians and Nebuchadnezzar of Babylon because of the predominance of idol worship that God found so abhorrent and the depth of depravity reached by the priests serving in the temple, referred to in chapter 3. It was a turning point in their relationship with their God.

God's anger with the house of Israel (all twelve tribes) was aroused because of the way they defiled the land by their own ways and deeds so they were scattered among the nations (Eze. 36:19, 20). They forgot that the land belonged to God even before the Canaanites live there. With the Lord's help Israel were conquerors overcoming those who had defiled the land before them, only for them in time to also defile the land; a land pivotal to God's plans for the salvation of the whole of mankind and the point of His coming again to the earth in triumph.

By the time of the exile the whole matter of sin within the human race was coming to a critical state where even God's chosen people, called to be His face to the other nations, had become as corrupt and godless as all the other nations around them. Just as the Canaanites got to a point of such depravity that God sent Israel into a land that belonged to

Him as creator of all things, to remove them, so with the descent into depravity of His supposedly God-focused priests who led the people into sin defiling His temple, God Himself took over by preventing the people having the freedom they enjoyed when they worshipped Him with true hearts. The warning Moses gave to the people before they entered the land concerning life and death and their right to live in the land:

> But if your heart turns away and you refuse listen [to God or be mindful of all his laws], being drawn away from God to bow down to other gods and serve them, I warn you now that you shall perish; you shall not enjoy a long and prosperous life in the land that you are crossing the Jordan to enter and possess (Deut. 30:17, 18).

The exile had been a wake-up call for the Jews. They had to realise that God would no longer tolerate their waywardness. They had tried His patience too far, and as His chosen people they had brought dishonour to His great name because of their waywardness so, to protect His great name, He withdrew His protection from them (vs. 21, 22).

> The word of the Lord came to me saying: mortal man, when the house of Israel lived in their own land, they defiled it with their ways and their deeds; their conduct in my sight was like the uncleanness of a woman in her menstrual period. Therefore, I poured out my wrath upon them for the blood that they had shed upon the land, and for the idols with which they had defiled it. So I scattered them among the nations, and they were dispersed through other countries; according to their ways and deeds I judged them. But when they arrived in the nations, wherever they went, they even profaned my holy name there, because it was said of them, 'These are the people of the Lord, and yet they had to go out of his land.' I had concern for my holy name, which the house of Israel had profaned among the nations to which they went. (Eze. 36:16 – 21).

The writer to the Hebrews wrote: *"It is a fearful thing to fall into the hands of the living God" (Heb. 10:31).* That might have been written about 2000 years ago but do not be fooled for God is the same yesterday, today and forever into eternity. It is essential that we take the warnings in the Bible seriously and do not take God for granted and we take care to uphold the supreme holiness of God's name and not bring it into disrepute, because He will not forgive us.

Sadly both by their alternative worship within the temple and their exile the whole of Israel had profaned His great name amongst the nations, because by the wholesale removal of all but a very few from the land the surrounding nations thought their God to be merely a tribal deity who was powerless to protect His land from invasion and His people from exile. Just as they were His witnesses, so are we.

However, in order to sanctify His name, and demonstrate to the nations His supreme power and authority over the earth and man (notice it had nothing to do with the spiritual state of His chosen people), He was to recover them from the nations and re-establish them in His land which He had promised to His friend Abraham. By the time of their return the land had been taken over by the people of Edom who believed it belonged to them, something they would regret because by doing so, and becoming enemies of Israel and Judah in order to possess the land, they had aroused the anger of God (Eze. 35; 36:1 – 8).

When the exiles returned to the land, it took time for the returnees to get into a routine of worshipping God in the rebuilt but far less glorious temple (see Haggai).

God's plan for the salvation of mankind started as soon as Adam and Eve were ejected from the garden. Now, with the return of the exiles and the erection of the new temple of Zerubbabel, the time prophesied by Daniel for the coming of the Messiah started ticking away.

In chapter 36 Ezekiel speaks about a time when the Jews would have their stony heart removed and a new heart given to them and a new spirit put within them (Eze. 36:26, 27). By putting His Spirit within them God would enabled them to walk in His statutes which illustrated the essence of Divine Grace. But it would not happen immediately for this promise was for the future, after the coming of the promised One, the Messiah, who would baptize with the Holy Spirit. This happened on the day of Pentecost when the disciples were together in Jerusalem after the ascension of the Messiah. But like all the promises of God, they are only effective for those who are willing to open themselves up to God: *"Behold! I stand at the door, knocking; if anyone hears my voice and opens the door, I will come in to him and eat with him, and him with me" (Rev. 3:20).* Thus the responsibility rests entirely with the individual responding to the call of God, not the other way around, and as only the willing will respond, many will go the way of eternal death.

The purpose of the redemption of Israel was to demonstrate to the world at large that their God was the one being on whom the worship of the human heart should be focused. Many national leaders recognized this fact, particularly Nebuchadnezzar. The effect was to an extent immediate because when a whole people were taken out of a land and the land given to another nation, in the case of Judah the land was taken over by the Edomites, it was very unusual for the original nation to regain their land and become a nation again. But for the Jews that was made possible only because of the power and authority of almighty God and the use He made of individuals such as Nehemiah and Ezra.

So how does all this link in with the trial of the Messiah?

God's plan of salvation for the world was progressive and unless we have some understanding of the way in which God demonstrated His power and authority through His chosen people over many generations we will never even begin to fully grasp what happened at the Passover when God offered His Son as the eternal sacrifice for sin. It cannot be taken out of context because that would render all that happened at that time meaningless.

These events must be viewed in the light of both the spiritual ignorance of the religious elite and life under pagan Roman occupation as it conflicted with the interaction of various religious beliefs in a fragmented Israel along with the inbred historical mindset of the Jewish people. An Israel that had previously angered God to the point where He removed the nation (both Israel and Judah) from His promised land into exile and then 70 years later caused them to return to their land and re-establish themselves in it, although this time it was to be without the complete freedom of self-governance they had previously enjoyed.

With the inbred sense of superiority within the Jewish mind, and the loss of faith of many of the Jewish people because of the ineffective spiritual leadership and the dominance of the oppressive man made oral law on daily life that had developed over centuries, the sudden appearance of hope, first in the form of John the Baptizer and then the obviously authoritative teaching of the Messiah, tensions between the Jewish religious leaders and the two, humanly speaking, unauthorized teachers arose, mainly because of jealousy (Matt. 27:18).

Suddenly, amongst all the difficulties of daily life, there came a gospel of hope, taught with an authority that completely outshone the uninspired teaching of the scribes and Pharisees. The officers then came to the chief priests and Pharisees, who said to them, "Why did you not bring him?" The officers answered, "No one ever spoke like this man!" The Pharisees answered them, "Have you also been deceived? (Jn. 45 – 52) Those given to teaching the word of God were so focused on the minutiae of the words of the Law of Moses that they were unable to stand back in order to understand what God was seeking to teach them through the Law. In it was the love and compassion of God shining through to help them understand their sinfulness and the means God had provided to help them receive forgiveness, which was sadly suppressed by the godless legal thinking of the lawyers and priests.

As Rabbi Aaron once told me, after his rabbinic training he understood what the scriptures said because he had been taught how to interpret them rather than being taught to ask God to interpret them to him. However, once he had experienced his 'epiphany moment', when he met with God and God became real and personal to him, God the Holy Spirit was able to interpret the scriptures to him in a way he had never experienced before, just like Paul. He was blown away with the joy of being able to understand the truth of God through inspiration and being able to grow spiritually.

The Messiah, whom they mistook as just a man from Nazareth in Galilee, undermined their religious authority, and His continuous criticism of them attacked their pride and vulnerability. In their inner conscience they were uncertain that what they taught was definitely true, but that uncertainty was suppressed. They must have realized that many of the rules and regulations they sought to enforce were impractical because they did not follow them themselves.

After the raising of Lazarus (read John 11) it became clear to the leaders of the Jews that He had to be silenced:

> *"So the chief priests and the Pharisees called a meeting of the council, and said, 'What are we to do? This man is performing many signs. If we let him go on like this, everyone will believe in him, and the Romans will come and destroy both our temple and our nation.' But one of them, Caiaphas, who was high priest that year, said to them, 'You know nothing at all! You do not understand that <u>it is better for you that one man die for the people than to have the whole nation destroyed</u>.' He did not say this on his own, but being high priest that year prophesied that Jesus was about to die for the nation, and not for the nation only, but to gather into one the dispersed children of God of every nation. So from that day on they planned to put him to death"* (Jn. 11:47 – 53).

The accusations of this man from the Gentile region of Galilee hit them hard, increasing their sense of vulnerability which in turn caused them to become angry and vindictive, hence their increasing efforts to gain the upper hand over this man they did not recognized as being God from God.

When Cain had his sacrifice rejected by God he became angry and refused to repent. These men knew about God from an academic and theological point of view. However, their vociferous opposition to Him gave witness to a hardness of heart towards the Lord, thus preventing them from being attracted to Him in their spirit like Nicodemus, indicating the lack of an enquiring mind and spirit. Their attitude towards Him would also suggest they had never had that experience of a personal spiritual meeting with God, that epiphany moment that Rabbi Aaron finally experienced when he received the gift of the Holy Spirit from God.

All the teaching they received had focused on the Law, not primarily on God. If we do not understand who God is and how we can make contact with Him as did the prophets of old and the disciples and other followers of Jesus, then there is no possibility of understanding what He has to teach us through His Word. *"You search the scriptures yet you do not realise just who I am because you are not God sensitive and the Holy Spirit is unable to prompt you into recognizing just who I am,"* is what I believe Jesus was saying to the scribes and Pharisees who were opposing Him.

It is important to consider these matters in order to understand what happened at the time of His arrest and ultimate crucifixion.

It was a volatile time with occasional outbursts of violence and cruel suppression. During the 400 years of God's silence there was a considerable amount of cruelty with despotic rulers as the accounts of life during the Maccabean period clearly illustrates. In one instance, recorded in Luke 13:1, it is reported that Pilate mixed the blood of some Galileans with sacrifices to Roman gods. Fear was pervasive and no less from the point of view of the Jewish authorities when considering doing anything that might inflamed the sensitivities of the general population.

The problem they had with the Messiah is that some believed He was a holy man and others believed he was a prophet and a few believed he was the Messiah because of the authoritative way He spoke on scripture, outshining the scribes and Pharisees, along with the miracles He performed. The authorities, ruling without the power they previously held over the population when the whole of Israel was a free, independent nation under God, were fearful of the people and the reaction of the Roman authorities should they cause a riot by arresting Him. God used this fear to prevent them doing anything to His Son until the appointed time.

Judas had accepted a bribe to betray the Messiah, because he wanted to force the Lord's hand to show Himself as the warrior Messiah, not realizing that his master had another work to do first. No one can force God to do anything that is not in His will to do! This sadly disillusioned man was the key to the start of the Lord's inevitable physical suffering.

So fearful were the authorities that anything should go wrong this time, that they sent a large armed force to arrest their Messiah in the darkness of night. Did the Messiah not say, *"... men love darkness rather than light because their deeds are evil"? (Jn. 3:19b)*. What is also interesting is that even though He had been a public figure for almost three and a half years, exposed to the view of thousands of people, Judas was required by the authorities to identify Him with a kiss. Agreed it was dark and there could have been other men who looked similar, so the kiss was to confirm they definitely arrested the right man, but such a procedure clearly illustrates their nervousness concerning this arrest. Satan must have believed he was finally succeeding after years of trying to have Him put out of the way, but he was only doing what God allowed Him to do.

After the intimacy the Lord had with His disciples explaining to them that he was going back to the Father and praying for them during a time of intimacy with His Father (Jn. 15 – 17), John then tells us about the Lord's arrest. The end was in sight. The Lord had suffered abuse and questioning about His authority and the subject matter of His message along with attempts by the authorities and local Jewish leaders to arrest or assassinate Him. Now their hatred of Him had come to fulfillment when God removed all protection from Him thus allowing the human authorities of His chosen people to do their worst.

Just try and imagine the burden, both psychological and spiritual, on the Messiah of being physically totally alone in the face of all the hostility and evil hatred, knowing all that would happen, yet with the glimpse of victory, willingly submitting Himself to all that was to happen, *"Father not My will but Yours be done"*. That is the supreme example of true surrender to the Father's will.

When the detachment of armed troops arrived in the Garden of Gethsemane, the Messiah, knowing all that would happen to Him went forward to meet them and ask whom they sought. It is interesting that when He replied, *"I am He"* at first they suddenly drew back, being in the presence of God incarnate. Leaving the disciples alone, for they were protected as the leaders of the future church of the Living God, the troops finally arrested our Lord and took Him to the High Priest and the leaders of the Jews who had already gathered like vultures at a killing.

Trial before the High Priest

The chief priests and the majority of members of the ruling body, the Sanhedrin, were those most incensed by the Lord's public attacks on them. With their hurt pride and anger at not being the main resource for all things religious (consider Matt. 23) and their inability to silence Him because of his popularity amongst the people, which showed just how precarious was their position of authority over the people, their desire to see Him eliminated dominated and corrupted their thinking, truth and honesty being banished from the proceedings.

Corruption amongst the priests prior to the exile to Babylon should have been eradicated by the time of their return to their land. The leadership of Nehemiah and particularly that of Ezra in his prayer of confession (Ezra 9), all of which the Jewish scholars studied, then the proclamation of the Mosaic Law to all the people (Nehemiah 8), the public confession of sins (Neh. 9) and their rededication to God by binding themselves with an oath, vowing to accept the curse of God should they fail to be obedient to God's law as given to them by Moses the servant of God (Neh. 10), all this should have laid the foundation for a new, more spiritually attuned Israel.

The people's solemnly promise to observe and do all the commandments of the Lord their Lord along with His ordinances and statutes was a well recorded and momentous time in their history which all subsequent generations should have taken to heart. The prophets Haggai and Zechariah were also active at this time. Sadly that was not to be as corruption and godlessness once again took control of the priestly class.

There have been many books written on the trial of the Lord before the high priest analyzing every detail, so there is no point in doing the same here. However, it is important to consider certain aspects of the trial which relate to the foregoing paragraphs.

The authorities found themselves faced with a very short time scale of 24 hours should they succeed in having Him condemned to death, because of the impending Passover celebrations which started at sunset. The rules required that all dead bodies had to be removed before it started. Indeed such was the urgency of the condemnation of the Messiah that the trial started immediately after His arrest even though it was late at night demonstrating that even in this God was forcing the religious authorities to work to His timescale.

It is important not to forget that the man we are talking about was not an ordinary man, but God incarnate. He knew all that was going to happen to Him, including the verbal abuse and scourging as well as the severe suffering He would experience when nailed to the wooden cross. Although He was God, He inhabited a human body with all the nervous systems that we have, therefore the pain He experienced would be no less than what the thieves crucified with Him experienced. What makes the Messiah so special, now that He rules with His Father in the heavenly places, is that He experience so much whilst on earth so that no one can say that He could not possibly understand what we are going through (Heb. 4:15, 16).

Imagine the creator of the world and of men being despised by those He had created and to whom He had come to preach the love of God, having to experience the oppressively evil and hateful atmosphere of the trial before the high priest, who was a man who was supposed to be the one most in contact with God.

Jesus having allow Himself to be arrested, because His time of sacrifice had finally come, as prophesied (Matt. 26:31, 32), all his disciples suddenly abandon Him, as He was led to the awaiting Caiaphas, along with the scribes, Pharisees and elders of the people.

How the antagonistic anti-God, anti-truth atmosphere must have jarred with the truth the Messiah spoke to the people. The judge and jury at this trial wanted their Messiah dead, therefore they used anyone willing to bear false testimony to speak out against Him. A useful trick is to take what has been said out of context. Satan is skilled at it.

When the Lord said, *"Destroy this temple and in three days I will raise it up"*, the Jews hearing that remark replied, *"It has taken forty-six years to build this temple and will You rise it up in three days?"* Sadly the religious elite were so focused on the physical that any reference to the spiritual fell on deaf ears, unable and unwilling were they to believe that the usefulness of the temple as God's house would soon come to an end for in future the Spirit of God was to live in the temple of the body of individual believers, the Messiah being the first of the new type of temple which would be rebuilt because from a physical body it was to become a spiritual body, a spiritual temple (1 Cor. 3:16; 15:42 – 53)

The Lord's statement, *"Destroy this temple and in three days I will raise it up"*, was clearly misquoted at the trial because of unbelief to become, *"If you destroy this temple, I am able to rebuild it in three days"*. Clearly this witness was far from the knowledge of God. To the woman at the well the Lord said, *"God is Spirit, and those who worship Him must worship Him in spirit and in truth"*. So what is the Lord Messiah saying? Thus far the Jews worshipped God through the sacrificial services in the temple and other worship services in the synagogue according to prescribed formats. Yet the essence of true worship was the spirit God breathed into man communicating with the Spirit of God in an act of adoration and praise. When the Messiah had offered the once and for all sacrifice for the sins of the whole world, those willing to repent and believe and seek and receive the Holy Spirit would become living temples of the Holy Spirit, the physical man made temple built primarily for the offering of animal sacrifices being of no more relevance

The corrupt facade of a trial the Messiah faced clearly shows just how far removed from their God the leaders of the people had become. But there is another reason. Through their obduracy, not only was the Son of God sacrificed, but after the disciples received the gift of the Holy Spirit and began preaching the message of salvation for all they became determined to crush the messengers of hope thus silencing the message of salvation through the Messiah whom they had murdered. In that they failed because it was broadcast by the power of God around the Gentile nations by those Jews who believed in Him, who became the remnant that was always focused on, and loyal to, God.

Going back to the trial, the high priest, being used to offenders groveling before him, was annoyed that the man before him said nothing as Isaiah had prophesied, *"As a lamb before her shearers is dumb so He opened not His mouth"*. What was the point? With truth having been denied entry into this trial, the Lord of all truth had nothing to say. He was surrounded by those whose motives and beliefs were more in line with the doctrines of Satan, not those of the God they purported to worship and serve.

Just as the Lord was facing this hostile court and witnesses He heard Peter deny Him three times and turned and looked at him. Peter, his brash exterior exposed for what it was, went away weeping, being changed at that moment into a deeper and more mature disciple.

So what made the Lord give them information that finally enabled them to bring accusations against Him for which the death penalty was the only sentence. The demand for a straight answer. *"I put you under oath,"* said Caiaphas to his Messiah, *"by the living God: Tell us if you are the Christ, the Son of God."* The Messiah had no option but to speak the truth. *"It is as you said,"* the Lord replied adding, *"nevertheless, I say to you, you will see the Son of Man sitting at the right hand of the Power on high and coming on the clouds of heaven"* (see Acts 7:55, 56).

Notice first the change of title from Son of God to Son of Man because it was as a man that He had come to the earth to give witness to His Father's love and in order to provide the perfect sacrifice for sins; then the prophetic note: *"nevertheless, I say to you, you will see the Son of Man sitting at the right hand of the Power on high and coming on the clouds of heaven."* Thus advertizing His second coming.

Firstly He was to sit at the right and of the Power on high (God the Father) (see Ps. 110:1, repeated in Matt. 22:44). Then at some future time He is to come on the clouds of heaven (Rev. 1:7; Acts 1:11). This was undoubtedly spiritual and prophetic language which, like their forebears, the high priest and other religious elite were unable to properly receive, let alone understand in their attitude of evil intent.

Within the charged atmosphere of the 'court room' evil forces were engaged in battle and Satan was not going to let the Lord escape his clutches. At this point the appointed minister of God, charge with directing the attention of the people towards God rose up, tore his clothes crying out his judgement, *"He has spoken blasphemy"*. How ignorant he was concerning the presence of God incarnate and how humble the Lord of glory was before those He had created, allowing them to have authority over Him on this occasion.

As the Lord said on the cross, *"Lord forgive them for they do not know what they are doing."* This is because of the hardness of their hearts towards their God and the person of His Son who was standing before them, they had allowed themselves to become tools of Satan in this intense spiritual battle, and therefore became totally ignorant of all that was happening and over which they unwittingly had no control. But it was necessary for the Christ to die for the people, so although tools in the hand of Satan they were involved in the plan of God to provide salvation to all men (Jn. 11:50)

With the finding of the high priest that the Messiah had spoken blasphemy, it was obvious those sitting in judgement would call for Him to be put to death, a sentence they had no power to carry out (Jn. 18:31).

It is interesting how callous the Jewish leadership was towards Judas who had realized that his plan for the Messiah to be forced to take up arms and become the warrior Messiah had failed and that instead He was condemned to death. Returning the thirty pieces of silver, the price for a servant gored by an ox (Ex. 21:323; Zech. 11:12, 13; Matt. 27:3 – 8), Judas then went and hanged himself unable to cope with what he had done.

Trial before Pilate

When morning came and the whole of the Jewish leadership, now determined to have the Messiah killed, the chief priests and members of the ruling body, had Him taken to Pilate the Roman governor for sentencing. The problem was that the governor preferred to do his own questioning.

It is important to remember the Jewish day went from sunset, around 1800, to sunset so the arrest and trials of the Messiah happened on Friday, the day before the start of Passover at sunset, the start of Saturday, the seventh day in the Jewish week.

John tells us that when they led Him to the Praetorium, it was still early in the morning, however the high priest and leaders of the Jews would not enter because they did not want to be defiled so that they might eat the Passover. So Pilate had to go out to them and the conversation went like this:

Pilate   What charges do you bring against this man?

The Jews   We would not have brought Him to you if He had not done something wrong.

Pilate   Then you take Him and judge him by your laws.

The Jews   But we are not allowed to carry out the death sentence.

Pilate then went back into the Praetorium to hear what the Messiah had to say, but exactly what happened we will never know because of the bits of information each of the gospel writers recorded. It is likely there were questions Pilate initially asked the Messiah in response to the many false accusations that were leveled against Him, such as perverting the nation and forbidding Jewish citizens from paying taxes to Caesar, with the Messiah refusing to answer them because there was not a grain of truth in them.

During this period Pilate, particularly in the light of the regal presence of the man before him, quickly came to realise that He only answered his direct questions but was completely silent when asked to respond to the accusations leveled against Him by the Jews, therefore the main problem the Jewish leadership had with this Man was that of jealousy (Matt. 27:18).

It also became obvious to Pilate the accusations had nothing to do with criminal activity he knew anything about. Rather, they seemed to be based on some particular interpretation of Jewish law of which he had no knowledge. Unfortunately as Governor of the region He was responsible for justice and he was the only one who could hand out the death sentence.

> **Pilate** *"Are you the King of the Jews?"*

> **Messiah** *"Are you speaking of your own initiative or has someone else told you?"*

> **Pilate** *"Am I a Jew? Your own nation's leaders have brought you to me so what have You done?"*

The interesting thing about this conversation is that Pilate did not have any preconceived ideas and genuinely wanted to know what was going on, which is why the Messiah responded to his questions, still preserving Isaiah's prophecy, *"As a lamb before her shearers is dumb so He opened not His mouth"*.

> **Messiah** *"My kingdom is not of this world. If it had been, my followers would fight to keep me from being handed over to the Jews. But my kingdom is not of this world"*.

It is interesting that deep spiritual truths were given by our Lord to non-Jews. The woman at the well was told about spiritual 'Living Water' and the need to worship the Father in spirit and truth, and now Pilate was being told about the spiritual kingdom of God which is outside of all that has been created and therefore eternal.

> **Pilate** *"You a king then?"*

Pilate genuinely wanted to know. In the oppressive and aggressive spiritually atmosphere that pervaded Jerusalem at that time, suddenly there was a moment of genuine interest in the truth.

Pilates wife had had a dream so she sent a message to him during the trial telling him to *"have nothing to do with that just and righteous man"*. The problem Pilate faced concerned the conflicting information he was receiving and the aggressive nature of the accusations from the Jewish leadership. As he was the only one with the authority to confer the death sentence, the final decision regarding the future of this *'righteous man'* was his and his alone.

Trial before Herod

When Pilate heard the Messiah was a Galilean (see Matt. 2:23), although He had not been born there, He came under Herod's jurisdiction, so Pilate quickly arranged for the Messiah to be seen by the king. This one act boosted Herod's sense of importance allowing the two men to become friends. Also for sometime Herod had wanted to meet with the Messiah because of all he had heard about Him and hoped He might perform a miracle for him to see. That, of course, was not what the Messiah was on earth for, to perform for kings.

The conversation between the Messiah and Herod, who probably wanted to use this moment to impress the Jews who had come to witness what went on, was one-sided with the Messiah saying not a word. Indeed the situation must have been something of a farce with the chief priests and scribes on the side lines shouting accusations and abuse with the Messiah standing in total silence before the king looking regal.

Herod, it seems, was wise enough to realise the hatred of the Jewish leadership towards this man was for apparently no good reason except jealousy. To put it another way, the Jews were like a pack of hounds snapping at their prey, being prevented from tearing Him to shreds with their own teeth.

Return Trial before Pilate

There is something of a conundrum in all this. Certainly Pilate had a problem. He realized early on that the Jews had brought this man to him out of jealousy. He also, both through his experienced of being in the presence of the Messiah compared to his experiences of criminally minded men that had been brought to him, along with the urgent message he had received from his wife, realized that this man was completely innocent of anything deserving death.

Yet unbeknown to him, Pilate had to pass the death sentence for the Messiah had to die, not because of the charges that had been laid upon Him by the Jews, but because he was the perfect Passover sacrifice, the new spiritual high priest after the order of Melchizedek who was both willing and able to present His own body as the sacrifice (Heb. 8:26 – 28; 9:11 – 14) as compared to all human high priests after the order of Aaron, sinful men who had to sacrifice animals.

One crucial factor in all this is the fact that Pilate got frustrated with the Messiah when He remained silent even though he had come to realise why.

Pilate *"Why do you not speak to me when I have the power to release you or have you crucified?"*

Messiah *"You could have no power at all over Me except it were given to you from above. Therefore the one who delivered Me to you has the greater sin."*

This would clearly have unnerved Pilate because, as Paul realized, both the Greeks and the Romans were very religious (Acts 17:22), they were also probably very superstitious, and the Messiah's reference to a heavenly being with absolute power over the proceedings would have had an impact on him, because, we are told, that from then on Pilate did all he could to try and have the Messiah released.

When the leading Jews realized what Pilate had in mind, for neither he nor Herod found any of the accusations against the Messiah worthy of the death sentence, they upped their anti by generating such a riot inducing atmosphere that to keep some semblance of peace he was forced to concede to their demands. It was truly demonic.

Pilate then called together the chief priests, the leaders, and the people, and said to them, 'You brought me this man as one who was perverting the people; and having examined him in your presence I have not found this man guilty of any of the charges you have raised against him. Neither has Herod, for he sent him back to us. Indeed, he has done nothing to deserve death. I will therefore have him flogged and release Him.'

Then they all shouted out together, 'Away with this man and release Barabbas for us!' (This was a man who had been put in prison for an insurrection that had taken place in the city, and for murder.) Pilate, wanting to release Jesus, addressed them again; but they kept shouting, 'Crucify, crucify him!' A third time he said to them, 'Why, what evil has he done? I have found in him no ground for the sentence of death; I will therefore have him flogged and then release him.' But they kept urgently demanding with loud shouts that he should be crucified; and their voices prevailed. So Pilate gave his verdict that their demand should be granted. He released the man they asked for, the one who had been put in prison for insurrection and murder, and he handed the Messiah over to be crucified as they wished. (Lk. 23:14 – 25)

After all the failed attempts to assassinate the Messiah or bring Him to 'justice', the Jewish authorities and the people gathered to watch the spectacle. Under the influence of Satan the authorities had became determined that this thorn in their side would die and now their efforts seem to be bearing fruit.

The atmosphere in the centre of Jerusalem was tense and oppressed by evil spiritual activity as the chief priests stirred up trouble and incited the people to demand the Messiah's death, completely contrary to their priestly function. Their king was supposed to be the living God, yet they cried out that they had *"no king but Caesar"*. Just like the priests of old who worshipped idols and the sun and insects believing God did not see them, so the priest's declaration concerning their faith in the living

God had no substance.

In order to avoid a major riot within the confines of the city, which his troops would have found difficult to contain, and with the accusation that if he did not accede to their demands he was not Caesar's friend, Pilate was forced to reluctantly concede to the demand of the Jews to have their Messiah crucified. Even the choice between a notorious murderer and the Messiah did not relieve the situation.

The power of Pilate to freely judge this case had been overwhelmingly usurped by evil forces with the principle of truth and justice being completely overthrown. Think about it. Here was a man used to pagan worship, who had abused the temple by having unlawful sacrifices offered there, so although there was an element of doubt in his mind about the legitimacy of the request from the Jewish authorities, there was little he could do if he was to avoid an outright riot in the centre of the city

The corruption of the priesthood had regressed to that of their forebears at the time of Jeremiah and Ezekiel and the exile.

Such was the evil spiritually impregnated atmosphere within the city that Pilate had no choice in this matter. Satan was being allowed by God to bring about the death of His Son (see Job 1:12; 2:6) in order to satisfy His wrath against the destructive and godless sin, which He abhorred, that had been introduced into the human race by Satan, and to also provide a means of eternal salvation for all mankind through the shed blood of the Messiah. This was God's grace being displayed to mankind, though only those willing to reach out to God can ever, in their own way, properly appreciate it.

CRUCIFIXION

Just consider that the means whereby man received complete forgiveness of sins was first mentioned when the Israelites were travelling in the wilderness. The people were continually complaining when things did not suit them demonstrating their complete lack of faith in God, even though He had proved Himself and His power over all that is both natural, spiritual, environmental and human. In fact God had clearly and publically demonstrated that nothing could stand up to the almighty power of the God of Abraham, Isaac and Jacob, the God who had called Moses to serve Him by leading His chosen people out from the oppression of the Egyptian Pharaoh.

During their journey in the wilderness God had supplied them with manna to eat which they could cook in a variety of ways and although it was the same day after day it was still food in a place where there was very little. What was particularly irritating was the fact that instead of asking God for a change of diet they complained:

"The people began to murmur against God and against Moses, 'Why have you brought us up out of Egypt to die in the wilderness?', they complained, 'For there is no food and no water, and we detest this miserable food'" (Num. 21:4, 5).

Yet at the appropriate time God had provided both, albeit after testing. And why continually harp back to their time in Egypt when the children of Israel cried out to God because of the arduous nature of their laborious and unrelenting burden under the whips of their task masters and the hot sun? At that time all they wanted was for their horrendous situation to end. With these thoughts in mind God's anger is understandable and justified.

He had rescued them from such a depth of slavery in Egypt that had prompted them to appeal to God for salvation, and He had done that in a spectacular way. So why were they complaining that having saved them and led them through the wilderness the food should be of a staple type of food? They were free and they had food. Could they not have gone to Moses and asked if God could give them a change of diet rather than this rebellious complaining?

Because of their complaints against Him, and the mention of returning to Egypt, God sent poisonous serpents amongst them and many died from being bitten. Again and again they had complained and suffered for it because of God's anger yet they persisted in their complaining so that in the end all those who had known slavery in Egypt died in the wilderness except for Caleb and Joshua who both entered the Promised Land. As soon as the people started dying they went to Moses and admitted their mistake of complaining, and to end the problem Moses was instructed by God to make a replica serpent and put it on a pole and raise it up so that the people could see it and be saved.

Rebellion is offensive to God because His supreme desire is to love mankind and bless them, but love cannot overcome persistent complaints and rebellions from people who will not learn and understand what is best for them. The supreme love of God is only effective amongst those who want to enter into a relationship with Him, be obedient to Him and serve Him.

The bronze serpent would have taken time to produce which meant that many died. It is also interesting that God had told the people not to make any graven image, but this was an exception because it had a meaning far beyond the immediate situation. The cause of death amongst the people was the venom of the snakes, so if a person was bitten all they had to do was to look at the image of the serpent on the pole and they would be saved from death. But they had to believe in the power of the serpent on the pole to be healed.

The Lord Jesus said:

> "… just as Moses lifted up the bronze serpent in the wilderness, so must the Son of Man be lifted up, that whoever believes in him may have eternal life" (Jn. 3:14, 15).

But what has the bronze serpent and Son of Man got in common? The bronze serpent represented the bite of the living serpents which caused the death of all those bitten and that death was compounded by the fact that the whole of mankind in under the sentence, issued by the Father, that the sin that is in our DNA causes spiritual death. Just as looking upon the bronze serpent and believing that it would heal them, so by taking upon Himself the sin of the whole world the Son of Man became sin for us if we (in our imagination) look upon the Son of man hanging on the cross and dying for us, we will be saved from that death sentence and be restore to spiritual life which leads to eternity.

Therefore just as the people who had suffered a bite from the serpent could look upon the bronze effigy of the serpent and be saved from death, the effect of the injected chemical being annulled, so by looking upon the Son of God as the Son of Man and Saviour, all those bitten and contaminated by sin could look on the sacrificed Saviour and by believing in Him be healed from their sin and receive the gift of eternal life.

From the very beginning God set the rules for the sin offering which was refined by the structured sacrificial services at the alter in the tabernacle courtyard. What was sacrificed had to be a male lamb and perfect in every way (Ex. 12:1 – 10; Mal. 1:8), not a bone was to be broken and it was to be all burned up. The supreme sin offering could be no different.

"For all have sinned," says Paul, *"and come short of the glory of God."* It was Adam, the man, the one first created who sinned, therefore all men have inherited that sin and separation from God through the male line, which is why the Son of God, who was perfect in every way and completely without sin, had to be born of a virgin and therefore uncontaminated by sin from a natural father. Also He had to be born of a woman because it was a body that was prepared for Him so that He could come down and be the perfect sacrifice for sin.

> *"... when the Messiah came into the world, He said,*
> *'Sacrifices and offerings you have not desired,*
> *but a body you have prepared for me;*
> *in burnt-offerings and sin-offerings*
> *you have taken no pleasure.*
> *Then I said, "Behold, I have come to do your will,*
> *because of what is written of Me in the scroll of the book"'*
> *(Heb. 10:5 – 7)*

God had no pleasure in seeing animals continuously slain, it was purely for the sake of man, and His love for man, that He allowed that means of atonement for the forgiveness of sin to continue because sin is so abhorrent to Him. Indeed it is the complete opposite to all that He is. But in the fullness of time, and in direct fulfillment of all the prophetic utterances of God throughout the history of the Hebrew people, the Israelites, the whole purpose of His coming is expressed in Hebrews as: *"Behold, I have come to do your will ... ",* that is the will of the Father.

The essence of the crucifixion is this, *"Sacrifices and offerings you have not desired, but a body you have prepared for me;"* and it was the Son of God in that body, prepared specially for sacrifice, that was to suffer on the cross for a total of six hours suffering all the pain that the criminals crucified with Him felt.

But that sacrifice and all the suffering beforehand at the mercy of the Roman soldiers with the crown of thorns and whips with fragments of bone woven into the thongs that reduced His back to a ploughed field, and His six hours of suffering on the cross, emphasized just how abhorrent sin is to the Father. That he should allow His only Son to come down to the earth from glory to live a life as a human being, to speak to the people about the love of God and then die in such a sacrificial way, also very clearly illustrates how much God loves man that He should want to save the man He had so lovingly created, from eternal spiritual death.

Man might think it was very costly in the lives of innocent animals, yet the sacrifice that the Son of God, who had become Son of Man, offered was far more costly. God Himself coming as a man and suffering and dying for created man. Amazing. Man was created by God as the pinnacle of His creation with the whole purpose of man being God's delight for eternity, therefore, with the introduction of sin, God introduced a means of rescuing mankind.

It is essential that the humiliation the Son of the living God experienced at the hand of sinful men is even partially understood for us to realize the cost of salvation God was willing to pay. God allowed Himself to be humiliated by those he had created, even those who had been chosen to be His priests; to suffer the intense pain of the tortuous lashings and then being nailed to the wood of the cross; the spiritual turmoil in being rejected by His Father, with whom He had been in continuous and complete unity from eternity. Allowing Himself to be put through such horrendous suffering cannot possibly be fully understood or appreciated by man. But such is the value God put upon the salvation of man that He, the creator of all that is, believed it was worth the price paid in both animals and the suffering of His Son.

The spiritual battle was now building up to its climax. The forces of evil were getting ready for the sweet smell of victory when the Son of God would die and they would be rid of Him forever. Or that is what they thought. The leading religious leaders were certainly well pleased that they had managed to get the death sentence passed and wanted the crucifixion to proceed with haste because of the impending Passover celebrations.

On the way to the cross, as the women wept for Him the Saviour told them to weep for themselves:

> "... 'Daughters of Jerusalem, do not weep for me, but for yourselves and for your children. For the days are surely coming when they will say, "Blessed are the barren, and the wombs that never bore children, and the breasts that never nursed them." Then they will begin to say to the mountains, "Fall on us"; and to the hills, "Cover us." For if they do this when the wood is green, what will happen when it is dry?"' (Lk. 23:27 – 31).

Completely unaware of the turmoil that would grip the nation after His death, resurrection and ascension, the chief priests and leaders of the people were in festive mood as their victim got nearer to the place of execution. Nor did they understand the full implication of what they were doing to their future role in the life of the nation and that of the temple when the Holy Spirit inspired disciples launched their campaign to publicize the good news of salvation once the price of sin had been paid in full.

The leaders, because of their spiritual detachment from God and all His teaching, succumbing to the authority of Satan because of that detachment, may have succeeded in bringing about the death of this irritant, but had they realized just who the irritant was they would have thought twice about what they were doing illustrating just how far from God they were.

Although The Messiah had to die for the salvation of mankind, thus freeing men from the embrace of Satan and all his evil forces and enabling man to again commune with God, the perpetrators of His death would experience a heavy cost for their efforts in bringing it about. *Then they will begin to say to the mountains, "Fall on us"; and to the hills, "Cover us."* The problems ahead of them were to be traumatic and life changing to the whole of the nation.

Not only would the Jewish authorities be unable to take control of the events after His death and the coming of the Holy Spirit in power and the subsequent activities of the disciples He inspired, on the reverse side neither would they be able to control the zealots who would become such an irritant to the Roman occupying forces that the whole nation would be in turmoil and the Roman forces would bring the rebellion to a violent end.

Jesus truly said,

> 'Daughters of Jerusalem, do not weep for me, but for yourselves and for your children. For the days are surely coming when they will say, "Blessed are the barren, and the wombs that never bore, and the breasts that never nursed."'.

There is, however, one other phrase He used which is most interesting. *For if they do this when the wood is green, what will happen when it is dry?'* What can this mean? Israel was only safe and secure when their attention was focused on their God and they were willing to come under His authority and rule, proclaiming Him, rather than Caesar, as their King. As soon as their attention was diverted to earthly matters, God inevitably withdrew His protection from them. In all their history that is one lesson they seemed not to have learned. Not only had they suffered from their lack of consistency in their relations with their God, but their children also suffered, so that even they were fodder for violent forces.

It can be said that if they were prepared to deal so aggressively with an innocent man that they did not recognize, but were willing to condemn Him to death, the green tree, what will be the effect of God's wrath on them when their continued disobedience and dishonest behaviour brought them only shame and dishonour, *(what will happen when it is dry?)*. The temple, that great and costly edifice which took 46 years of hard labour and the deaths of many slaves to construct and which they so admired, was eventually to be left in ruins.

The Messiah knew all that would happen and all that He would have to endure in the forthcoming final spiritual battle of His mission on earth. Already racked with pain from the flogging from those that had mocked Him, and the crown of thorns being forced upon his scalp, he would also be tired through a lack of sleep as that night He had endured trial after trial. He was assisted with carrying the cross by a bystander, a man from Cyrene named Simon, to ensure His body did not give out before they had a chance to see Him crucified.

In all the intensity of the events that happened in the crowded confines of Jerusalem, we need to pause for a moment and consider again just who we are remembering. This man was God, the Word made flesh who in the beginning was responsible for creating all things, the I AM, ever the same now clothed in a human body but still God and still eternal, whose Spirit was indestructible.

At anytime He could have called upon legions of angels to rescue Him from the hands of men; but He had come on a mission to save mankind from eternal death by sacrificing the body Mary had provided for Him, even though that meant enduring excruciating pain and looking like a defeated man. All this He went through because He was willing to submit to the scorn and insults of sinful and errant men He, as a member of the Divine Trinity, had been responsible for creating, knowing that ultimately He would have the victory. As He said to the chief priest:

62 And the high priest arose and said to Him, "Do You answer nothing? What is it these men testify against You?"
63 But Jesus kept silent. And the high priest answered and said to Him, "I put You under oath by the living God: Tell us if You are the Christ, the Son of God!"
64 Jesus said to him, "It is as you said. Nevertheless, I say to you, hereafter you will see the Son of Man sitting at the right hand of the Power, and coming on the clouds of heaven."

By putting Him under oath, Jesus had to confess that He was the Son of God, which confession sealed the death sentence.

The pain He endured through the scourging and the crown of thorns, and the tiredness He experienced because of the continuous trials He was forced to go through, as He was paraded from one human authority to another, was severe and real. However the worse pain was to come when His executioners drove the crudely formed nails into His wrists and ankles and His Father turned His back on His Son.

Being necessarily cut off from His Father as He took upon Himself the sin of the world, that was the cruelest of all the experiences He was forced to endure. Then the final insult. Being crucified between two convicted criminals, both of whom were, by the admission of one of them (Lk. 23:40 – 43), worthy of death.

Holy Spirit

To understand not only what went on during the actual crucifixion but also the manner in which the effectiveness of the shed blood of the Messiah is applied to the individual repentant sinner, it is important to appreciate the spiritual aspect of the events that occurred for three hours in which the Messiah suffered alone on the cross, being separated during that time from His Father.

During the Lord's time on earth the whole identity of the Trinity can be seen separately yet working together in harmony and in three completely different dimensions. After all the Father remained in His place of abode beyond the created heavens, the Son was in a human body and the Holy Spirit was the unseen intermediary between the two and the active power source for the miracles. During the First Testament times the role of the Holy Spirit amongst men was severely restricted, only dealing with those chosen servants of God, such as Abraham, Moses, David and the prophets.

The Jews had been taught that their God was One and therein lies a problem because, as I have pointed out previously, in the second verse of Genesis it says that the Spirit of God, not God Himself but His Spirit, hovered over the empty and formless mass that was the embryo earth. In another part we are told that God never leaves His abode *"No one has ever seen God. But His Son, who is Himself God and is close to the Father's heart, He has told us about Him" (Jn. 1:18)* and *"Not that anyone has seen the Father, only I who was sent from God have seen the Father" (Jn. 6:46).* The Son reveals the Father to us and this is explained when Philip said to Jesus, *"Lord show us the Father and we will be satisfied".* In reply Jesus said to him, *"Have I been with you all this time, Philip, and you still do not know me? Whoever has seen me has seen the Father. How can you say, "Show us the Father"?" (see Jn. 14:8, 9).* This is a very difficult concept to grasp, but the saying, 'you have seen one you have seen them all', is true.

A member of the Godhead [not an angel] visited man in the Garden of Eden and this is considered to be the Son of God for it was to be the Son that was designated to be the one who was to come to earth in human form. It is also accepted that He came in the form of Melchizedek when He met with Abraham, and Abraham gave him tithes for it is a lesser man who gives tithes to a greater man. Such is the bond between the members of the Godhead that seeing one you have seen them all, because they are one as we shall see we below.

It is not strictly correct to refer to God as a trinity because of the unique oneness of God; the theology of the Trinity is merely a means for man to even begin to understand the uniqueness of the God of Israel — which is another factor believers from the Gentile nations must understand. With God, Israel must come first for He chose them as His priestly nation and all believers from other nations become members of the spiritual nation of Israel when they are baptized into the faith of Jesus as saviour.

Let us consider the matter of the tribe of Israel and the new Israel a little more deeply. This was the start of Israel being transformed from the physical nation to a spiritual nation. The physical nation was born from Abraham, its chosen founder, and developed throughout its history. After it had been established as a nation it was given ownership of the Promised Land with its capital being Jerusalem, its temple dedicated to the God of Israel, with priests in the line of Aaron officiating at the altar of sacrifice and in the holy place with its candelabra, table of showbread and altar of incense.

But what happened when the Messiah died. The earthly temple was made redundant by God the Holy Spirit tearing the curtain separating the holy place, where the priests officiated daily, and the most holy place where only the high priest was allowed to enter once a year on the day of atonement. This meant that the earthly had been succeeded by the heavenly because the original temple in heaven, of which the earthly was merely a copy, became the main focus for true believers.

No longer was the Holy Spirit involved with the temple made by human hands. The Lord had told the leaders of the Jews, *"Destroy this temple and I will raise it up in three days" (Jn. 2:19)* and the reason for that was that the whole basis of Israel's relationship with God was no longer the physical ritual of the temple, but spiritual.

To the woman of Samaria the Lord said *'If you knew the gift of God, and who it is that is saying to you, "Give me a drink", you would have asked him, and he would have given you living water'* or rather spiritual refreshment from the Holy Spirit because *"the water that I will give will become in them a spring of water gushing up to eternal life."*

When the Saviour ascended into heaven, He promised to released the Holy Spirit into the hearts and minds of believers, no longer confined to the temple, but through baptism was to be found in all those who truly believed, both Jew and Gentile, rather than just those physically born as Israelites, so that Abraham became not exclusive to the Jews but, as Paul wrote to the Galatians, *Understand, then, that those who have faith are children of Abraham* no matter whether they are Jew or Gentile.

This becomes clearer when we read what the Lord said to the woman:

'Woman, believe me, the hour is coming when you will worship the Father neither on this mountain nor in Jerusalem. You worship what you do not know; we worship what we know, for salvation is from the Jews. But the hour is coming, indeed is now here, when the true worshippers will worship the Father in spirit and truth, for the Father seeks such as these to worship him. God is spirit, and those who worship him must worship him in spirit and truth.' (Jn. 4)

This means that Israel has been changed and is being prepared for life after the earth has completely disappeared (see 2 Peter 3).

No one who despises Israel can be of God. Although the physical nation has sinned and gone away from God many times, and we have to ask ourselves the question, "what man has not sinned?" yet God has never completely abandoned it for salvation is still, and will always be, of the Jews, for the simple reason Jesus was completely Jewish, being the 'Son' of David and even now is the King of Israel and high priest according to the priesthood of Melchizedek.

When Jesus said to the woman at the well in Samaria that salvation was of the Jews He was speaking the truth because He Himself was and is true salvation for all mankind. As He is the only way to God, because no one can approach the Father except through Him, the Messiah of Israel and saviour of all who believe and an integral part of God.

Already we have a record of three aspect of God; Father, Son and Holy Spirit, so how can three be one? It is this fact that emphasizes the uniqueness of the God of Israel and singles Him out from all the other gods that have ever been worshipped in the course of human history.

We have already considered the different roles of each member within the One God. Their unity, their oneness is all to do with their reliance upon each other because each one supports the other two, and each one is reliant upon the other two; what is more their roles do not conflict, rather they compliment each other and the unifying element is a love so powerful, so all encompassing, so self-sustaining that it far exceeds anything that man can possibly comprehend. Three individuals working as one integral, inseparable unit, uniquely coordinated with one purpose. There is no other god like the God of Israel.

The only conclusion to which we can legitimately come, even though the word Trinity is used in this book, is that God is One and because one is only divisible by itself it remains one.

The Holy Spirit was the first to fully engage with the creation at the very beginning and took control of the formless embryonic earth to bring about the created environment we have today according to the will of the Father and the word of the Son, much of it outside the reach of man because no man has ever seen, nor is it possible for him to ever see, the full extent of the creation. The responsibility of the Holy Spirit was also to take care of the planet on which man was to be created.

In my book The Origin of Life I wrote this:

"Consider if you will.... a giant bubble, which we will call the envelope, but instead of this envelope containing air it contains the whole of creation"

It was in the 'bubble' containing the creation within the limitless space God occupies that the Holy Spirit exercised His power to control the evolution of the creation.

Throughout the history of man, particularly in relation to the Hebrew nation of Israel, the Holy Spirit was a key player in providing visions and dreams and the prophets with power. Consider Elijah preventing the rain falling for three and a half years and Elisha feeding a hundred men with twenty loaves of bread (2 Kgs. 4:42 – 44) and causing Naaman, the Syrian army general, to be healed in the river Jordan (2 Kgs. 5), to name but three.

It was the Holy Spirit, using His creative powers under the guidance of the Father, that first barren Elizabeth became pregnant with a son and six months later Mary was able to become pregnant even though she was a virgin. He guided the wise men to the new born Messiah in Bethlehem and warned them to return home by a different route. Crucially, however, the Holy Spirit was with the Son before the world began and continued to be with the Son without measure all the while He was living on the earth because God, although three persons, cannot be separated; they are one.

What is significant is that it was the Holy Spirit who provide the Son with knowledge of all that was happening around Him. It was the Holy Spirit who stilled the storm at the Messiah's command and caused people to be healed, informed the Messiah what people around Him were thinking, as the example below illustrates, and so much more.

"… some people brought a paralyzed man lying on a bed. When Jesus saw their faith, he said to the paralytic, 'Take heart, son; your sins are forgiven you.' Then some of the scribes said amongst themselves, 'This man speaks blasphemy.' But Jesus, <u>perceiving their</u>

thoughts, said, 'Why do you think evil in your hearts? For which is easier, to say, "Your sins are forgiven", or to say, "Stand up and walk"? But so that you may know that the Son of Man has authority on earth to forgive sins'. Speaking to the paralytic he said 'Stand up, take up your bed and go to your home.' In response the man stood up and went to his home. When the crowds saw it, they were filled with awe, and they glorified God, who had given such authority to men (or human beings)" (Matt. 9:2 – 8).

The concept of God consisting of three individuals is not an easy one for today's believers to understand, so it is understandable why so many Jews found it so difficult to believe that the human being before them was the Son of God, a full member of the Godhead yet living on earth amongst them. After the healing of the paralytic the multitude of onlookers "… *glorified God, who had given such authority to human beings" (Matt. 9:8).*

Even the Jewish ruling council headed by the chief priest could not believe how God could be standing before them when all they saw was a human being. "*This man speaks blasphemy" (see Matt 26:65),* cried the high priest before the council to which in unison the members shouted back that He was guilty of death.

How could He be God as a living breathing human being when remembering the scriptural record of the environmental eruption over Mount Sinai at the time of the giving of the law because of the awesome and all powerful presence of God? Moses met with God in the tent, although God was spirit and had no physical form. All the prophets spoke of how God spoke to them but there was no one there in physical form except when God sent an angel to appear before them. We know it as a miracle, but at the time the Jews were confused, although those that met with Jesus were astonished by Him and all that He said and did (Jn. 1:45 – 51).

Although it had been confirmed time and again throughout scripture that to God nothing is impossible, yet for the Son, when He was clothed in human flesh, to refer to Him who is in His heavenly home outside of the creational 'bubble' as His Father, and to the omnipresent Holy Spirit as the one who was to be sent down from heaven to start His full ministry amongst believers after the Son had returned to His Father, stretches the imagination of the human mind to breaking point. The words omnipresent, omnipotent and omniscient also are words that describe aspects of God that are very difficult for us to understand, except to suggest that God is beyond and above our comprehension.

The One God represents three distinct persons, each with their own task, yet so united that they cannot be separated. It was and is a massive ask. It is understandable that God released information about all the members of the Divine Trinity only gradually, with Daniel being possibly the first to have a vision of the Son of God (Dan. 7:13, 14).

As has already been discussed God and the Spirit were revealed from the beginning of Genesis, although it was not until Moses that a third member of God, which inevitably became a Divine Trinity in the minds of men, was revealed.

When Moses told the children of Israel that they should look out for One that was to come the idea that He would be none other than the Son of God was not evident:

> *"The Lord your God will raise up for you a prophet like me from among your own people; you must listen to that prophet. You petitioned the of the Lord your God at Horeb on the day of the assembly when you said: 'If I hear the voice of the Lord my God any more, or ever again see this blazing fire of his presence, I will die.' Then the Lord replied to me: 'They are right in what they have said. I will raise up for them a prophet like you from among their own people; I will put my words in his mouth for he shall speak to them everything that I command [Jn. 5:19 - 47]. I myself will hold accountable anyone who does not take notice of the words that the prophet shall speak in my name." (Deut. 18:15 – 19)*

Compare what Moses said to what Peter said on the day of Pentecost, remembering that the promised Prophet is by this time also known as the Son of God and Son of Man:

> *Moses said to the fathers, "The Lord your God will raise up for you a Prophet like me from your own people. You must listen to whatever he tells you. And it shall be that everyone who does not listen to that prophet will be utterly destroyed from among the people." (Acts 3:22, 23; read 16 - 26)*

These are harsh words yet Simeon and Anna knew because the Holy Spirit identified the infant Jesus when they met Him in His 'human mother's arms' in the temple, but both of them had become intimate with God and therefore spiritually aware.

We have the advantage of the scriptures and many authoritative and well versed spiritually attuned scholars to assist our understanding of this matter so that we can follow the full narrative from Genesis through Revelation, which those living at the time of the Lord's coming did not have. But even that does not make the task any easier. So credit for their God focused lives must go to those, such as Simeon and Anna, who were sufficiently sensitive to the Holy Spirit that He was able to reveal to them the long promised Messiah even when He was a baby. Others came to believe in the Messiah during His ministry because of their openness to the Spirit of God, possibly because their heads were not filled to bursting point with a surfeit of learning and human opinion.

The difficulty is compounded when it comes to understanding the cross. It was when Christ died and actually shed blood from His wounds, particularly from the spear piercing His side, that the salvation process was started, with its fulfilment coming when He rose from the dead, thus defeating the permanency of physical and spiritual death, which potentially permanently separates a man from God, and then ascended into heaven.

Although the scripture tells us that God the Father could not look upon sin, and the Lord Jesus Christ became sin for us by taking upon Himself the sin of the whole world, the Holy Spirit was there with Him, not assisting Him but acting as a witness to the sacrifice so that He could apply the efficacious effects of the blood of Christ to those who come to believe that Jesus is the anointed One sent from God to save us from our sins.

Crucially we are told that the blood of bulls and goats and the ashes of a heifer could only cleanse men's bodies, their flesh, from the defilement caused by sin, which was needed continually because men sin continually. But consider how much more effective and powerful the blood of the Messiah, the Christ, who through the power of the Holy Spirit offered His own pure spotless body to God, is able to cleanse not just the flesh but the conscience of the truly repentant sinner from sinful acts by being the perfect sacrifice for sin (Heb. 9:13 – 15).

Let there be no doubt, the Messiah was God in the beginning. As John wrote, the eternal Word was in the beginning with God, and indeed was God, so that nothing that was created was created without His direct involvement. In Him was life and that life was the light of men. He was God in Mary's womb and became flesh through her. Even as a child growing into a man He was God, in fact the Messiah was never not God.

When the Messiah was baptized by John in the river Jordan the Holy Spirit came down as a dove to signify the divinity of the Messiah, an act that made clear that as part of the divine Trinity He was filled with the Holy Spirit without measure. Actually the Spirit had never left Him, could not leave Him, so the symbol of the dove was, I believe, for the benefit of the onlookers as a sign that He really was not only from God but also God Himself.

The holy Trinity is God. Indeed not one of the three can be fully separated from the other two, so all the while the Messiah was on the earth His link with the Father was through the Holy Spirit, the three working together in continuous harmony. It is a precious example to us of what God is able to do for us. Having been in existence for eternity, the

Trinity that is God, is sufficient unto itself and has no need of assistance because it is the source of all that is.

Whilst the Messiah hung on the cross, however, the Father could not look upon the Son in whom He was well pleased, because of the sin the Son took upon Himself. This is what made three hours of His time on the cross particularly painful and traumatic for the Messiah, the Son of God was temporally separated from the Father.

Crucially it was the Holy Spirit who was with the Son witnessing the act of sacrifice who subsequently has been able to apply the blood of the Lamb of God and cause it to wipe clean the history of sinfulness of the repentant sinner, not once, but be a constant cleansing power all the while the sinner is repentant and fully focused on serving God with his whole mind, heart, soul and strength.

Messiah

Confined to His human body with its feelings and emotions, the Messiah had not looked forward to this moment. In the Garden of Gethsemane He cried out to His father about removing *'this cup from Me'*, quickly reassuring His Father that He was willing to go through with it because it was the Father's will that He should *'die for the people'* (Jn. 11:50). That was why He had come and it was in fulfillment of God's plan of salvation the Godhead had decided upon from the beginning. What is also interesting is that such was the impact on His body and the severe emotional and spiritual stress He experienced at that time in the darkness of the Garden of Gethsemane, that as He considered all that He was to endure He sweated great drops of blood, a natural phenomenon for anyone under very severe stress.

As the method of death of the Messiah had been decided on by God, and the Son, who would have realized how agonizing it would be, the question must be asked why was that particular method chosen? The answer would seem to be that it was gruesome enough to emphasize just how repugnant sin was to God and how seriously He took the need to provide an antidote to sin, a means of forgiving the curse of sin that would do a thorough job of deep cleansing within the soul and spirit of the repentant sinner. As Charles Wesley wrote, it was to *"be of sin the double cure, cleanse me from its quilt and shame"*, which means the sinless Messiah, by taking upon Himself the sins of the whole world, became sin for us sinners and by taking on that rebellious nature towards God and overcoming it, not only could the repentant sinner be cleansed from all sin, but sin was also be deprived of its power over all those who turn their lives over to the Lord Jesus Christ, the Messiah to the Jews.

A number of events occurred that separated His death from that of all those others crucified for wrong doing over which the chief priests and leaders of the people had no control.

Place of crucifixion — was in a prominent place by a busy thoroughfare outside the city walls because those who passed by shouted abuse and shook their heads in mockery (Matt. 27:39). It had to be in a spacious area because His supporters were able to witness the event at a distance (Matt. 27:55), although near enough for Him to command John to take care of Mary, the mother who bore His human body.

It was also the place where the chief priests and leaders of the people were able to vent their anger and hatred of Him by flinging abuse at Him.

> *"You claim you can destroy the temple and rebuild it in three days; well if you are the Son of God then come down from the cross and save yourself."*
>
> *"He saved others yet he cannot save himself. "*
>
> *"If He is the King of Israel; let him come down from the cross now, and we will believe in him."*
>
> *"He trusts in God; let God deliver him now, if he wants to; for he said, "I am the Son of God.""*

All this abuse from unbelievers towards the Son of Man who, according to scripture, was providing mankind with the means of eternal salvation. Because of the need to inter the body of the Lord quickly the tomb needed to be fairly near the site of the crucifixion.

Earlier before Pilate, the crowd had already taken on the responsibility for His death for when Pilate absolved himself from his death (Matt.

27:24), in unison those who had gathered to see the spectacle shouted, *"We will take responsibility for His death, we and our children" (Matt. 25:25).* This had been said in the highly charged atmosphere generated by Satan and stoked up within the enclosed, oppressive spiritual atmosphere of Jerusalem by the chief priests and elders of the people. It is most likely that members of the crowd could almost taste the spiritual atmosphere, so intense would it have been.

What is clear, and that applies to many who celebrate Easter year after year, is that neither the priests, whose job it was to interpret the scriptures, nor the people, who themselves should have personally sought after the knowledge of God, seemed to properly understand all that was happening but were being carried along by the events.

It is easy for us to study the scriptures and read all the prophetic passages regarding the Messiah's sacrifice and listen to Handel's 'Messiah' and other oratorio's, and music which sets the atmosphere for the celebration of Easter, but how many seek for a fuller, deeper spiritual understanding of all that the Messiah did and suffered during His ministry and on the cross for our salvation? How many of those who call themselves believers ever read the scriptures and study them to gain the knowledge of God, just as those in Jerusalem shouting at the Messiah should have done. It was their ignorance that played into the hand of God to allow the murder of His Son.

It is possible for the annual programme of the Christian year to be observed in a mechanical and clinical way and therefore be unfulfilling except in a human sense because the pageantry and pleasurable music and singing has the potential for the individual participant to dispense with the need for them to become spiritually involved with God.

The purpose of this book is to demonstrate that there is far greater spiritually fertile substance within the scriptural text to excite and focus the reborn human spirit on deeper spiritual truths than most people would believe. Indeed, contained in the historical events and prophetic announcements leading up to the birth, ministry and sacrifice of the Messiah, along with the details of the trial and crucifixion, there is a treasure trove of inspirational knowledge to excite the spirit and inspire the soul.

The notice — Pilate demonstrated his angst and anger at being forced by the Jewish religious leadership to condemn to death a man whom he considered innocent. As the time for Him to be sacrificed for sin had come the Lord told him, he had no control over the situation and that the man *"who brought Me to you has the greater sin"*. However, Pilate, being a pagan, had no knowledge of truth (Jn. 18:38), and found himself quickly loosing control of the whole situation.

When it came to finally conceding defeat and authorizing the crucifixion, he felt compelled to demonstrate his power over the Jewish religious leaders who had so aggressively undermined his authority, by having a notice written in several languages and fixed on the cross above the Messiah to emphasize his disagreement that He was deserving of death. Yeshua (Joshua or Jesus) of Nazareth, King of the Jews.

This angered the Jews who wanted the wording changed, but Pilate was adamant, *"what I have written I have written"*, and so the notice stayed and was recorded for posterity to describe exactly what he was, but not King of the Jews only but the King of all those who believe and will enter into the kingdom of heaven.

Forgiveness — *"Am I a Jew?"* Pilate asked Him. *"Your own people and their chief priests and leaders brought you to me. But I do not understand why. So I am asking you, what have you done?"*

Because this matter was all wrapped up in Hebrew history and theology, it was not surprising that this whole matter of the priests requiring the man standing before him to be condemned to death was beyond Pilate's comprehension; *"But I do not understand why"*. Indeed it was a mystery to all those who had no knowledge of the Hebrew scriptures, particularly for non-Jews such as Pilate and Herod. Even those accusing Him of the offense of blasphemy had got to the stage of being out of their depth because from the cross the Lord uttered those words of Divine grace *"Father forgive them for they do no know what they are doing"*. For this reason Satan was able to take control.

Knowing this, and the fact that it was necessary for Him to die for the sins of mankind, the Messiah forgave those responsible for His execution, particularly the soldiers who were only following orders. As has already been discussed the problem with Judas was that he, like Cain (Gen. 4:3 – 16), certainly by his actions, seemed far from understanding God's plan and purpose for the Messiah and therefore decided to follow his own thoughts and ideas without reference to God even though he came under the influence of the Word of Truth made flesh along with the other disciples. By the time he realized that it was not possible for him to force his master to do what <u>he</u> wanted Him to do, it was far too late. So distressed was he by the turn of events he had initiated, that he returned the money the temple authorities had given to him and committed suicide.

In contrast, the end of life spiritual rescue of a criminal crucified alongside Him emphasizes the Messiah's claim to seek and save those that are lost and willing to repent and believe in Him. One of the criminals, cynical and far from God, added to the abuse of the onlookers by challenging Him to rescue the three of them from their crosses. The other admitted that his deeds had been evil and he was rightfully suffering for them, acknowledged that the Messiah was innocent of all charges, and, with great foresight, asked Him to remember him when He entered His kingdom. At that moment the man was forgiven his sins and would indeed enter heaven with Him.

Darkness — God is light and in Him there is no darkness at all. Turn away from the light and there is nothing but darkness. As the Son of God, Messiah to the Jews, hung on the cross, for three hours God turned His face away causing darkness to cover the face of the earth. It was necessary for God to demonstrate to those instrumental in having His Son crucified that they were dealing with God Himself (see Acts 5:29 – 39).

Surely the people would have found it strange for normally bright sunlight at noon to be absent all the while the Messiah was alive and suffering on the cross? The vociferous reaction of the excited crowds at the public trial, when they shouted for the man to be crucified, and then the probably rowdy processional journey to the site of the public crucifixion, is likely to have suddenly been dampened when an eerie and oppressive darkness enveloped them. The unnatural environmental event whilst the man was suffering on the cross must have had a profound impact on many observers and passers by.

Messiah cries out — We cannot possibly appreciate the trauma the Messiah went through on the cross as He was counted among the transgressors. What with the crudely fashioned nails of beaten metal piercing His human flesh through the wrists and ankles and hammered through them into the wood, and the pain of hanging on those nails on the cross in an extremely difficult twisted position, His bent legs forced to one side by the nail through the side of His foot, yet a worse spiritual trauma for a spiritually sensitive man was to come when His Father turned his face away so that for three hours there was separation between the Father and the Son.

> *"From noon until three in the afternoon darkness covered the whole land. About three o'clock Jesus cried with a loud voice, 'Eli, Eli, lema sabachthani?' that is, 'My God, my God, why have you forsaken me?' ….. Then Jesus cried again with a loud voice and His body breathed its last and His Spirit left the body." (see Matt. 27:45, 46, 50).*

Those three hours were the crucial time when the Messiah accounted for the sins of the whole world by taking them upon Himself, during which time He was separated and alone, the Holy Spirit merely being a witness to His agony and sacrifice, unable to lessen the trauma of the human pain and spiritual isolation of the Messiah.

Temple curtain torn in two — such was the height of the building containing the holy place and holy of holies that there was no possibility of any man being able to reach the top of the curtain separating the two rooms, a curtain which was made of thick highly embroidered material that was impossible to tear. Descriptions of the veil can be found in Alfred Edersheim's Life and Times of Jesus. Its purpose was to prevent all but the high priest gaining access to the presence of God, and he was only allowed to enter just once per year on the Day of Atonement with blood from an animal sacrifice on his hands.

Therefore, for the curtain to be ripped in two, no matter in which direction (top to bottom, bottom to top), such an event had to be an act of God, although how it was known the curtain was miraculously torn in such a fashion is unknown except a priest had been in the Holy Place at the time. Although the sequence of events cannot be identified, the rending of the curtain certainly indicated the irreversible change in the manner of man's relationship to God that had been completely changed with the completion of the sacrifice of the Son of God.

One thing is for certain, at that point the Holy of Holies, which had not contained the Ark of the Covenant with its Mercy seat lid since its disappearance at the sacking of the temple by Nebuchadnezzar, was no longer separated from the holy place allowing access to more than just the annual visit by the high priest with the blood of sacrifice on his hands.

This was God signaling the end of His requirement for the man built temple in Jerusalem. Indeed, as the woman at the well was told by our Saviour, from henceforth the Father would speak not with the high priest once a year, but directly with anyone who accepted His Son as their Lord and Saviour and willingly worshipped Him as their God.

All true believing individuals would each become a temple of the Holy Spirit, with the individual temples being brought together to become one living holy temple for the living God (Eph. 2:19, 22). Such a unifying of Jew and Gentile could only have been achieved through the Messiah having done a work of reconciliation which has brought them together through spiritual rebirth and conscience cleansing forgiveness by the application of the blood of Messiah by the Holy Spirit to those who have believed.

This is the working of the Holy Spirit, through the sacrifice of the Son of God with the authority of the Father.

Earthquake — throughout the history of the Hebrew people God has used environmental activity to emphasize His influence on events (Isa. 29:6 – Ariel [vs 1] is Jerusalem the city of David; Amos

1:1). Consider for instance the environmental activity over Mount Sinai during the giving of the Law and the marriage of Israel with their God, and Elijah's experience on Mount Horeb when there was high winds, and an earthquake and then fire before he heard the still small voice of God.

It is interesting that a pagan army officer realized the meaning of the earthquake after the period of three hours of darkness between noon and three o'clock in the afternoon saying, *"truly this was the Son of God"*. Surrounding the cross were the forces of evil, but on the cross and protecting the Son of God was the Holy Spirit and the forces of God, for Satan was limited to what he was able to accomplish, just as he was limited in what he could do against Job.

Tombs opened — The collective events that happened around the time of the Messiah's sacrifice and death must have concerned the chief priest and leaders of the people. But particularly when the tombs were opened by the earthquake and out came the spirits of long dead saints of God to give witness to the fact that the man crucified on Calvary really was the Messiah of God offering Himself up as the eternal Passover Lamb of God, in the strange and somewhat overwhelming physical and spiritual atmosphere of environmental activity of midday darkness and the earthquake outside Jerusalem's city walls. We are not told of the immediate affect this had on the ordinary population, but it could well have been an underlying reason why so many were added to the church just fifty days later on the Day of Pentecost. In those days memories were exceptionally good.

Witness of the Centurion — Here was a man of unknown nationality, serving in the Roman army merely doing his job. Gruesome though it may be, it is unlikely to have been the first crucifixion he had attended in that capacity. What made this event unusual was the strange atmosphere and combination of environmental events and spiritual pressures along with the presence of the Holy Spirit in that place which made him respond as he did.

The arrest, trial and crucifixion of the Messiah had to be accomplished in a very short timescale because of the official Passover when no bodies were to be left hanging.

Time	Event	References
Previous events	Last supper	Matt. 26:20 - 30; Mk. 14:17 - 26; Lk. 22:14 - 38; Jn. 13:21 - 30
	Garden of Gethsemane	Matt. 26:36 - 46; Mk. 14:32 - 42; Lk. 22:39 - 45
	Betrayal and arrest	Matt. 26:47 - 56; Mk. 14:43 - 52; Lk. 22:47 - 53; Jn. 18:1 - 11
	Trial before Caiaphas	Matt. 27:1, 2; Mk. 15:1; Lk. 22:66 - 71
6 a.m.	1st Trial before Pilate	Matt. 27:11 - 14; Mk. 15:2 - 5; Lk. 23:1 - 5; Jn. 18:28 - 37
	Trial before Herod	Lk. 23:6 - 12
7 a.m.	2nd Trial before Pilate	Lk. 23:11
	Sentenced to death	Matt. 27:26; Mk. 15:15; Lk. 23:23, 24; Jn. 19:16
8 a.m.	Journey to Calvary	Matt. 27:32 - 34; Mk. 15:21 - 24; Lk. 23:26 - 31; Jn. 19:16, 17
9 a.m. 3rd hour	Nailed to the cross	Mk. 15:25; Lk. 23:34
	Soldiers cast lots	Mk. 15:24

Time	Event	References
10 – 12 a.m.	Insulted and Mocked by:	Note: The Messiah hung on the cross for six hours
	Those passing by	Matt. 27:39, 40
	Leaders of the Jews	Mk. 15:31
	Soldiers	Lk. 23:36, 37
	One of those crucified	Lk. 23:39
	Criminal saved	Lk. 23:40 -43
	John appointed to look after Mary	Jn. 19:26, 27
Noon 6th hour - 3 p.m. 9th hour	Darkness covers the land until the ninth hour	Matt. 27:45; Mk. 15:33
	Messiah cries out to the Father	Matt. 27:46
	Becomes thirsty	Jn. 19:28, 29
	Said, "It is finished"	Jn. 19:30a
	Said, "Father, into your hands I commit My Spirit" and died	Lk. 23:46

Now let us try to relate that into the days of the week. According to Leviticus 23:5 Passover is to be held on the 14th day of Nissan.

In the year of 2015 the first day of the month of Nissan, which is the first month of the ecclesiastical year for Israel, started on March 21st and ended 30 days later on April 19th. This means that the 14th day of Nissan was on Friday April 3rd. However, in the year of our Lord's death it was on a Wednesday, therefore we can say that the Messiah and His disciples ate their Passover meal on **Tuesday the 13th day of Nissan**, after which He went with His disciples to the Garden of Gethsemane (in which there was a cave containing a press to extract the oil from olives), at the bottom of the Mount of Olives. It was there in the garden that Judas betrayed the Messiah.

The first trial of the Messiah was held secretly in the night time hours **(1830+ hrs) of (Tuesday/Wednesday) 14th day of Nissan**. By 0600 hrs He was standing first before Pilate then before Herod. By approximately 0700 hrs He was back before Pilate when the wrangling over the application of the death sentence took place between Pilate and the leaders of the Jews.

He was crucified at 0900 and from Noon (6th hour) to 1500 (9th hour) darkness fell as the Father turned His back on His Son, or rather, because He is Spirit, He separated Himself from His Son. The Messiah finally said that the task He had been given to do had been accomplished (it is finished) and gave up His Spirit, or rather His eternal Spirit left His body, thus causing His body to die because he had the power to give up His earthly life whilst maintaining His Spiritual life:

> *"for this reason the Father loves Me, because I lay down my life in order that I might take it up again. No one can take it from Me, but I lay it down of My own accord. I have power to lay it down, and I have power to take it up again. I have received this command from my Father."*
> *(Jn. 10:17, 18).*

Having anything to do with a corpse would make a Jew unclean and unable to be involved in the set annual celebrations. The Passover was counted as a Sabbath day on which no work was done and the leaders of the Jews were concerned that neither the Messiah's body nor the bodies of the two criminals could remain on the crosses on Passover, hence the legs of the two criminals were broken to speed their death.

What is particularly interesting is that the Messiah had to die on the 14th day of Nissan, the day God set for the celebration of Passover. It was essential that as the perfect Passover Lamb He died on that day, yet the leaders of the Jews were preparing to celebrate Passover on the following day the 15ᵗʰ day of Nissan thus treating the day of the crucifixion as the day of preparation (Mk. 15:42), the Passover being considered a Sabbath day. This is because in that year the Passover was celebrated on two consecutive days, which meant that the Messiah died on the day of Passover set by God and the leaders of the Jews, who were responsible for His death, conveniently celebrated it the following day. For one explanation of why that might have been see the web site below:

http://www.puritanboard.com/showthread.php/59717-Why-Did-Jesus-Eat-the-Passover-Before-All-Israel-Ate

By the ninth hour the Lord knew that He had accomplished all that He had come to achieve, through His suffering on the cross as prophesied. As soon as He died He knew that the Father's charge for sin against men would be lifted for all repentant sinners whose lives are changed by the cleansing of sin through the application of His blood, and the rebirth of the spirit in man by the power of the Holy Spirit.

The instruction for the first Passover lamb required that its bones should not be broken (Ex. 12:46), therefore the Messiah was seen to die (Jn. 19:28 – 30) and John was an eyewitness to all that happened.

When the Jews asked for the legs of the men to be broken to hasten their deaths (Jn. 19:31 – 37) the Lord was already dead and to confirm that fact a soldier jabbed a sharp spear into His side.

To emphasize just how in control of His body the Messiah was the scriptures tell us that 'He gave up His Spirit' (Jn. 19:30), which meant that His eternal Spirit, which could never die because He was God incarnate, left His human body. As a conscious act 'He gave up His Spirit' or rather just as He had entered the body whilst in Mary's womb so He left that mature body which, as a result, died and this was proven by the separated blood and plasma flowing out of the side of His body when it was pierced by the soldier's spear. The 'tent' in which He had lived for 33.5 years, and by which He was recognized, had been 'vacated'.

As soon as the two other men had died the bodies were removed from the crosses. From His nighttime arrest to His death at the ninth hour (1500 hrs) in the afternoon, all was accomplished in a single day, giving time for His body to be put into the rock tomb, originally prepared for a rich man (Is. 53:9), before the start of the special Sabbath. The chief priests and leaders of the Jews could well have left the scene with mixed feelings after experiencing all the events that surround the site of the crucifixion because of what was said and by whom and the unnerving environmental activity. Those whose hardness of heart dominated their thoughts and actions would probably have gone away pleased with their efforts, whilst others could well have been questioning what forces had been at play over the previous few hours and what the events meant to their faith in God.

TOMB & RESURRECTION

The reason the Bible is worth studying is that just as God is complete in Himself, so the scriptures are complete in themselves, with the First Testament laying the foundations for all the events of the Second, which are the fulfillment of the First Testament prophecies God gave through the prophets of old, with some yet to be fulfilled. Even the timing and manner of the Messiah's entry into Jerusalem was correctly prophesied. So too the entombment of His body (Is. 53:9). Therefore, in spite of the fact that at least four hundred years separates the two testaments, neither is complete without the other (Part 1 and Part 2) and, because of the outstanding prophecies still to be fulfilled from both testaments, neither can be neglected.

What is also interesting is those involve in the writing of the Second Testament.

- Matthew, a hated, self-serving tax collector working for the Romans and considered a traitor but chosen by Jesus to be a disciple.

- Mark, who was not a disciple but saw the Messiah during his ministry was nearly grabbed by the mob after His arrest. A cousin of Barnabas, although he went with Paul and Barnabas to Antioch he deserted them at Perga to return to Jerusalem which upset Paul, although their relationship changed later on when he was well spoken of by Paul. Much of Mark's gospel comes from the teachings of Peter.

- Luke was a Gentile doctor who served Paul and did a great deal of research which resulted in his gospel, written as a letter. It would have been written with as much accuracy as was possible in those days providing more persuasive evidence that the Second Testament is to be believed. What is more the sequel of the gospel, the book of Acts continues to account for what happened after the Lord's death and resurrection, and the unstoppable spread of the message of salvation around the world empowered by the activities of the Holy Spirit.

- John the favoured disciple, previously a fisherman.

- Peter, an unrefined fisherman chosen by the Lord to be a fisher of men and given a lead position amongst the disciples, *"feed my sheep"*. Prone to mistakes yet he was a leader within the new church and the first to evangelize the Gentiles

- James – the Lord's brother conceived and born in the natural way of mankind.

- Paul, a Pharisee of Pharisees, obviously very well educated in the Hebrew scriptures having studied under the highly respected Gamaliel. After the death of the Messiah he was very active in trying to stop the spread of the gospel causing the death and imprisonment of many believers until the risen Lord met him on the road to Damascus and turned his life around. Through the enlightening of the Holy Spirit which opened up the scriptures to him to reveal the true meaning of the First Testament scriptures in regard to the coming of the anointed one, He became as ardent a disciple of the risen Lord as he had been as an opponent of the early church.

Many decry the validity of the Second Testament, and yet those who wrote it were ordinary people who had been with the Lord and were writing from the heart about all that they had actually seen, heard and experienced, providing us with eyewitness accounts and with extraordinary power to convey the truth of all that the Lord Jesus said and did through the empowerment of the Holy Spirit. What is more, of those who have read their accounts and letters millions have been brought to such an understanding of God in Christ that they have given their hearts and lives to the Saviour, many even willing to die rather than give up their faith, which suggests the testimony of those involved with the Messiah and the spread of the gospel as recorded in the Second Testament must be sound. After all how could it have been possible for so many to have thought up such a plot that agreed so fully with the First Testament, including one man who was the Lord's physical brother, James, having been born of Mary and Joseph.

Thus the effect that the gospel has had on a vast number of people around the world since His ministry in Israel, and the work of the Holy Spirit within the hearts of believers since, means that the accounts in the Second Testament must be true. Not only that but for over 500 people to have seen the risen Lord as well as those closest to Him experiencing not just His intimate presence but also further teaching, the case for the risen Lord is proven beyond reasonable doubt, not forgetting those that witnessed His ascension into the sky and the coming of the Holy Spirit in power as promised. All this adds up to a powerful message that only a fool would disregard it (Ps. 14:1; 53:1).

Death of the Messiah

To all intents and purposes, certainly as far as the crowds surrounding the site of the three crucifixions were concerned, the 'King of the Jews' was dead. The disciple John, along with other followers, including the Lord's human mother, was a witness to it. There is also the word of the centurion, confirmed by the soldier's spear, that not only had he died, with blood and water giving final proof of His death, but that He was from God.

The sign above the Messiah's head revealed the truth of who He was although the chief priests and leaders of the Jews were not prepared to accept it, even though they were the ones who studied the Hebrew scriptures in minute detail along with the writings of rabbis throughout the ages, the thoughts of whom seem to have taken precedence over that of holy writ. And that perhaps was their problem.

Their studies could well have dwelt far too much on the letter of the law and what the rabbis of old understood to be the meaning of those scriptures, rather than being able to freely meditate on the law in order for them to understand the spirit of the law as revealed to them by God. The mental attitude they should have had was 'what was God teaching them that would enable them to get closer to Him and learn of Him so that they were more able to serve Him'.

With an earth bound mind and intellect and an analytical brain they were unable to meditate on the word as Asaph had done. At a time of deep distress He recalled all that God had done in the past (Ps. 77) causing his nights to be filled with joyful song. Then when everything seemed to go wrong, as it does for all of us from time to time, he meditated within his heart on the scriptures and on his relationship with God.

It was because Asaph was so focused on God that, through his God-sensitive spirit, he was able to consider his relationship with God in those difficult times, asking himself if the Lord had rejected him forever. It would appear that it was that close, whole-person relationship he had with God that he was able to praise Him whose ways are holy in spite of his immediate troubles:

I will call to mind the deeds of the Lord;
I will remember your wonderful deeds of old.
I will meditate on all your work,
and ponder on your mighty deeds.
Your ways, O God, are holy.
What god is so mighty as our God?

You are the God who works wonders;
you have displayed your might among the peoples.
With your strong arm you redeemed your people,
the descendants of Jacob and Joseph.
Selah
(Ps. 77:11 – 15)

Hindsight is very important to believers, as it was for Asaph, because by that means they are able to see the hand of God in their lives and therefore praise God for all the blessings He has bestowed on them. But Paul, writing to the believers in Rome says, *"we know that all things work together for good to those that love God, who are called according to His purpose for them." (Rom. 8:28).*

Even when things appear to go wrong, it has been my experience that God is in them too, for at times of seeming disaster God is causing us to change direction or learn something new, experience something that is essential for our spiritual growth and the growing of our faith and trust in Him, so that He can do a further work in us and lead us onto a new way or new work that relies on that experience, that testing. The essential feature is that we are focused on God and never give up on Him for He will never give up on us.

Consider what another Psalmist wrote about having tried his best to find God, a search of the spirit, he writes, *"… please do not let me wander from your commands, for I have hidden your word in my heart that I might not sin against you …" (Ps. 119:10, 11).* That is the only way to keep close to God and allow Him to influence our thinking.

With all the wrong things that were done to the Messiah, our Lord, the purpose of the Lord's coming to the earth was ultimately to die for the nation of Israel! (Jn. 11:51). Not for that nation only but for all mankind to which the good news of eternal salvation would soon be spread. It is the six hours of His physical suffering on the cross, and particularly the three hours of spiritual suffering, when He was separated from His Father, that was the greatest burden He was prepared to take upon Himself in order to save mankind from sin and the Devil.

The exact location of the tomb is disputed with two sites becoming visitor attractions for the pilgrim and tourist alike. But the site of the actual tomb is of little consequence because His body is not there, rather it is the account of all that happened to the Messiah, to God made man, that is of greatest importance.

It is at times of great significance that true friends come to the fore and offer their services. We have learned much from the secret meeting of Nicodemus with the Messiah and now another senior figure in the life of the nation came forward to offer his services.

> *Joseph of Arimathea, a respected member of the council, who was himself waiting expectantly for the kingdom of God, taking courage went into Pilate and asked for the body of Jesus.*
>
> *Then Pilate, amazed that he might already be dead, summoned the centurion, and he asked him whether he had been dead for some time. When he learned from the centurion that he was dead, he granted the body to Joseph.*
>
> *Then Joseph bought a linen cloth, took down the body, wrapped it in the linen cloth, and laid it in a tomb hewn out of the rock. He then rolled a stone against the door of the tomb. Mary Magdalene and Mary the mother of Jesus saw where the body was laid. (see Mark 15:43 – 47)*

Joseph of Arimathea is recorded as being a man waiting for the kingdom of God (God focused), a member of the council who is unlikely to have consented to the crucifixion, a rich man who had become a disciple of the Messiah though secretly. With the Lord's death and nowhere to bury His body, Joseph was forced out of hiding and senior enough to be able to go to Pilate to ask for the Lord's body to be given into his charge.

With the help of other disciples, including the women, the Lord's body was carefully and lovingly removed from the cross, wrapped in linen cloth and taken to a newly hewn rock tomb nearby and His body laid there.

The leaders of the Jews

The hard heartedness of the majority of the religiously minded Jewish leadership knew no bounds. To them the strict observance of the Passover ritual was of paramount importance. In accordance with what God said about crucifixion (hanging on a tree - Deut. 21:22, 23), that the body must be removed before the end of the day, the Jews dutifully requested that the bodies of the three men should not be left on the crosses the following day (Jn. 19:31 – 37). There seemed to be no compassion so long as the legal, ritual requirements were observed, so the body of the Son of God was hastily removed and unceremoniously transferred to a private tomb.

Suspicious to the last, they were concerned that something might happen to the body when interred in the grave, possibly at the hands of the disciples, so they again petitioned Pilate.

> *The next day, that is, after the day of Preparation, the chief priests and the Pharisees gathered before Pilate and said, 'Sir, we remember what that deceiver said while he was still alive, "After three days I will rise again." Therefore command that the tomb be made secure until the third day; otherwise his disciples may go and steal him away, and say to the people, "He has been raised from the dead", making the last deception worse than the first.' Pilate said to them, 'You have a guard of soldiers; go, make it as secure as you can.' So they went with the guard and made the tomb secure by sealing the stone and setting the guard. (see Matt. 27:62 – 66)*

Notice how they accused the Lord of being a deceiver and promoted the deception that they would eventually use, *'the disciples came and stole Him away making out that He had risen from the dead'.*

Suspicious and without a shred of God consciousness in spite of the environmental and spiritual events that had occurred during the crucifixion and following the death of their Messiah, and the tearing of the curtain between the holy place and the holy of holies which fact they kept secret, they were concerned that the disciples or some other group would try to steal the body and claim He had risen just as He had publically promised He would. These were religious people who wanted to engineer all that happened to their nation, in spite of their restricted powers because of their subjection to the Roman occupying forces and the fact that they were supposed to be the servants of God rather than acting as though they were God.

At this point it is worth differentiating between the religious leaders and those who live a life of faith. The strictly religious man (both men and women are included) is one who is focused purely on the ritual in the worship of their particular god, believing that they communicate with their god through that ritual according to the particular holy book they use. The man of faith, on the other hand, focuses on the person of their God (the God of Israel being the only true God). In seeking to worship Him from their hearts in adoration and deepening belief and faith, entering into spiritual intercourse with Him, spirit to Spirit, the man of faith might find a prescribed form of formal worship helpful. However, although that form of ritual can be very helpful to some, it must be tempered with worship from the heart because it is into the heart of a man that God looks.

Not only was the very heavy round stone sealing the entrance of the tomb itself sealed to the surrounding rock by the priests, but a guard was placed by the tomb to prevent the body being stolen (Matt. 27:66). Speculation would suggest that the leading Jews would have been nervously keeping an eye on the tomb throughout the celebrations and would have been relieved as each hour passed with nothing happening.

The timing of the crucifixion was specific. Not only did the Messiah die on the 14th day of Nissan according to the command of God, but the resurrection occurred on what was to the Jews the first day of the week. Their seventh day was the Sabbath (from sunset Friday to sunset Saturday) which God declared was a day of rest because after the creation God was said to have rested on the seventh day.

The first day of the week (sunset Saturday to sunset Sunday) was a new beginning, the old is passed and the new begins, and the whole purpose of the death of the Lord was to provide mankind with an eternal salvation that was completely separate from the old animal sacrifices with an earthly high priest confined to the man built temple in Jerusalem, especially when the man behind the latest manifestation of Moses' tabernacle, which took 46 years to build, was a tyrant. In fact none of the king Herods who ruled in the Holy Land were particularly pleasant men. One tried to kill the infant Jesus but only succeeded in killing a large number of innocent boys under the age of two. Another had John the Baptizer beheaded because of a very foolish promise to his daughter Salome who danced before him. Yet another died because he was publically described as a 'god' and accepted the accolade.

The Messiah was crucified and buried on the Thursday evening and rose in the early morning of our Sunday, therefore He was in the tomb for three days. Then, before sunrise on the third day, remember that the Jewish day started at sunset the day before so this was well into their 'day', and the first day of the week (our Sunday), there was a great earthquake and, to the amazement and horror of the guards, an angel came down from the sky and single handedly rolled back the heavy stone. The guards would have been unlearnéd men unused to the spectacular things of God and therefore terrified, unable to understand what was going on with this spiritual incursion into the human world.

Such outstanding spiritual events affect different people in different ways. Just as with the raising of Lazarus many believed, others immediately reported back to the Pharisees all that the Messiah had done. It is interesting that Matthew reports that only some of the guard reported to the chief priests all that had happened, although we do not know what percentage of them did so.

The chief priests inevitably reacted in the way of unbelievers, although not having the faintest idea of what exactly happened they wanted to make sure their made-up understanding of events were fed to the public at large by paying the guards to start the rumour that His disciples had come during the night and stolen His body whilst they slept, promising to ensure they would not get into trouble should the governor hear about it. In reality it was their problem alone and therefore of no real concern of the governor (Matt. 27:65, 66).

Just consider what the guards were told to say for a moment. If they were asleep, how would they have known it was the disciples who had come to steal His body, and in any case did the guards know who His disciples were? These were likely to be unschooled on the meaning of the events of the last 3.5 years, and totally ignorant of their relevance to the Jewish mind. Sadly it is a rumour that has been perpetuated down through the centuries to this very day, blinding the eyes of many Jews, and others to the truth concerning the coming of their Messiah, depriving them of eternal salvation.

Messiah in the Tomb

So what happened whilst the body of the Messiah was in the tomb? What lessons can we learn from the time the Messiah was out of sight?

Noah alone was noticed by God as being righteous and of a character that enabled him to become God's representative on earth, just as the prophets such as Elijah and Jeremiah were. Noah alone was sufficiently and determinedly focused on God to do the work God gave him to do. Whilst building the ark and preaching about the forthcoming catastrophe (before any 'Word of God' was written or printed, which indicated just how strong was his faith) and the need for the people to reach out to God, Noah was reviled and mocked.

The spiritual blindness of the godless causes them to despise what they consider to be other than 'normal' because their earth bound way of thinking prevents them from seeing further than the immediate and what they believe and understand is 'real'. The truth and reality of God is beyond their comprehension, and ours to some extent.

Peter tells us that the Messiah visited the spirits of those imprisoned at the time of Noah (1 Pet. 1:19 – 21). Whether some realized their mistake and sought God once Noah had entered the Ark and the rains began to fall or not we will never know in this world, however it can be conjectured that the Lord announced His victory over sin and the reality of the power of God to all those who had died and possibly the salvation available to those who had called out to God at the time of the flood.

The referendum and elections in the UK (2014/15) clearly demonstrated that there are some individuals who are aggressively vocal in attacking the opposing parties whilst supporting their own point of view, Indeed I have experienced most unfortunate aggressive and abusive language on social media myself. The party they supported did not win possibly because the silent majority had no intention of being bullied and because of the confidential nature of the voting system it allowed that majority to vote for what they believed in, not the way the aggressive campaigners wanted them to vote.

Such could well have happened at the time of Noah when the more timid and less confident members of the population did not want their beliefs to be generally known, and therefore paid with their lives when the waters overcame them. Such thoughts are born out by the example of both Nicodemus and Joseph of Arimathea who were secret disciples of the Messiah whilst being member of the Sanhedrin and on the council of Jewish elders. Only at a critical moment were they forced into revealing their position.

We are dependent not upon the will of men but the will of God, which is not always clear to the finite minds of men. With regard to suffering, Peter says that even if we suffer for doing right, and it is the will of God that we suffer, then we will be blessed. Why should this be?

Firstly because evil is in the world, introduced by Satan who seeks aggression and chaos and the destruction of all that God saw was good, and none of us can avoid it. This is because at the moment Satan is the prince of the power of the air. Although the Messiah has gained the victory over death, that is the death of the spirit of man, the time of Satan's power on the earth has not yet come to an end.

Secondly because our faith is much more precious than gold, God is therefore prepared to allow us to undergo trials and tribulations in order for that faith to grow and mature in order for it to become strong because He loves us so very much.

What if during our lives our faith was not tested, that we had an easy uneventful life. What would that do for us? For a start we would not be put in a position to have to trust God for anything, with the obvious danger of considering ourselves self-sufficient, therefore why would we need God at all? I say this as one who has been tested over many years. Imagine being out of work with more funds going out than were coming in, which was our experience for 23 months? In fact my wife and I thought we would have to sell up and move to a much cheaper property, until God stepped in and told us that we would not have to move; and we didn't. That was just one of many testing times.

Until Mary agreed to edit this book I was on the verge of abandoning the project because I felt very uncomfortable in my spirit about it; I can be a little too positive about the Lord sometimes. After the influence of Mary's more careful approach, the rough edges and more strident wording have been removed and the text made more explanatory and therefore far more positive. It took her many hours over many weeks to read through the draft and she deserves much praise for her forthright and carefully worded comments, which all challenged me to do more research and to explain things in a clearer and far more positive way.

For our faith to grow strong it has to be tested, just as gold is purified by fire, being heated to melting point to remove all impurities. God knows us better than we know ourselves. He knows the state of our hearts and what He needs to do to bring us into a deeper spiritual relationship with Himself. The will of God, therefore, is to prepare us for heaven mentally and spiritually by whatever means is necessary and it is up to us to respond. All those who in times of difficulty, like Noah and the prophets, reach out to God to seek His help and guidance will become stronger in faith and become disciples and spokesmen for Him, being trained by God using the evil that has become endemic in the world. Those who do not even listen to God, or complain about testing and trials will remain in darkness, and forever away from God.

John's Revelation of what will happen in the future makes it clear that the situation on the earth will only get worse before the final battle that will see Satan judged and sent to the lake of fire along with all those who have opposed God. The only way believers will not only survive but blossom in their relationship with Him is to accept the trials and tribulations they experience and allow their faith in God to grow and become strong (Rom. 8:28).

During the three days the Lord's body laid in the tomb, God the Holy Spirit made it into a spiritual body into which the Spirit that was the Son of God, Son of man re-entered to be seen and recognized by the disciples. Paul to the Corinthians speaks of two bodies: the material body made from the dust of the ground and the spiritual body that we will all be given when we are brought alive from the dead. For us it will be at the sounding of the trumpet when the dead are raised and this corruptible puts on incorruption, and this mortal puts on immortality (read 1 Cor. 15:35 – 58). Then the death sentence uttered by God in the beginning will be made null and void because of the sacrifice of His Son and the transformation of His body from being a mortal body to a spiritual and incorruptible body. Then risen He became the eternal High Priest after the order of Melchizedek (Heb. 7, also read the Appendix in The Tent of the Meeting about Melchizedek), combining for the first time the roles of King and High Priest.

Resurrection

When the Lord asked for the stone covering the entrance to the tomb where the body of Lazarus had been laid to be removed, Martha immediately protested because after four days the body would have started to decay and stink (Jn. 11:1 – 38). Jesus replied, *"Did I not say to you that if you believed you would see the glory of God?"* The Lord had full confidence in His Father and the Holy Spirit and because of their eternal intimacy and interdependence, the Lord knew all that was to happen, and was able to demonstrate the power of the triune God without any nervousness, which showed because the people were amazed by the power and authority of His teaching.

Previously the Lord had said to Martha, a very practical woman, that He was the resurrection and the life. Is it any wonder, therefore, that He had power through the Holy Spirit to cause Lazarus to rise from the dead? Lazarus, when commanded to come out of the tomb did just that to the astonishment of all those present.

But did you notice the reaction of certain members of the crowd? Although on the evidence before them many were prepared to believe in Him, remarkably there were others so steeped in earthly wisdom that they were blind to the miracle that had been performed before their very eyes. They did not seem to be even remotely curious about the how and why and what it meant from a spiritual point of view. The fact that the Lord did something completely out of the ordinary had to be reported to the Jewish religious leaders, like informers amongst the people.

Rather than praising God, they immediately reported back to the Pharisees who merely saw it as a threat to their godlessness and their established way of religious life, which is extremely sad. Remember the amazing reaction to the Christ child by Simeon and Anna, and the curiosity of the despised tax collector Zacchaeus, who wanted so desperately to meet the Lord, and the trust of the woman who touched the hem of His garment that she might be healed.

If the Messiah claimed to be the resurrection and the life, and that He had the power to lay down His life and then to take it up again, demonstrating that He was able to not only raise the widow's son to life but dramatically raise His friend Lazarus also, what was preventing Him from raising Himself up from the dead with the assistance of the Holy Spirit? Nothing. Absolutely nothing!

During His time in the tomb His Spirit was alive visiting the souls in prison as has been considered above. But, come the end of the three days He was due to spend there, the body so carefully laid in the tomb was transformed, not in order to come alive as did the body of Lazarus in a physical sense, but to miraculously become a spiritual body that was able to walk through doors when they were shut and locked, and in preparation for His entry to the place where His Father dwelt, outside of creation. Just as God is a Spirit, and the Son was an unrestricted Spirit until He took on a human frame, so in order for Him to return to be with His Father, His human body had to become a spiritual body.

What is interesting to ponder is having heard that their Lord had risen from the dead from the women who had gone to embalm His body, with some of the disciples having seen the empty tomb and heard what the angels had said, and Mary giving witness to actually speaking with Him, there was still an aura of unreality amongst them. Imagine then the effect on His disciples when He suddenly appeared to them in that upper room in Jerusalem where they were hiding away, coming through the door as though it was open when it was securely locked, and when He allowed Thomas to 'put his hand into His side' and for Him to even eat fish to prove that He was not an apparition.

The two on the road to Emmaus did not notice anything familiar about the stranger who came alongside them on the way until they saw the manner in which He broke the bread and then He was gone. These were all witnesses to prove that He had risen from the dead and before He rose up into the sky He was seen by 500 people who gave credence to His resurrection. Thus the lies perpetrated by the religious leaders were completely ridiculous but sadly believed by so many Jews over the years

Firstfruits

The celebration of firstfruits was one of the main events in the Jewish religious calendar. It called for the first of the harvest to be offered to God in recognition of His provision, *"when you harvest your crops, select for me a choice sample of the first portion of the harvest. Take the grain to the priest who will lift it up to Me so that it may be accepted on your behalf."* *(Ex. 23:19; Lev. 23:10).* The feast was a thanksgiving offering to God for His loving provision of food from the land for the people of Israel which was used to support the priests who were dedicated to His service and could therefore not work for themselves.

The programme was as follows:

- Passover   14th day of Nissan

- Feast of Unleaven Bread   15th day of Nissan

- Feast of Firstfruits   21st day of Nissan

These were referred to as one feast with the remaining main annual feasts being Pentecost, Trumpets and the Day of Atonement.

To the Corinthians Paul explains the importance of the spiritual aspect of Christ's resurrection and ascension (see 1 Cor. 15:20 – 23, 42 – 53 for the biblical text) thus:

> *"By the body of Christ being raised from the dead, He became the firstfruits of all those who have died (spiritually fallen asleep), the first of all those who through faith are due to be raised to eternal spiritual life. Since death came into the world through the actions of the first man Adam, so the resurrection of the dead has come through another Man who is Christ Jesus (the Messiah).*
>
> *Because we are all naturally related to the first man Adam, we will all die, it is the natural process. However, all those who are spiritually related to the other man Christ, the Messiah, through repentance and faith, will be awoken from that spiritual sleep and given new spiritual bodies in which they will be presented to God. Now Christ, who was God made man, died and became the first to be <u>raise to life again</u> but in a spiritual body prepared for entry into the heavenly realm where God dwells."*

Of this matter of the spirit returning to the body we have many examples, one being in the First Testament when Elijah restored the widow's son to her (1 Kgs. 17, esp. vs. 20 - 22). At the time of the famine that covered the land when Ahab was king the Lord hid Elijah first by the brook Cherith and then in the town of Zarephath where he lodged with a widow. During his stay the widow's son died and she pleaded with the prophet concerning her son, so Elijah sought God to return the lads 'soul', which was his character, and his 'spirit', which was the God breathed and therefore God-ward part of him, back to his body.

By the Messiah physically dying and then, instead of His Spirit falling asleep as all the spirits of men do after leaving their bodies (dust returning to dust), returning to His body that had become a spiritual body in the tomb, the Messiah became the first man to immediately rise from the dead, therefore He was the firstfruits of those who believe and will one day enter into the heavenly realm with new spiritual bodies (1 Cor. 15:35 – 58).

The Women

It is interesting that according to the Gospel narrative it was the caring women that were concerned about the preservation of the body of their Lord, who first, and very bravely because of the animosity of the Jewish leaders towards the Lord, ventured to the tomb. Their concern was in keeping with the role God gave Eve when she was created from the rib of Adam. It is worth mentioning here that the role of women was to be that of supporting the men, not as servants but as equal before God, and also as bearers of children, home-makers and nurturers of their children, certainly in the early formative years.

However, modern life now requires adjustments to what is described in the scriptures. For example one of my sons became a house-dad until his children went to school because his wife earned more than he did and they lived considerably nearer her work place than his. He did learn how to drive commercial vehicles in that time and started to earn extra money driving large articulated vehicles, at night and at weekends when his wife was at home to look after the children.

The women followed the men carrying the body of the Messiah and witnessed the manner in which it was laid in the tomb, then spent time and effort in preparing spices before resting on the Sabbath day according to God's command. Then very early the next morning a number of the women went to the tomb and, according to Matthew, experienced the earthquake and the angel descending from heaven and the stone being rolled back to reveal an empty tomb. The effect of these events and the presence of the shining angel on the guards was to fill them with terror although only some of the guards went to tell the Jewish authorities what had happened, so some might have been in awe of the events rather than terrified.

On the other hand the angel (Luke mentions two) calmed the women's fears by telling them that the Messiah was not there because He had risen, and then inviting them to go into the tomb to see where

His body had been laid. Then he urged them to go and tell His disciples that He had risen from the dead and would go before them into Galilee and they were to meet Him there. Luke also tells us that the angel(s) reminded the women that the Messiah had told them that He would be crucified and on the third day rise again.

There seems to be some confusion about exactly what happened and when it happened because each gospel gives a slightly different account of the events. Suffice it to say that an angel (or angels) came and moved the heavy disc shaped rough hewn stone from the mouth of the tomb to reveal that it was already empty, the Lord having already risen from the dead. The removal of the stone was not to allow the Messiah to leave the tomb, rather it was to allow His followers, such as the women and Peter, to enter it and observe the discarded grave clothes that had been so lovingly wrapped around His dead body when it was taken down from the cross.

One particular touching moment was when Mary stood weeping outside the tomb after everyone else had left. According to Mark it was Mary Magdalene for out of her the Messiah had cast seven devils, therefore she who had been of greatest need and had received the greatest release had the greatest desire to know the whereabouts of His remains. She stooped down to confirm that the grave clothes were laid aside with the cloth that had been around His head lying separately, they being of no further use.

Then she saw two angels in the tomb sitting where the body and head of the Messiah had been, and they asked her why she was weeping? Explaining to them that all she wanted to know was where His body now lay, she seemed to have a feeling that someone else was there and turned around to see the figure of a man. The man asked her the same question as the angels to which she gave the same answer saying that she wanted to know where He had been taken so that she could look after the body. It was at that moment that the Messiah spoke her name. *"Mary"*.

What immediately followed must have been a very brief moment of incredulity before she could focus her mind on analyzing the fact that the voice was familiar and then the recognition of just who it was who had spoken to her. *"Rabboni!"* (teacher). What a joy the realization of knowing He was alive must have been for her. She wanted to touch Him but He asked her to refrain from the embrace she had been used to giving Him. He was in transit, soon to return to His Father and our Father.

What is particularly sad, yet to an extent understandable, is the disbelief of those she told about the Lord's resurrection. It had taken her time to realize that the man before her was the risen Lord, and she was in His presence.

Even though the disciples had been told by the Lord that He would rise again on the third day, yet they did not really believe Him. So why should they believe Mary or anyone else who had told them the same thing? Finally it was impetuous Peter who ran to the tomb only to find it empty and marvelled. The two believers walking to Emmaus did not recognize the Lord as He walked with them some distance. It was only the way He broke bread that made them realise who it was, and then He quickly vanished.

But it was to the women that the Lord revealed Himself first for it was they who had ministered to Him during His ministry.

All the witnesses to the Lord's resurrection were ordinary people who were very saddened by the loss of their Lord, and very practical people, not given to fanciful thoughts and ideas, therefore their witness can be taken at face value. Why would the religious leaders create an alternative explanation that had no credibility if they did not fear He had actually risen from the dead, a fact that they could not handle because in doing so they would have to accept they had condemned an innocent man to death, and the Son of God at that.

Priest and King

Aaron became the first God appointed high priest of the new nation of Israel. With his sons he was responsible for ministering to God on behalf of the nation and for the proper running of the temple complex and all its services. Once a year, on the day of atonement, he was to appear before God in the holiest place with sin covering animal blood on his hands to seek forgiveness for himself and the sins of the nation.

The transformation of the body of the Messiah has already been discussed, but there was another transformation that took place in the tomb that is very significant. The Messiah, speaking to the Samaritan woman at the well, told her that God was no longer interested in those who worshipped at the various centres of worship, rather he was looking for all those who wanted to worship Him in spirit and in truth, that is worship Him spirit to Spirit in truth (Jn. 4:23, 24), for God will not tolerate lying and cheating.

The prophet Malachi reprimanded the priests for sacrificing animals that were anything but pure and perfect (Mal. 1:7 – 11) thus dishonouring His name, and as has previously been discussed the reason for the nation's time in exile was because of corruption amongst the priests while they were supposed to be ministering before the Lord in the temple in Jerusalem (Eze. 8:15 - 16).

With the sacrifice of the Messiah and the opening up of the Holy of Holies, which had already lost its furniture of the Ark of the Covenant and the Mercy Seat, which Jeremiah told the people must not be made anymore (Jer. 3:16), the Holy of Holies had lost much of its importance. What was in the Ark but the ten commandments, the written law that was the foundation of Israel's relationship their God, their contract of marriage with Him. Jeremiah later prophesied to the people *"... but this is the covenant that I will make with the house of Israel after those days, says the Lord: I will put my law in their minds, and I will write it on their hearts; and I will be their God, and they shall be my people ..." (Jer. 31:33).* No longer did the words of the covenant need to be engraved on slabs of stone. God, throughout the life of the nation, had taught them through their various experiences of Him that He wanted to deal with them as individuals, not just as a nation. Over the years of their history it became clear that the nation of Israel was to be transformed into a spiritual nation. No longer was there to be a reliance on the slabs of stone with the engraved law, rather God wanted them to learn the law and then apply it to their hearts and lives. Moses told them that God did not want them to rely on the outward physical sign of their membership of the nation of Israel, but that circumcision had to be spiritual, of the heart, that inner spiritual person whose belief in and commitment to God was in spirit and in truth.

Ultimately, when the Messiah said that there were other sheep that were not of the fold of Israel, He meant that the new spiritual Israel would consist of both Jews and Gentiles. True believers for which His kingdom was the essential ingredient of their lives.

With the rending of the curtain separating the Holy of Holies from the Holy Place the importance of the Holy of Holies to the functioning of the temple year completely lost its importance so that even ordinary priests could enter without fear. God was no longer dwelling in that place. Rather He was dwelling in the hearts of believers who became the new temples of God.

Because the Messiah came to emphasize the importance of the spiritual aspect of worshipping God, and the need to sacrifice animals had been made redundant with the sacrifice of the Lamb of God, which was the once for all sacrifice for sin, the role of the human high priest had also been made redundant. Now instead of the Aaronic high priest appearing before God once a year in the Holy of Holies to plead for the forgiveness of sins of the people and nation, a new advocate had been appointed who was not only able to sympathize with our weaknesses, but was Himself pure and perfect in every way (Heb. 4:15) who has become our advocate, not confined to the temple in Jerusalem, but living with God the Father in the heavenly places (1 Jn. 2:1, 2).

Just as God appointed Aaron as the first human high priest in Israel, and over time many men held that holy office, with the death of God's Son that office became redundant with the opening up of the Holy of Holies, so God the Father needed to appoint a new spiritual high priest who would minister before Him on behalf of the people on earth. What is so unique about the appointment of the Messiah to that role is that rather than sacrificing animals with their blood on His hands to appear before the man made mercy seat in the presence of God in the man made temple, the Messiah had His own blood on His hands and His side to appear, not in a man-made structure but before God the Father in person in His holy abode.

Also, the high priesthood was not according to that of Aaron but of Melchizedek (Ps. 110:9). But who is this Melchizedek? (See Genesis 14)

Lot had been captured and Abram, along with a number of local kings, had rescued his nephew. After the victory the King of Sodom offered the spoils to Abraham, however: unlike Lot Abram did not trust the King of Sodom and would take nothing from the spoils of war, accepting only that which his men had eaten and a tithe to the King of Salem, lest at any time the King of Sodom should claim that he had helped him get rich. His witness to the King of Sodom was that he had lifted up his hands to the "Lord God Most High Maker of heaven and earth" promising that he would not take so much as a thread or shoe fastening from the spoils that he had brought back.

The most significant occurrence in this drama is the first appearance of the priest king Melchizedek, who was both King of Salem (later to be called Jerusalem) and priest of the Most High God. He came out to Abram with bread and wine for his sustenance. In a book (the Bible) in which symbolism plays such an important part, the offering of bread and wine, although given for sustenance at that time, will inevitably be seen as significant considering the later connection between this king and the Messiah. Abram in giving the king a tenth of all the spoils he had taken also has implications for the authority and standing of the Aaronic priesthood in relation to the priesthood of Yeshua. Because Aaron had yet to be born of a descendent of Abram and because Melchizedek was honoured by Abram as his senior, Melchizedek was also senior to Aaron which means that the priesthood of Melchizedek was greater than that of Aaron. According to the writer of the Hebrews the uniqueness of this king is that he was without father or mother and without ancestry, beginning of days or end of life, but resembling the Son of God he continues to be a priest without interruption and without a successor.

This meeting would have implications on the new covenant between God and mankind when the Messiah to the Jews came as prophesied in Yeshua (Jesus). He became a priest after the order of Melchizedek, that is a uniting of the roles of king and priest in one man, being also king of righteousness and also king of peace. (extract from The Origin of Life : God's Relationship With Man in Genesis)

What is of particular importance is that the Messiah could not have been appointed by His Father to a position that had previously been held by created man, seeing He was God incarnate and above man (consider the exalted position of the Messiah - Heb. 1). He was not of the tribe of Levi and therefore not eligible to serve as a priest, rather He was of the tribe of Judah, the kingly and superior tribe. With the Lord being born into the tribe of Judah and of the lineage of king David, His appointment as the chosen and higher, spiritual high priest final brought together the roles of king and priest in one man, and the kingship back to God.

It is reasonable to say that the appearance of Melchizedek was the second time the Son of God appeared on earth. The first was to walk with Adam in the Garden and the second was to meet with Abram and establish on earth a union of King and High Priest, a uniting of roles that no living human being was allowed to accept, as the account of king Uzziah so graphically illustrates (1 Chron. 26:16 – 21, cf. Ex. 28:36 – 38).

Pilate had already inspirationally established that the Messiah was the King of the Jews because of the notice he had had nailed to the cross above His head. With His resurrection in a transformed spiritual body, having won the victory over death, the Messiah assumed the title of High Priest after the order of Melchizedek, the order He had established in the beginning when He ministered to the first Hebrew and Father of the nation of Israel, Abram. No wonder He was able to say, "Abraham rejoiced to see my day, and was glad he saw it." (Jn.8:56).

Consider what Peter wrote on this subject:

> *For Christ also suffered for sins once for all, the righteous for the unrighteous, that He might bring us to God, being put to death in the flesh, but made alive by the Spirit, by whom also he went and made a proclamation to the spirits in prison, who in former times were disobedient, when God waited patiently in the days of Noah,*

during the building of the ark, in which a few, that is, eight souls, were saved through water.

And baptism, which this prefigured, now saves us (not as a removal of dirt from the flesh, but the answer of a good conscience towards God), through the resurrection of Jesus Christ, who has gone into heaven and is seated at the right hand of God, with angels, authorities, and powers made subject to him. (1 Pet. 3:18 – 22)

God's Refining Fire

Herein lies a paradox. With no memory and no understanding or experience of life all children need to be taught and to learn about life as a human being. The Messiah, however, was no ordinary child. From the age of 12 He was able to debate with the best minds in the temple regarding the law and the prophets, this was because the Messiah was not dependent upon His human brain but the knowledge of His Spirit which had been with God and was an integral part of God. He was/is the Word of God the Father, therefore nothing was written without His direct involvement, so when He came to the earth and took on the form of a baby He already had infinite knowledge to confound even the most prominent, self-confessed experts in the law.

From the start he knew all that would happen to Him even the sacrifice He was to make when nailed to the cross. What is of particular importance to us is that He stayed the course and rose victorious from the grave. He was successfully tested in the Garden of Gethsemane and is an example to all of us.

The Jews, because they were so far from God, did not realise that first must come the sacrificial servant Messiah rather than the victorious Messiah they thought they so desperately needed. But consider the tabernacle made under Moses' leadership. Within the curtained off courtyard, just inside the entrance was the altar of sacrifice because the first and foremost requirement as far as God is concerned is to deal with the problem of sin (my book 'The Tent of the Meeting : Illustrating God's Plan of Salvation' explains the importance of the layout of the tabernacle complex).

The leaders, and particularly the teachers of the Law and Pharisees, as has already been made clear, were far from knowing God let alone having a spiritual understanding of Him or a relationship with Him. It is only necessary to read about Nicodemus and his secret meeting with the Messiah to realize just how little he understood of how far he was from knowing the truth about God, but at least he was prepared to find out.

Consider what Malachi declared:

> *Behold, I am sending my messenger to prepare the way before me, and the Lord whom you seek will suddenly come to his temple. The messenger of the covenant in whom you delight. Behold, He is coming, says the Lord of hosts.*
>
> *But who can endure the day of his coming, and who can stand when he appears? For he is like a refiner's fire and like launderers' soap; he will sit as a refiner and purifier of silver, and he will purify the descendants of Levi and refine them like gold and silver, until they present offerings to the Lord in righteousness. (Mal. 3:1 – 3)*

This story was discovered on the internet and concerns the refining of silver:

> 'Some time ago, a few ladies met in a certain city to read the scriptures, and make them the subject of conversation. While reading the third chapter of Malachi they came upon a remarkable expression in the third verse:
> *"And He shall sit as a refiner and purifier of silver."*
> One lady's opinion was that is was intended to convey the view of the sanctifying influence of the grace of Christ. Then she proposed to visit a silversmith and report to them what he said on the subject.
> She went accordingly and without telling the silversmith the object of her errand, begged to know the process of refining silver, which he fully described to her.

"*But Sir*" she said, "*do you sit while the work of refining is going on?*"

"*Oh, yes, madam,*" *replied the silversmith; "I must sit with my eye steadily fixed on the furnace, for if the time necessary for refining be exceeded in the slightest degree, the silver will be injured.*"

The lady at once saw the beauty, and comfort too, of the expression, "*He shall sit as a refiner and purifier of silver.*"

Christ sees it needful to put His children into a furnace; His eye is steady and intent on the work of purifying, and His wisdom and love are both engaged in the best manner for them. Their trials do not come at random; "the very hairs of your head are all numbered."

As the lady was leaving the shop, the silversmith called her back, and said he had forgotten to mention that the only way that he knows when the process of purifying is complete is when he sees his own image reflected in the silver....'

Author Unknown

The Messiah was expected at any time. There were many clues provided by God for the chief priests and leaders of the people as to His arrival but no one seemed to be spiritually sensitive enough to recognize the Lord's hand in the events leading up to His arrival and certainly not when He came to His temple. The witness of Zechariah when he was ministering in the temple and came out to the people dumb, or the pregnancy of the barren Elizabeth whose son was called John against the accepted tradition of naming the first child. And what about the arrival of the wise men who asked where the Messiah was to be born, or the shepherds who witness the angelic choir and told others all that had happened, or when John started his ministry of announcing the Messiah's coming as a man whose shoe fastening he was not worthy of undoing. Simeon recognized Him and so did Anna, but no one else did.

"*But who can endure the day of his coming, and who can stand when he appears?*" Consider how He stood out from the crowd and taught with such authority that His teaching outshone that of the Scribes and

Pharisees. Consider the condemnation the leaders received from Him, the disruption of the money changers' tables in the temple courts. None of the Jewish authorities were spared His righteous judgement, nor were they able to stop Him until His time for arrest had come.

"For he is like a refiner's fire and like launderers' soap;" with a refiner's fire relating to the smelting of ore to extract pure metal and the launderers' soap being the strong soap used to bleach the impurities from cloth to make it white. His was a purifying ministry making those who responded to Him ready for the kingdom that He was bringing in. He was the shepherd of those sheep that heard His voice and followed Him, entering into the sheepfold for which He is the door.

The disciples were the leaders of those who had purified themselves through His blood and entered into a new relationship with God, and this new movement was not based on the temple in Jerusalem, but through the baptism in the Holy Spirit they themselves became temples of the Holy Spirit worshipping God in the Spirit and in the Truth of the word of God.

The church is meant to be a spiritual church for Jew and Gentile believers who are no longer strangers and enemies but fellow citizens, purified in the refiners' fire and with the launderers' soap to become members of the household of God, built upon the foundation of the apostles and prophets, with the Messiah being the chief corner stone, in which the whole structure, is fit together to become a holy temple in the Lord (see Eph. 2:19 – 21).

PENTECOST

The English word "Pentecost" is a transliteration of the Greek word *pentekostos*, meaning "fifty" and comes from the ancient Christian expression pentekoste hemera, which means "fiftieth day."

However the origin of Pentecost comes from God's instructions to the Children of Israel in the book of Leviticus regarding the offering of the first fruits of the harvest to God:

> The Lord spoke to Moses: Speak to the people of Israel and say to them: When you enter the land that I am giving you and reap its harvest, then you shall bring the sheaf of the first fruits of your harvest to the priest. He shall raise the sheaf before the Lord, so that you may find acceptance; on the day after the Sabbath the priest shall raise it. On the day when you raise the sheaf, you shall offer a lamb a year old, without blemish, as a burnt-offering to the Lord. …..
>
> And you shall count from the day after the Sabbath, from the day on which you brought the sheaf of the wave-offering, seven Sabbaths; they shall be complete. Count fifty days to the day after the seventh; then you shall present an offering of new grain to the Lord. (Lev. 23:9 – 12; 15, 16)

Everything done and said in the First Testament had meaning for the work of the Lord Messiah. As God had given the land to the Israelites He expected them to offer to Him the first fruits of the harvest as their landlord and provider. The harvested seed had died and then sown at the appropriate time and because of the rains and the good soil it sprouted and produced a harvest. The first ingathering of the harvest was to be presented to God in thanksgiving. But it was also to have a spiritual connotation through Christ, the Messiah:

> *"... now Christ has been raised from the dead, the first fruits of those* (truly committed, spiritually reborn believers in the Lord, the God of Israel and His Messiah) *who have died physically. For since death came through a human being, the resurrection of the dead has also come through a human being; for as in Adam all die, so in Christ will all be made alive. But each in his own order: Christ the first fruits, then at his coming those who belong to Christ"* (see *1 Cor. 15:20 – 23)*

All that the leaders of the Jews had been told by the Messiah during His ministry and at His trial was inevitably coming to pass. Consider when he went into the temple and drove out the commercial enterprises, those selling oxen, sheep and doves and those changing commercial currency into the temple coinage for huge profit, saying, *"Take these things away! Do not make My Father's house a house of merchandize"* (Jn. *2:16)*. In doing so He became the refiners' fire, telling them that they had changed the whole purpose of the temple from that of being a means of allowing believers in their God to worship Him in the spirit, rather than the earthly human way of pagan worship of other nations, into a money making exercise.

The whole purpose of the temple along with its dedicated priesthood was that it was to be the centre of the worship and adoration and glorification of God. Situated from the very start in the centre of the nation, it was where the nation was to focus its attention on their God (Ps. 119:1 – 8), and not just any God, but a God who had proved

Himself time and again by blessing and protecting them all the while they were open to His voice and obedient to His command. The temple was the place where God's spiritual presence dwelt amongst His chosen people, and where that presence was given physical expression.

After the Lord's rampage through that holy place, His disciples remembered the scripture, *"Zeal for your house has consumed Me."* But what was the reaction of the ruling classes? *"By what sign can you show us the authority you have for such an action?"* His reply: *"Destroyed this temple (meaning His body) and I will restore it in three days."* By their reaction the leaders of the Jews did not understand what it meant, but those in whom the Holy Spirit later took up residence did, because its meaning was spiritually discerned.

Unwittingly they did destroy it, by nailing Him to a cross to die and in three days His body was restored to life. Sadly, not only did they not believe what happened, but by spreading pernicious rumours did all they could to prevent their own people from believing in Him as their Messiah.

At His trial the Messiah told Caiaphas the high priest, *"... hereafter you will see the Son of man sitting at the right hand of the Power and coming on the clouds of heaven ... "*, prophesying His ascension into heaven to return to His Father, and His coming again in victory. So far from the Spirit of God were they that they were unable to accept what He had told them, yet before the day of Pentecost He had ascended into heaven through the clouds in order for the Holy Spirit to come down in power to take His place on earth on that very day to empower those willing and able to be truly born again in the Spirit, and to minister to and support all such believers wherever they might be (Jn. 16:5 – 15)

> *"Now I am going to him who sent me; yet none of you asks me, "Where are you going?" But because I have said these things to you, sorrow has filled your hearts. Nevertheless, I tell you the truth: it is to your advantage that I go away, for if I do not go away, the Helper (Holy Spirit) will not come to you; but if I go, I will send him to you."*

The work the Messiah had come to the earth to do had been completed. Through His death and resurrection He had provided the antidote to sin enabling anyone wanting to be reunited with the creator God to do so. But that was not the end of God's work amongst mankind, indeed it was just the beginning. Although the ultimate sacrifice for sin had been offered and accepted by the Father, the message of the good news had to be broadcast around the world so that all men might know the truth that had the power to set them free from the world of sin and the power of Satan.

For a person to be born afresh of the Holy Spirit they needed to know about it and also know how to become one in Christ, the Messiah. That was the job of the Holy Spirit of God.

Previously the Holy Spirit had been strictly limited to what He was able to do until the suffering servant Messiah came. With the return of the Son of God, Son of Man and saviour of the world to the heavenly place to be with His Father, He was able to send the Holy Spirit to the earth in power to work through all that have committed themselves to God the Father through the Son by the power of the conscience cleansing power of the shed blood of Messiah.

So what did the Messiah say was to be the role of the Holy Spirit:

"And when he comes, he will convict the world concerning its sin, and (lack of true godly) righteousness, and (faulty) judgement: about sin, because they do not believe in me (being ignorant of the truth and purity of God); about righteousness, because I am going to the Father and you will see me no longer (no longer have the example of the pure right-ness of God that He provided which was far greater than merely being without sin, the pure salt that savoured the world of men); about judgement, because the ruler of this world has been condemned (indeed the whole world, order corrupted by sin introduced by the first man Adam and perpetuated the active work of Satan and his demonic forces which, through His sacrificial death and resurrection, has been condemned and its adherents and servants sentenced to the lake of fire). I still have many things to say to you,

but you cannot bear them now. When the Spirit of truth comes, He will guide you into all the truth; for he will not speak on his own, but will speak whatever he hears from the Father, and he will declare to you the things that are to come. He will glorify me, because he will take what is mine and declare it to you (for I am the way to God, the truth of God and the life of God which is eternal). All that the Father has is mine. For this reason I said that he will take what is mine and declare it to you" (Jn. 16:5 – 15 my interpretation).

No man can overcome the power and authority of God, even though many have tried. The leaders of the Jews were beside themselves trying to cover up His resurrection. Yet worse was to come.

It is interesting that after a night of fishing in which nothing was caught the Lord, although they did not at first know it was Him, told the disciples to cast their net on the other side of the boat, which they did and immediately the net was so full of fish that they could not get it onboard the boat. John instantly realized who it was that had spoken to them and called out *"it is the Lord"*. Peter had been so engrossed in what He was doing that he did not consider who it was that had called to them. However, John instinctively recognized his Master and called out to the others who it was on the shore. As soon as he heard John's call, Peter could not help himself but instinctively dived overboard to go to Him (Jn. 21:6, 7).

When the Lord spoke with His disciples after the meal He had prepared for them, He first challenged Peter with the question, *"Simon, son of Jonah, do you love Me more than these?"* the Lord having noted his prompt action of seeking to reach the Lord as soon as he was told it was Him on the shore. Peter, still deeply embarrassed by his denial of his Lord such a short while ago, could only muster the replay that he had affection for Him in a brotherly way. It was the third time the Lord asked that question of Peter, that he confessed that the Lord knew all things, even the things deep within his heart. And it is interesting that the Lord commissioned Peter first to *"Feed My lambs"* and then to *"tend My sheep"*, which meant for him to act as the shepherd of the flock, which he did as leader of the new Christian church in Jerusalem until his death on a cross in Rome.

Although they met with the Lord on the shore of Galilee, they were still not empowered for the task before them of spreading the gospel of God's full and free salvation. It was not until they had gathered in Jerusalem, had witnessed the Lord returning to His Father, God going back to God, with the commission that they were to go out into the whole world and preach the gospel, baptizing new believers in the name of the Father and the Son and the Holy Spirit, had received the prophetic announcement that He would return in the same manner that God sent the Holy Spirit in power.

Finally the new period of grace was announced when the Holy Spirit revealed Himself by empowering the disciples. With His 'appearance', Pentecost had fully come. The time between the offering of first fruits and Pentecost having been set by God at the beginning, at the time fixed by God the Father, the Holy Spirit descended on those who truly believed on Him in their hearts by faith and through the disciples spoke to all those in Jerusalem for the annual celebrations. The Holy Spirit speaking through Peter convicted 3,000 souls who asked what they had to do to be saved from their sinfulness.

With this sudden eruption of spiritual activity displayed through the one time timid disciples, along with many signs of supernatural power, such as the healing of the lame man by the gate beautiful, and the bursting forth of great numbers of new believers, the authorities became more and more troubled. The disruption of normal religious life throughout the country with the outbreak of powerful preaching and miraculous healing by ordinary men, some of them common fishermen (Acts 4:13), became a thorn in the side of the leaders.

Awe came upon everyone, because many wonders and signs were being done through the apostles. Now all who believed were together and had all things in common; selling their possessions and goods and distributing the proceeds to all who were in need. Continuing daily together in the temple, they broke bread at home and ate their food with gladness and simplicity, praising God and having favour with all the people. And day by day the Lord added to their number those who were being saved. (Acts 2:43 – 46)

From the point of view of the authorities, the whole situation was getting out of their control. Far from having rid themselves of a man who was undermining their authority, there was now an explosion of events purporting to have been initiated by the very man they thought they had silenced by killing Him. Suddenly there was a new and dynamic movement in city which demonstrated a togetherness and gladness amongst the believers at having found salvation that had not been seen before. This was a new thing that the Holy Spirit was doing and those around the new believers rejoiced in it, no doubt asking them what it was all about, with some asking how they could also receive what they had.

The warning by Gamaliel to the members of the Sanhedrin that they needed to be careful not to be found fighting against God was accepted but still, after beating them, they ordered the apostles not to continue to preach in the name of Yeshua whom they referred to as the Messiah (Acts 5:33 – 42).

But a Pharisee in the council named Gamaliel, a teacher of the law, respected by all the people, stood up and ordered the men to be put outside for a short time. Then he said to them, 'Men of Israel, consider carefully what you intend to do to these men. For some time ago Theudas rose up, claiming to be somebody, and a number of men, about four hundred, joined him; but he was killed, and all who followed him were dispersed and disappeared. After him Judas the Galilean rose up at the time of the census and got people to follow him; he also perished, and all who followed him were scattered. So in the present case, I tell you, keep away from these men and let them alone; because if this plan or this undertaking is of human origin, it will fail; but if it is of God, you will not be able to overthrow them, in fact you may even be found to be fighting against God!' They were convinced by him, and when they had called in the apostles, they had them flogged. Then they ordered them not to speak in the name of Jesus, and let them go. (Acts 5:34 – 40)

There is one other point that needs to be considered regarding the members of the council and that is that we do not really know the thoughts of each individual. It could be that some did not fully go along with the more vociferous hardliners but were not prepared, perhaps because of fear of what might happen to their position on the council, to stand up against them like the well respected Gamaliel. However notice the reaction of the council to the witness of Stephen, when it says, they gnashed their teeth at him and then *'with one accord'* cast him out of the city and stoned him to death, even though it was illegal for them to do so (Acts 7 especially verses 54 – 59). There seems little doubt that the council acted in unison for it says that they acted *'with one accord'*.

With the knowledge of what God was doing through them, and having been strengthened with the power and insight of the Holy Spirit, the disciples and those who had followed the Lord during His ministry could not help but promulgate the good news of eternal salvation because it had changed their lives so dramatically and powerfully.

After all the training they had personally received from the Messiah, and having received the promised Holy Spirit, they were beginning to realise what He had been saying and through the inspiration and the ability of the Holy Spirit to expound the scriptures to them (as He did to Paul), all the teaching they had received was beginning to make sense impelling them to preach the gospel of God's eternal salvation in Yeshua Messiah, Christ Jesus our Lord.

"… I have said these things to you so that when the time comes for their fulfilment you may remember that I told you about them. 'I did not say these things to you from the beginning, because I was with you. …. Nevertheless, I tell you the truth: it is to your advantage that I go away, for if I do not go away, the Helper will not come to you; but if I go, I will send him to you.
And when he comes, he will convict the world about how wrong

they are about sin, about its lethal effect on the spirit within man, along with righteousness and judgement: about sin, because they do not believe in me, being made blind to the truth through the sin of unbelief; about righteousness, because I am going to the Father and you will see me no longer; about judgement, because the ruler of this world has been condemned and those who follow him and serve him will be condemned along with him". (See Jn. 16:4 – 11, includes some of my words)

It was clearly the empowerment of the promised Helper in the otherwise ineffectual disciples and other believers that resulted in an increasing number of the general population believing that the crucified Yeshua (Jesus) of Nazareth really was the Messiah and that He had died in order that believers could be cleansed of their sin and given a new and eternal life in God. Such was the power of the Holy Spirit working through all believers that the authorities were becoming deeply troubled, particularly when they were being blamed for crucifying the promised Messiah and, according to Stephen before the Sanhedrin, that the Messiah was already seated before the Power on high as He said He would be to Caiaphas at His trial.

God used the clampdown on those who believed in the new 'Way' to cause the believers to be scattered around the world to spread the message they had so willingly and fully received. The sadness of those imprisoned for their faith would turn to joy when they were rewarded when they entered heaven, just as the Messiah had promised.

So what is this all about? Consider Paul's experience on the Damascus road when he met with the risen Christ. With the blinding white light of God shining directly on Him, a light brighter than the sun shining in its full strength, he was stopped in his tracks and put on the defensive.

"Saul, Saul," called a voice out of the blinding light, *"why are you persecuting Me?"* The focused hatred in his heart for the followers of the Way and the desire to put an end to the whole movement was suddenly dissipated. *"Who are you, Lord?"* Saul, a leader amongst his people,

asked. Suddenly he was in a position where he did not know what was happening to him.

The Messiah, whom Saul had rejected as an imposter, along with the other leaders of the Jews, now identified Himself, not as a man among the people, but as the risen exalted Messiah He had claimed to be, now truly the King of the Jews. *"I am Jesus of Nazareth whom you are persecuting through My followers."* Whatever was happening in the heart of Saul that caused him to so hate the followers of the Messiah and willingly witness Stephen being stoned to death illegally, we will never know. He had genuinely believed he was doing God's work in persecuting all those who believed that Jesus the Nazarene was the Messiah.

> *"As for yourselves, beware; for they will deliver you over to councils; and you will be beaten in synagogues. You will be brought before governors and kings because of me, as a testimony to them. And the gospel must first be proclaimed to all the nations.*
>
> *When they bring you to trial and hand you over to the authorities, do not worry beforehand, or premeditate about what you are to say; but say whatever is given you at that time, for it is not you who speak, but the Holy Spirit. Brother will betray brother to death, and a father his child, and children will rise against parents and have them put to death; and you will be hated by all because of my name. But the one who endures to the end will be saved." (Mk. 13:9 – 13)*

Now, to be suddenly challenged in this spectacular way, far from habitation and by the voice of the very man he did not believe was the Messiah and whose followers he was fighting, will have come as a complete shock that was to so dramatically affect his future relationship with God and his service for Him.

Paul had amassed considerable knowledge of scripture having been taught by Gamaliel and through his own personal study. But that knowledge was contaminated by the earthly thinking of the ancients.

Consider what was said earlier about Rabbi Cohn:

Rabbi Cohn, accustomed to the intricate and often veiled polemical treatises of the Talmud (collection of ancient texts written by men), now found himself strangely captivated by the clear and soul-satisfying declarations of the Word of God, and it was not long before he began to question in his mind the reliability of the Talmud, seeing that in matters so vital it differed from the Holy Scriptures.

Paul could well have had the same problem and certainly Rabbi Aaron told me that through his rabbinic training he thought he knew how to interpret scripture, but it was not until he experienced his epiphany moment that the scriptures suddenly became clear to him so that he discovered new things in them each time he read them.

As far as Paul was concerned, it was not until after he had had time to reason within his mind, being prompted and enlightened by the Holy Spirit, during the three days he suffered total blindness, that he was in a fit state to receive the baptism of the Holy Spirit. That was the moment Ananias laid hands on him. At that moment not only did he have his physical sight restored to him, he was also filled with the Holy Spirit as the disciples had been on the day of Pentecost. He was then immediately baptized in water.

The truths contained in all the stored knowledge of the scriptures in his memory, that had been hidden from his understanding for so long, was suddenly unlocked for him by the Holy Spirit, allowing him to better understand all that had been prophesied about the Messiah. The reason why all the letters he wrote are so important is because they clearly show how God opened his eyes to the deeper meaning of scripture that had previously been hidden from him in order to assisted him in teaching the young church the deep spiritual truths in the Hebrew scriptures that had for so long eluded him.

Once the Messiah, having finished the task the Father had given to Him had been accomplished, had returned to heaven, the Holy Spirit was empowered to live within and work with all true believers, developing the teaching the Messiah had given them in order for the message of salvation to be taken to those unsaved people who were/are searching for the truth.

Throughout my books the term 'true believers' is used and in a number of places this has been expanded, but this seems to be a good time to explain the meaning behind it.

It is written that many are called by few are chose. The reason for this is that the offer of eternal salvation is freely offered to all, but this salvation is only confirmed in those who are willing to not just believe in God through the sacrifice of the Lord Jesus Christ, the Son of God/Son of Man but also to commit themselves to God as required by the first commandment:

> *"'Teacher, which commandment in the law is the greatest?' He said to him, "You shall love the Lord your God with all your heart, and with all your soul, and with all your mind." This is the greatest and first commandment. And a second is like it: "You shall love your neighbour as yourself." On these two commandments hang all the law and the prophets.'" (Matt. 22:36 – 40)*

Consider carefully what the Lord said to the disciples as He sent them out to the lost sheep of Israel:

> *"'Everyone therefore who acknowledges me before others, I also will acknowledge before my Father in heaven; but whoever denies me before others, I also will deny before my Father in heaven. 'Do not think that I have come to bring peace to the earth; I have not come to bring peace, but a sword. For I have come to set a man against his father, and a daughter against her mother, and a daughter-in-law against her mother-in-law; and one's foes will be members of one's own household. Whoever loves father or mother more than me is not worthy of me; and whoever loves son or daughter more than me is not worthy of me; and whoever does not take up the cross and follow me is not worthy of me. Those who find their life will lose it, and*

those who lose their life for my sake will find it. (Matt. 10:32 – 39)

The reason for the conflict within families and society is because sinfulness is not restricted to those who have a criminal nature, but even those who think they are good are challenged by the righteousness of those who have been changed through the baptism of the Holy Spirit. Satan does not mind those who attend church but have no real passion for the gospel. On the other hand he hates those who have had a personal experience of the risen Lord through the Holy Spirit and are on fire for Him, because they want to tell others of the transforming power of the good news of Christ and want them to know all about it.

As soon as the disciples received the fullness of the Holy Spirit they could not hold back proclaiming that new found knowledge. Consider the reaction of some in the crowd about them being drunk, and the reaction of the authorities who tried to crush the eruption of preaching and teaching.

Consider what Jeremiah said:

> *Your words were found, and I consumed them,*
> *they became a joy to me*
> *and the delight of my heart;*
> *for I am called by your name,*
> *O Lord, God of hosts.*
> *I did not join in the company of merrymakers,*
> *nor did I rejoice;*
> *under the sense of your presence I sat alone,*
> *for you had filled me with indignation*
> *regarding their sinful behaviour.*
> *(Jer. 15:16, 17)*

The above experience of Jeremiah is very important to us for it tells us a number of things:

- The effect the words from God had on him when he received them, *"they became a joy to me and the delight of my heart"*, but does the word of God have the same effect on us?

- His relationship with God because of those words, *"for I am called by your name, O Lord, God of hosts."* When you accepted the message of God's salvation into your heart, were you prepared to accept God's calling into His service?

- The effect of those words from God on his attitude to those around him, whose focus was on the lighter things of the world, *"I did not join in the company of merrymakers, nor did I rejoice;"* are you full of earthly merriment or has your idea of being merry changed since you put your trust in God?

- The effect the presence of God (Holy Spirit) had on him, *"under the sense of your presence I sat alone, for you had filled me with indignation regarding their sinful behaviour"*, but how has the effect of God's presence changed your lives or have you not had that personal life changing experience of God?

Jeremiah lived at a time when God was preparing the nation to go into exile because they had deserted Him and worshipped other gods, and Jeremiah was at the forefront of passing on God's prophetic words regarding their future punishment:

> *O Lord, you drew me to yourself,*
> *and I was attracted to you;*
> *you have overpowered me*
> *with your love and presence,*
> *and you have prevailed upon me to serve you.*

Jeremiah was called by God to serve Him at a time he would have been called to serve in the temple, (Jer. 1:4 – 10). Sadly the message God gave him to give to the people was undoubtedly unpalatable, but like the Lord Jesus he was determined to fulfill God's instructions to him. However it was not an easy life for him because of the opposition he experienced from a people who did not want to accept what God was planning for them and Jeremiah was responsible for telling them:

I have become a laughing-stock all day long;
everyone mocks me.
For whenever I speak, I must cry out,
I must shout, 'Violence and destruction!'
For the word of the Lord has become for me
a reproach and derision all day long.
So I said, 'I will not mention him,
nor speak any more in his name.'
But his word was within me,
in my heart like a burning fire
shut up in my bones;
I am weary of holding it back,
and I cannot.

Jeremiah's task was to speak the words God gave him to speak which were not pleasant at that time. He got to a point where he just wanted something more palatable to say to the people, but it was the attitude of the people towards their God that was defining what Jeremiah was required to say.

In the UK today there is much errant teaching within the churches with many going along with the mood of society even though it is contrary to scripture and that sets the people against God, the very problem Jeremiah experienced for it was the Holy Spirit that was giving him the words to speak. Sadly, the message he had to give caused many, even those of his own family, to speak out against him. But did the Lord not warn us about such things?

For I hear many whispering, mocking:
'Terror is all around!
Denounce him! Let us denounce him!'
All my close friends
watch for me to stumble.
'Perhaps he can be enticed,
and we can prevail against him,
and take our revenge on him.'
But the Lord is with me like a mighty warrior;
therefore my persecutors will stumble,
and they will not prevail.
They will be greatly shamed,
for they will not succeed.
Their everlasting confusion will never be forgotten.
O Lord of hosts, you who test the righteous,
you see the heart and the mind;
let me see your retribution upon them,
for to you I have committed my cause.
(see Jer. 20:7 – 12)

The reason I have mentioned the problems Jeremiah had as he preached the words God gave him for the people is because believers today will experience pressure to conform to the social and moral standards of the more vociferous members of the population when the Holy Spirit is giving them a different message to pass on to others.

We either enter into a relationship with God through our Lord Jesus Christ, or we go the way of the world. The choice is ours but there can be no 'sitting on the fence'. The life of the believer in Christ is not easy because the more active they are in the Lord's service the greater will be the opposition from the world of Satan who will use every means, fair and foul, strangers and family members who are not believers to undermine them, which is why all believers need to understand the example of our Lord who, although He is a God of love and came to serve, the world must conform to Him, not Him to the world and we must do likewise. We will not overcome sin unless we focus our attention on our Lord and commit ourselves to Him.

What primary example did the Lord Messiah give to those who met with Him?

Although He was God, He served all those He met, even to the washing of the disciples' feet. He consistently said that He was about His father's business. It might seem hard to digest what He said about the relationship with our human family, *"For I have come to set a man against his father, and a daughter against her mother, and a daughter-in-law against her mother-in-law; and one's foes will be members of one's own household. Whoever loves father or mother more than me is not worthy of me; and whoever loves son or daughter more than me is not worthy of me; and whoever does not take up the cross and follow me is not worthy of me."* But what did He mean when He said it?

"God is love and in Him is no darkness at all." God IS love. Indeed we are unable to love with the same intensity that God loves us, unless that is, we have the Holy Spirit living within us so that He can display the love of God in us, however attenuated that show of love might be. Therefore we can only understand what the Lord is telling us by accepting that individually we have no option but to commit ourselves completely to God first and foremost.

Our individual relationship with Him should take first place <u>all the time,</u> but sadly our feebleness often gets in the way. However, through our personal commitment, God is able to give us a love for others that we would not have had had He not taken central place in our lives. I love my wife not because of any physical attraction, although that is obviously very important, but I have found that just by thinking of her and looking at her, a sense of love for her wells up almost uncontrollably within me. That is God given love. There are people who I have been led to deal with, especially prisoners I met as a prison visitor, who could be referred to as not my type, but who need the help or encouragement that is in my power to provide.

None of us can have true love for others without having first bound ourselves up in our commitment to God and His infinite love as our first priority. Only then can the Spirit of God work in our hearts to not only enhance that personal love and commitment to Him and His service, but enable Him to fill us with that love He has for all who are seeking for salvation, whether or not they know that for which they are seeking. God sees into our hearts and knows those that are truly His, that is those who have a heart for Him.

It is only through the power of the Holy Spirit within us that we are able to serve God and others. I have visited prisoners as a prison visitor because of what the Lord said about being in prison but *you did not visit me*. That was the call which allowed me to visit and encourage many men, particularly those serving long sentences, over many years.

Here is a question that we need to ask ourselves, "Do we mention the name of Jesus Christ and willingly, and openly acknowledge Him as our Lord and Saviour in our ordinary daily life?" In other words are we willing to acknowledge our faith in God, or do we prefer to keep it a secret? How many of us read God's word and pray daily that we may be obedient to the will of God in our lives and ask for God to help and guide us in all that we do and say? It is not easy to be up front about our faith without 'pushing it down other peoples throats'. Just to acknowledge that we are believers is important, for surely the Lord said that if we do not acknowledge Him before others then He will not acknowledge us before His Father

The Methodist covenant prayer, prayed on the first Sunday of each new year, needs to be considered carefully before being repeated:

I am no longer my own but yours.
Put me to what you will; rank me with whom you will.
Put me to doing; put me to suffering.
Let me be employed for you, or laid aside for you; exalted for you, or brought low for you.
Let me be full; let me be empty.
Let me have all things; let me have nothing.
I freely and wholeheartedly yield all things to your pleasure and

disposal.

And now, glorious and blessed God, Father, Son, and Holy Spirit, you are mine and I am yours. So be it. And the Covenant which I have made on Earth, let it be ratified in Heaven.

Amen.

Could you commit yourself to praying this prayer, really mean it with all your heart and ask God to ratify it and honour it as well as to enable you fulfil that commitment?

Let me admit that for me this prayer is not one I am prepared to pray on the first Sunday of every year; the reason for that is because it has become my daily prayer, my minute by minute spiritual oxygen. It has been made the basis of my life for much of my life, and has been prayed frequently. It has to be admitted that along with that prayer I am constantly saying sorry to the Lord for all my failings because it is not until I am admitted into His rest that I will be fully refined in the furnace of life, as has been discussed above with all its testing

Without the living Saviour being at the centre, and the focal pint of my life, then it is of no value whatsoever because I believe that it is only in Christ that we are of use in His service. Fortunately I am far from being alone in this and of such are the children and servants of God, the true believers.

We have considered the importance of the ascension of the Messiah to the coming of the Holy Spirit in power and that the only way in which we can be effective in God's work on earth is to commit ourselves without reservation to Him and His service even as Isaiah did (Isa. 6).

But there is more to it than that for the simple reason this is the whole purpose of Easter. It is only through the death, resurrection and ascension of the Messiah, the man we call Christ Jesus our Lord that we can be saved to the uttermost, but, having had our conscience cleansed by His blood through the act of the Holy Spirit, we must enjoy the growth of our reborn spirit through our obedience to the word of God for us as we feed on the spiritual Word of God (Matt. 4:4), and through prayer and, being awake to His voice, receive guidance and commissions by which we can serve Him in newness of life in the power of the Holy Spirit as did the disciples and so many others.

Being blind to, or ignorant of the word of God and deaf to His call – that still small voice of God that Elijah heard – has the potential to make our relationship with God ineffectual. For all new believers and those starting out in the faith, that commitment to His word and prayer needs to be the aim. Life in the Lord is not easy for there are many times when we do not seem to hear anything from Him; no still small voice, no scripture jumping out at us and with plenty of questions in our mind begging for answers. David had the same problem as all of us do today. Yet this is where faith comes in which had been identified as the **F**antastic **A**dventure **I**n **T**rusting **H**im. In my experience it is a fantastic adventure that is only successful when we put our full and unerring trust in Him no matter how difficult the circumstances we experience.

VICTORY OF EASTER

In a vision, when testifying before the Sanhedrin, Stephen saw the Lord standing at the right hand of God (Acts 7:55). The apostle John had the privilege of being taken up in the Spirit into the dwelling place of God to meet with the Messiah he had known and had served before and after Pentecost.

In taking 'A Fresh Look At Easter' we have considered not just the weekend of Good Friday to Easter Sunday, but also important prophecies and events leading up to it and the events immediately after it, all of which help our understanding of everything that happened during that crucial weekend and the implications intrinsic to those happenings.

The necessary fragmentation of the celebrations of Christmas, Easter and Pentecost is understandable because believers celebrate the individual events approximately when they were believed to have happened. However to try to understand the importance of all that our Lord Messiah achieved during the original weekend of events, and the implications for us now, it is essential to consider the impact of the 'before', 'during' and 'after' as a whole.

The call *"Christ is risen!"* and the response *"He is risen indeed!"* is a powerful declaration of our belief that He defeated death and that through His victory we have eternal life. However, that is all very well but we also need to move on if we are to mature in our Christian life.

The writer to the Hebrew Christians remonstrated with them that they were not growing and maturing in the faith. He wrote:

"For though by this time you ought to be teachers, you still need someone to teach you again the basic elements of the oracles of God. You still need milk, not solid food; indeed everyone who continues to rely on a diet of milk is still baby and unskilled in the word of righteousness. But solid food is for the mature, for those whose faculties have been trained by practice to distinguish good from evil." (Heb. 5:12 – 14)

That was some condemnation from the writer of the book sent to those who at first believed in the Messiah but then got stuck on the elementary principles of the faith, which is about sins forgiven and being born again. In chapter 6 the writer goes on to say:

"… leaving behind the basic teaching about Christ, let us progress towards perfection, not laying again the foundation of repentance from dead works and faith towards God, or instruction about baptisms, laying on of hands and the resurrection of the dead, and eternal judgement.

It is possible for us to do this, if God permits, and move forward in the faith.

But it is impossible to restore again to repentance those who were once enlightened, who experienced the heavenly gift, have known the presence of the Holy Spirit, and have enjoyed all that the good word of God has to offer and the powers of the age to come, and then turned away from that whole experience. Indeed by rejecting all that they had learned and experienced it is impossible for them to go back to the moment when they first realized that they could have their sins forgiven. By rejection their salvation through Christ they are in effect bringing to naught all that the Son of God achieved on the cross and are holding him up to contempt as being just another criminal.

Ground that absorbs the rain falling on it repeatedly, enables it to produce a crop useful to those for whom it is cultivated, receives a blessing from God, so are they who receive the word of God with gladness and allow it to work within them. But those ho reject Christ are like ground that produces thorns and thistles, making it worthless and on the verge of being cursed; its end is to be burned over." (my interpretation of Heb. 6:1 – 8)

Constantly going over and over the basics of the faith will not allow anyone to grow. Confining believers to a constant diet of the gospels without expanding the diet to include the solid teaching of the understanding of how we must approach God and the experiences of the Israelites in the First Testament, along with the teaching of Paul and the revelations of John, and particularly the teaching regarding the baptism and influence of the Holy Spirit in the Second Testament, is a most unfortunate spiritual diet that will not build the spiritual muscles so necessary for our faith.

No one is able to become a professional at what they are doing without studying their subject either academically or through practice. My maternal grandfather could not read or write, yet as a miner there was nothing anyone could teach him about coal mining, in fact the pit bosses would ask him for advice. My father-in-law left school at 14 and was brilliant at mathematics but had no paper qualifications yet was a much sought after builder because of his willingness to learn and put the fundamentals into practice. He had learned to build to a very high quality so that people were prepared to wait for him to do their work. I have never been able to quote scripture like others, yet the Lord had enabled me to preach and teach and write books.

Unless learning about deep scriptural truths leads the individual into a growing understanding of the things of the Spirit and thereby cause them to enter into a increasingly meaningful and maturing spiritual relationship with God, the time spent in church services and other church organized meetings are of little or no value. It is the feast of rich fare that believers need to look for, which may at first cause spiritual indigestion but will, if willing to prevail and engage in further study, yield rich rewards and a productive and meaningful spiritual life.

We need to heed the warnings of the apostles concerning the worsening world situation, such as the coming of the man of perdition or lawlessness mentioned by Paul to the church in Thessalonica (2 Thes. 2:1 – 12). Just as there are counterfeiters as exposed by the BBC programme 'Fake Britain', so there counterfeiters and liars, wolves who want to scatter the flock of God Paul warned the leaders of the Ephesian church about (Acts 20:29, 30). Peter tells us to be sober and vigilant because our adversary the Devil walks around like a roaring lion seeking whom he may devour (1 Pet. 5:8 – 11). John writes to warn believers about the antichrist, or the counterfeit Christ taught by those raise up in the church, who may have gone out from the church but have never been part of the church because they have never met with or acknowledge the living Christ (1 Jn. 2:18 – 24).

Spiritual warfare is a reality. Paul wrote to the Ephesians advising them to put on the whole armour of God in order that we may be able to stand against the wiles of the evil one (Eph. 6:10 – 18). We know that Eve was deceived but Adam sinned. With all the knowledge available to us in the scriptures we would be exceptionally stupid to neglect all the warnings and not arm ourselves against attack. I have had demonic spirits in my house on more than one occasion and had to order them out in the name of Jesus. Although at first they resisted they had to go, because the Lord Jesus is victor over sin and the Devil.

During Easter we remember the death and resurrection of the Messiah, and then His ascension back to the Father. Moving on, and momentarily seeing through the spiritual eyes of Stephen, we see the Lord at the right hand of the Father (Acts 7:54 – 60; cf. Dan. 7:13, 14). Then in the book of Revelation we read about John's experiences whilst imprisoned for his faith on the island of Patmos. John's initial experience whilst 'in the Spirit' on the Lord's Day, when he heard a loud voice behind him, leads the believer into a new world of the Spirit in which the hidden treasures of the complete word of God are revealed, and new spiritual truths are revealed.

"Then, when I turned to see whose voice it was that spoke to me, I saw seven golden lampstands, and in the midst of the lampstands I saw one like the Son of Man, clothed with a garment down to His feet and with a golden sash across his chest. His head and hair were white as white wool, white as snow; His eyes were like a flame of fire. His feet were like burnished bronze, refined as in a furnace, and His voice was like the sound of many waters. In His right hand He held seven stars, and from His mouth came a sharp, two-edged sword, and His countenance was like the sun shining in its full strength. (Rev. 1:12 – 16)

This 'seeing' was not physical but spiritual for his worship in the Lord was so deep that the Holy Spirit led him into deeper spiritual communion with his Lord. This was the ascended Messiah he was seeing and hearing, and such was His glory that John could only use language that inevitably revealed the extra-ordinary nature of the vision he received.

"When I saw him, I fell at his feet as though dead. But he placed his right hand on me, saying, 'Do not be afraid; I am the first and the last, and the living one. I was dead, and see, I am alive for ever and ever; and I have the keys of Death and of Hades."

The importance of what John was to write about was what was to happen in the future in order to prepare those truly committed to God through the sacrifice of the Messiah and who had been reborn and energized in the Spirit for the future both immediate and long term.

"Now write what you have seen, what is, and what is to take place after this. As for the mystery of the seven stars that you saw in my right hand, and the seven golden lampstands: the seven stars are the angels of the seven churches, and the seven lampstands are the seven churches." (Rev. 1:12 – 20; — see my books Letters to the Seven Churches in Revelation, and Seeing into the Future : Understanding the Revelation of John)

God has moved on from the crucifixion, just as He moved on from the plagues and the exodus, moved on from the crossing of the Red Sea to established the children of Israel in the Promised Land, moved on from the establishing the nation in the land to training them and preparing them for the coming of His Son. Our Promised Land is the New Jerusalem that will appear out of heaven, a place where we will be found clothed in a spiritual body that God will provide for each one of us. But first we must face the remainder of our life here on earth and the warnings and encouragement of the message of Revelation is there

The First Testament tells us about how sin came into the world, about the evil one and how he seeks to influence nations and individuals. But it also tells us how God deals with nations and with individuals such as Abraham, Joseph son of Jacob, Isaiah, Jeremiah and many, many more. Example, after example, after example are there for our benefit. Consider King David and all that he wrote and that was written about him and his relationship with his God, and all the other writers of Psalms. And what about the teaching of Solomon in the book of Proverbs?

Moses was a murderer, David had Uriah murdered in order for him to have his wife Bathsheba, Solomon finally fell for worshipping gods because he disobeyed the commandments and married too many foreign women who worshipped other gods. All flawed characters whom God used to his glory. Rahab was a citizen of the condemned city of Jericho, and Ruth a Moabitess, a nation that had opposed Israel and was condemned for it, yet both women were remarkable ancestors of the Messiah.

The Second Testament teaches us about the arrival, life and death of the Messiah and all He taught about the Father; also how we need to react to His loving gift. With reference to the First Testament, in the Second we are able to learn the truth about the conquering of sin and why true believers will be able to meet with the Lord in the place the Messiah has gone to prepare for us. All the teaching in this book has been garnered from both testaments with nothing added or subtracted. However, we need to be conscious of the fact that we too are flawed and constantly in need of forgiveness and guidance by the Holy Spirit.

But there is more to the Second Testament than most believers are willing to accept. Do we accept that the Bible is the word of God? Or do we question everything in it? Surely it is best to accept it all. I understand Sir Isaac Watts once said, "The parts of the Bible I can understand I accept, the parts I do not understand I accept by faith." Even if he did not say those words they make sense to me, indeed for me, the Bible is our handbook to enable us to know God, and an instruction book on how we need to live our lives. Pour doubt on its contents and the whole book becomes suspect and therefore ineffective. What is the point of each person picking out the bits they believe and discarding the rest? Just because we are all flawed, it does not mean that the Bible is flawed.

Consider if you will the testimony concerning the book at the end of the Bible (Rev. 22:18, 19). Who is prepared to say that those words have no meaning?

This is an extract of the preface to my book 'Seeing into the Future : Understanding the Revelation of John":

It is important to realise that the Bible as we know it is an intrinsic whole. Remove the first chapter of Genesis, or consider the creation and the fall of man as myths, as some would have us believe (2 Tim. 4:4), and the book of Revelation becomes total nonsense, an insoluble riddle. Do away with the book of Revelation, or treat it as though its whole purpose was for the time it was written and not for the future that was still to come, and is still to come, and you make nonsense of the promise of the appearance out of heaven of the New Jerusalem, and we would still be asking questions about what happens after we die. Such questions are also relevant to those who will be living when the world comes to an end as prophesied in the Second Testament.

The Book of Revelation provides the Bible, for which Genesis is the beginning, with an end without which the Bible would be incomplete. It is like a belt, which is only of use when there is a buckle at one end into which the other end fits with the holes that allow the pin of the buckle to retain the belt in place. Do away with the means of fixing the belt in place at one end or the other and the belt is useless. So it is with this Word of God, which is such a treasure to those who would be saved, for the two ends fit together so seamlessly that the whole Bible becomes a complete and integrated whole, allowing sense to be made of all that is in between.

Along with the news of the eternal position of the Lamb of God and His involvement in the final stages of the life of the earth; the book of Revelation also contains warnings of what is to come and how we must prepare ourselves for the disruption to the lives of all people through the final activities of the evil one during the time of the end of the world, indeed of all creation.

> "Then I saw in the right hand of the one seated on the throne a scroll written on the inside and on the back, sealed with seven seals; and I saw a mighty angel proclaiming with a loud voice,
> 'Who is worthy to break the seals of the scroll and open it?'
> And no one in heaven or on earth or under the earth was able to open the scroll or to look into it. And I began to weep bitterly because no one was found worthy to open the scroll or to look into it.
> Then one of the elders said to me, 'Do not weep. See, the Lion of the tribe of Judah (Gen. 49:8 – 12), the Root of David (Is. 11:10), has conquered, making Him worthy to break its seven seals and open the scroll.'
> Then I saw between the throne and the four living creatures and among the elders a Lamb standing as if it had been slaughtered, having seven horns and seven eyes, which are the seven spirits of God (reference to the Holy Spirit) sent out into all the earth. He went and took the scroll from the right hand of the one who was seated on the throne. When he had taken the scroll, the four living creatures and the twenty-four elders fell before the Lamb, each holding a harp and golden bowls full of incense, which are the prayers of the saints. They sing a new song:

'You are worthy to take the scroll
and to open its seals,
for you were slain and by your blood
have redeemed us to God
from every tribe and language
and people and nation;
you have made them to be
a kingdom and priests to our God,
and they will reign on earth.'
Then I looked, and I heard the voice of many angels surrounding
the throne and the living creatures and the elders; they numbered
myriads of myriads and thousands of thousands, singing with full
voice,

'Worthy is the Lamb that was slaughtered
to receive power and wealth and wisdom and might
and honour and glory and blessing!'
Then I heard every creature in heaven and on earth and under
the earth and in the sea, and all that is in them, singing,

'To the one seated on the throne and to the Lamb
be blessing and honour and glory and might
for ever and ever!'
And the four living creatures said, 'Amen!' And the elders
fell down and worshipped." (Rev. 5 – for a more comprehensive
understanding of this chapter see my book "Seeing Into The Future
: Understanding the Revelation of John")

This passage is pregnant with First and Second Testament theology and can only be properly understood in relation to the word of God as a whole, for it is a word that is full of spiritual food for the spiritually reborn!

Consider what the Messiah said to Caiaphas and all the priestly and lay leaders of the people before whom He was on trial. When put under oath by the high priest the Messiah had no option but to admit that He was the Son of God adding *"nevertheless, I say to you, you will see the Son of Man sitting at the right hand of the Power on high"*.

Whilst on the island of Patmos the apostle John was caught up in the Holy Spirit and taken to the place of God's abode. There he saw someone sitting on a throne surrounded by worshippers and in His hand was a scroll with seven seals which no one seemed to be worthy of opening. John wept, but one of the twenty-four elders comforted him *'See, the Lion of the tribe of Judah, the Root of David, has conquered, making Him worthy to break its seven seals and open the scroll.'*.

It is the Messiah the elder was talking about. The man who stood trial before the worldly Caiaphas, the man whipped and made fun of by the Roman soldiers and on whose head they placed the crown of thorns. This is the man upon the cross calling out to His Father in pain and agony, and the man who gently called Mary's name when she was asking where His body lay. This is the same one who commissioned the disciples and then rose up through the clouds and out of the envelope of creation (see "The Origin of Life") to return in a spiritual body to His Father, the first fruits of all those who have died in the faith.

This final chapter is all about the need for the believer to progress beyond the parables and the crucifixion if they are to grow spiritually, and thus be empowered to teach others about what they truly believe, which is part of the commission for all true believers.

Sadly too many do not have clear knowledge to give an explanation for the reason for their faith or the experience of being born of God spiritually and therefore able to live in the Spirit of God. All believers need to have some knowledge and understanding that God can draw upon to give them the words that will enable them to convey to others why they believe as they do however weak or uncertain their faith.

There is a lot of imagery in Revelation which puts many believers off studying the book. But through prayer and meditating on the word, along with the use of various Bible translations and reference books, and books such as 'Seeing into the Future : Understanding the Revelation of John', it is possible for God to speak to us though what John recorded and it will enable us to better face the future during the increasingly difficult years that lie ahead.

> *'Worthy is the Lamb that was slaughtered*
> *to receive power and wealth and wisdom and might*
> *and honour and glory and blessing!'*
> *Then I heard every creature in heaven and on earth and under the earth*
> *and in the sea, and all that is in them, singing,*
> *'To the one seated on the throne and to the Lamb*
> *be blessing and honour and glory and might*
> *for ever and ever!'*

This is the victory of the suffering servant Messiah, this is what the crucifixion was all about, this is why the Messiah faced all the terror and the evil forces arrayed against Him during that time on earth, in order that those willing to believe in Him may be given a new spiritual life in Christ Jesus and enter the rest He has gone to prepare for them. As far as Satan is concerned, he was defeated for all time on the cross and at the glorious resurrection.

> *Then I saw an angel coming down from heaven, holding in*
> *his hand the key to the bottomless pit and a great chain. He seized*
> *the dragon, that ancient serpent, who is the Devil and Satan, and*
> *bound him for a thousand years, and threw him into the pit, and*
> *locked and sealed it over him, so that he would deceive the nations*
> *no more, until the thousand years were ended. After that he must be*
> *let out for a little while.*
> *(Rev. 20:1 – 3)*
> *When the thousand years are ended, Satan will be released from*
> *his prison and will come out to deceive the nations at the four corners*
> *of the earth, Gog and Magog, in order to gather them for battle; they*
> *are as numerous as the sands of the sea. They marched up over the*
> *breadth of the earth and surrounded the camp of the saints and the*
> *beloved city. And fire came down from heaven and consumed them.*
> *And the Devil who had deceived them was thrown into the lake of*

fire and sulphur, where the beast and the false prophet were, and they will be tormented day and night for ever and ever.

Then I saw a great white throne and the one who sat on it; the earth and the heaven fled from his presence, and no place was found for them. And I saw the dead, great and small, standing before the throne, and books were opened (the record of all that each person has done in life). Also another book was opened, the book of life (containing the names of all those who have truly believed and accepted the Christ as their Lord and Saviour). And the dead were judged according to their works, as recorded in the books. And the sea gave up the dead that were in it, Death and Hades gave up the dead that were in them, and all were judged according to what they had done. Then Death and Hades were thrown into the lake of fire. This is the second death, the lake of fire; and anyone whose name was not found written in the book of life was thrown into the lake of fire. (Rev. 20:7 – 15)

Let us be in no doubt that God will carry out His judgement on the earth, and man has no power whatsoever against Him. We all do well to study the Bible as a whole and not select the bits we think we find easy to understand in order for us to fully believe and also for us to be able to make a spontaneous and clear declaration of our belief to anyone who asks.

EPILOGUE

Throughout this book we have learned some amazing things about the God we purport to worship, His eternal existence and unimaginable power which He used to bring about the appearance of the heavens and the earth and how He is able to control it and bring it to naught at His command and according to His good pleasure. After all the power He owns is greater than anything He has created and therefore, just as a model maker, or builder can reduce what they have constructed to its component pieces or destroy it completely, so can He.

Yet this God, this supreme power is driven by love, hate being totally foreign to Him. Being three persons living and working in total harmony, it is the intrinsic supreme love of God that binds them together in an eternal bond of unity. And so it was that when God made man, love was the basis for God's design of man along with the desire to be united with him in a unity, a oneness similar to that which binds the three persons of the Trinity together, so that God and man would live together in total harmony.

Sadly man's rebellion in the beginning spoilt all that and caused a rift between God and man that could only be bridge by the sacrifice of God's Son who came in love and died because of love.

Hymns are sung in churches and Christian meetings that tell of God's love to us and the need for us to love God, but sadly it is clear that those who receive that gift of love, which is eternal salvation, want to be saved but are not necessarily willing to really commit themselves to God in the same way that God commits Himself for the benefit of man. To so many the thought of giving themselves completely to God for Him to guide and direct them in His service is anathema to them, at least that has apparently been the response of some to my commitment.

We sing that the love of God is greater far than tongue or pen can ever tell, and about how Love Divine excels all other love and yet a friend of mine asked some long term believers if they would be prepared to give themselves into God service without any conditions attached. A look of horror was seen in their faces. But we accept that God is a God of love and that man was made in love and for love in order for men to live in love and harmony with both God and man. If that is so then why the look of horror? Do they not fully believe that God is the source of all love? Then why do they not trust Him to guide and direct them on the basis of His love for them?

Consider the supreme lengths to which God was willing to go, even allowing the sacrifice of the physical life of His only Son, not for Himself but for our salvation? He is the good shepherd who loves His sheep and willingly gave His life for them, therefore surely it is right to surrender our lives completely to Him and trust that He will look after those that love Him, because that is not only what He has promised to do, but also has the power to do; *"Come unto me all you who are weary and carrying heavy burdens, and I will give you rest (Matt 11:28).* So why are some so reticent – *"Yet you refuse to come to me to have life" (Jn. 5:40),* when there is a bountiful supply of examples in the First Testament of God doing just that in dire circumstances.

Surely God wants to give us abundant life (Jn. 10:10b), for that is why He came, and the abundant life He is able to give is both physical and spiritual which leads us to eternal life.

The question needs to be asked again, "Why are those who call themselves true believers so against completely abandoning their lives to the very God who has saved them from eternal death, by causing them to be born anew spiritually and giving them a hope that is both certain and sure?"

Surely it is no good going to church and singing the hymns and praying prayers and celebrating communion if in their heart they are resisting committing themselves completely to Him? Do not forget the scripture which says that many are called but few are chosen.

The decision on how far to commit oneself to God is a strictly personal one, but I know that the only way I have grown ever closer to God is by surrendering myself completely to God and submitting myself to His will unconditionally.

APPENDIX A

Prophecy	First Testament reference	Fulfilment
The battle between Satan and the Messiah would cause the end of Satan whose head would be crushed	Gen. 3:15	Jn. 8:44; Acts 13:10; 1 Jn. 13:8; Rom. 16:20; Rev. 12:7 - 17
The currency of blood	Gen. 9:4 – 6; Lev. 17:11	Matt: 26:28; Lk. 22:20; Jn. 6:54 ; Heb. 9:14, 22
Abraham was father of all Hebrews and the spiritual father of all believers	Gen. 12:3; 18:18	Acts 3:25, 26; Gal. 3:14
Melchizedek - Priest & King blessed Abram and therefore Aaron	Gen. 14:18 - 20	Heb. 10
Judah was the patriarch of the tribe of kings	Gen. 49:10	Matt. 1:2; Lk. 3:33; Rev. 5:5
Messiah would be a prophet like Moses	Deut. 18:15 – 19	Acts 3:22, 23
The form of His death	Deut. 21:22, 23	Matt. 27:22, 23; Acts 2:23; 3:13, 14
The Messiah was to be the Son of God Himself	Psalm 2:7	Matt. 3:17; Mark 1:11; Luke 3:22

Prophecy	First Testament reference	Fulfilment
The Messiah will be raised from the dead (resurrected). He defeated death so that it would hold no power over those who believed in Him	Psalm 16:10, 11	Matt. 28:5 - 9; Mk. 16:6; Lk. 24:4 - 7; Jn. 20:11 - 16; Acts 1:3; 2:32

The Messiah's crucifixion experience is remarkably foretold by King David in Ps. 22. It includes a number of prophetic statements, which can be confirmed in Matt. 27:34 – 50,.

Prophecy	First Testament reference	Fulfilment
My God, my God, why have you forsaken me?	Ps. 22:1	
Sneered at and mocked	Ps. 22:7	Lk. 23:11, 35-39
Pierced through hands and feet	Ps. 22:16	Lk 23:33; 24:36-39; Jn. 19:18; 20:19, 20, 24-27
His bones will not be broken (a person's legs were usually broken after being crucified to speed up their death as were those of the two thieves)	Ps. 22:17; 34:20	Jn 19:31-33,36
Men will Gamble for the His clothing	Ps. 22:18	Matt. 27:35; Mk 15:24; Lk. 23:34; Jn. 19:23,24
He will be accused by false witnesses	Ps. 35:11	Matt. 26:59, 60; Mk. 14:56,57
He will be hated without a cause	Ps. 35:19; 69:4	John 15:23-25

Prophecy	First Testament reference	Fulfilment
He will be betrayed by a friend	Ps. 41:9	Jn. 13:18,21
He will ascend to heaven (at the right hand of God)	Ps. 68:18	Lk. 24:51; Acts 1:9; 2:33-35; 3:20-21; 5:31,32; 7:55-56; Rom. 8:34; Eph. 1:20, 21; Col. 3:1; Heb. 1:3; 8:1; 10:12; 12:2; 1 Pet 3:22; Rev. 1:11 – 20
He would be given vinegar and gall to drink	Ps. 69:21	Matt. 27:34; Mk. 15:23; Jn. 19:29,30
Great kings will pay homage and tribute to the Messiah	Ps. 72:10, 11	Matt. 2:1-11
He is referred to as "the stone the builders rejected" who will become the "head cornerstone"	Ps. 118:22, 23; Is. 28:16	Matt. 21:42,43; Acts 4:11; Eph. 2:20; 1 Peter 2:6-8
He would be a descendant of David	Ps. 132:11; Jer. 23:5, 6; 33:15, 16	Lk. 1:32,33
He would be a born of a virgin	Is. 7:14	Matt. 1:18-25; Lk. 1:26 – 35
His first spiritual work will be in Galilee	Is. 9:1-7	Matt. 4:12 – 16
He would make the blind see, the deaf hear, etc.	Is. 35:5-6	Cf. Matt. 11:3 – 6; Jn. 11:47

Prophecy	First Testament reference	Fulfilment
He would be beaten, mocked, and spat upon	Is. 50:6	Matt. 26:67; 27:26 – 31
The "Gospel according to Isaiah"	Is. 52:13 – 53:12	Matthew, Mark, Luke, John
People will hear and not believe the "arm of the LORD" (Messiah)	Is. 53:1	Jn. 12:37, 38
He would be rejected	Is. 53:3	Matt. 27:20-25; Mk. 15:8 – 14; Lk. 23:18 – 23; Jn. 19:14, 15
He would be killed	Is. 53:5 – 9	Matt. 27:50; Mk. 15:37 – 39; Lk. 23:46; Jn. 19:30
He would be silent in front of his accusers	Is. 53:7	Matt. 26:62,63; 27:12 – 14
He would be buried with the rich	Is. 53:9	Matt. 27:59,60; Mk. 15:46; Lk. 23:52, 53; Jn. 19:38 – 42
He would be crucified with criminals	Is. 53:12	Matt. 27:38; Mk. 15:27; Lk. 23:32,33
He is part of the new and everlasting covenant	Is. 55:3-4; Jer. 31:31 – 34	Matt. 26:28; Mk. 14:24; Lk. 22:20; Heb. 8:6 – 13
He would be our intercessor (intervene for us and plead on our behalf)	Is. 59:16	Heb. 9:15

Prophecy	First Testament reference	Fulfilment
He would make the blind see, the deaf hear, etc.	Is. 35:5, 6	Many places. Also see Matthew 11:3-6 and John 11:47
He would be beaten, mocked, and spat upon	Is. 50:6	Matt. 26:67; 27:26 – 31
The "Gospel according to Isaiah"	Is. 52:13 – 53:12	Matt., Mk., Lk., Jn
People will hear and not believe the "arm of the LORD" (Messiah)	Is. 53:1	John 12:37,38
He would be rejected	Is. 53:3	Matt. 27:20 – 25; Mk. 15:8-14; Lk. 23:18-23; Jn. 19:14,15
He would be killed	Is. 53:5 – 9	Matt. 27:50; Mk. 15:37 – 39; Lk. 23:46; Jn. 19:30
He would be silent in front of his accusers	Is. 53:7	Matt. 26:62, 63; 27:12 – 14
He would be buried with the rich	Is. 53:9	Matt. 27:59, 60; Mk. 15:46; Lk. 23:52, 53; Jn. 19:38 – 42
He would be crucified with criminals	Is. 53:12	Matthew 27:38; Mark 15:27; Luke 23:32,33
He is part of the new and everlasting covenant	Is. 55:3, 4; Jer. 31:31 – 34	Matthew 26:28; Mark 14:24; Luke 22:20; Hebrews 8:6-13

Prophecy	First Testament reference	Fulfilment
He would be our intercessor (intervene for us and plead on our behalf)	Is. 59:16	Heb. 9:15
He was to have two missions	Is. 61:1-3 (first mission ends at ". . . year of the LORD's favor")	First mission: Lk. 4:16-21; Second mission: to be fulfilled at the end of the world
He would come at a specific time	Dan. 9:25-26	Gal. 4:4; Eph. 1:10 It was this calculation that the leading academics of the day did not take into consideration when witnessing all that their Messiah did. Had they thought more about the miracles He performed and His teaching, they might have received understanding as Nicodemus did.
He would be born in Bethlehem	Mic. 5:2	Matt. 2:1; Lk. 2:4 – 7 The leaders of the Jews did not investigate the life of the Lord
He would enter Jerusalem riding the colt of a donkey	Zech. 9:9	Matt. 21:1-11

Prophecy	First Testament reference	Fulfilment
He would be sold for 30 pieces of silver	Zech. 11:12,13	Matt. 26:15; 27:3 – 10
He would be forsaken by His disciples	Zech. 13:7	Matt. 26:31,56
He would enter the Temple with authority	Mal. 3:1	Matt. 21:12; Lk. 19:45

There were so many events in the life of their Messiah that fulfilled scriptural prophecy to the letter, which should have enabled the scholars and religious leaders to have identified who He was. But the blindness of those who confessed to be 'religious leaders' was in part because He was not the person they were expecting to see, which prevented them from recognizing Him.

Appendix B

Numbers in Scripture

It is clear when reading through the Bible that certain numbers are used frequently and are inevitably linked in reference to some aspect of God, of man and of creation in general. We are told that although God is *three* persons (a Trinity), Father, Son and Holy Spirit, yet they are *one* because they are bound together with a love so strong that complete unity is inevitable. God IS Love, is the source of all love, therefore there can be no disagreement within them because working together in complete harmony is normal.

Here is a tabulated help with the spiritual significance of numbers which will assist with the reading of the word and help identify God in prophecy because of the spiritual significance of the use of numbers:

One   Unity and commencement — which speaks of God from before the beginning of creation

Two   Difference — (1) for two unconnected individuals to agree in evidence before a court of law, their joint testimony is conclusive; (2) two individuals will oppose, cause enmity and division. Consider how by adding the word double the meaning of a word such as mind or minded, is completely change. People can be described as being two-faced.

Three	Completeness — it takes the minimum of three lines to complete a plain figure; it is also easy to associate three with God because He is a trinity. The fundamental work of creation was completed on the third 'day', where there was light and dark, sky and earth and oceans and land. The succeeding 'days' are a counterpart being the embellishment of the work done in the first three. Resurrection is also implied because the land rose up out of the deep on the third 'day', and the Lord Jesus rose from the dead on the third day. Consider the number of times God caused something to happen on the third day.
Four	Creative works — 3+1 with reference to the material and terrestrial creation; the sun was in position and glowing, the moon also was positioned with the earth tilted and spinning to allow the sun to shine on half the earth during daylight hours and the moon to reflect the sun's light to the earth during the night. This was the first moment when time was initiated.
Five	Grace — 4+1 it was on the fifth day that God created all the living things that inhabit the oceans, the land and the sky along with the ability to pro-create. Five is the leading factor used in the construction of the tabernacle.
Six	Human number — it was on the sixth day that God created man and the hours of the day are multiples of six.
Seven	Spiritual Perfection — seven is the hall mark of the Holy Spirit. It was the Holy Spirit who hovered over the chaos of the earth at the beginning and breathed into man's nostrils the breath of spiritual life raising him above all God's other creatures. It was the Holy Spirit who caused all God's commands to become reality. God rested on the seventh 'day' having completed the work of creation. Seven is the number regulating the incubation and gestation in all living creatures.

Eight	Resurrection, regeneration — the first day of the week when Christ rose from the dead. A new first, beginning and commencement. In Hebrew letters also represent numbers and the Greek word for Jesus equals 888. Eight and its multiples are a significant part of all that has to do with the Lord's names, people and works.
Nine	Finality and Judgement — 3x3 with three being Divine Completeness. Nine, its factors or multiples relate to all cases relating to judgement.
Ten	Ordinal Perfection — after nine, ten is a new start.
Eleven	Disorder, disorganisation — with the death of Judas Iscariot the twelve disciples became 11 until Matthias was added to their number.
Twelve	Governmental Perfection — Notice how God had Jacob sire 12 sons to establish the 12 tribes of Israel. When the men of Benjamin were almost wiped out during the era of the judges how every effort was made to repopulate the tribe. Our Lord chose 12 disciples. 12 is also in evidence in measurement of time and matters governing matters in the heavens and the earth.
Thirteen	Rebellion — and all aspects of it. The first occasion it is used is in Genesis 14:4 where various nations came together to rebel against the suzerainty of Chedorlaomer and the kings that were with him.
Forty	Divine Order— when applied to earthly matters. Elijah went 40 days and nights without food or water as he travelled to the mount of God, Jesus did the same after which He was tempted by Satan

3, 7, 10 & 12 are four perfect numbers the product of which is 2,520, the Least Common Multiple of the ten digits governing all numeration. It can be divided by each of the nine digits without remainder and is the number of chronological perfection, 7 x 360.

Numbers play a significant part in the work of God in the world and we do well to consider them.

Appendix C

Thoughts on the Trinity

This was on an email from my Jewish friend:

> Bit complicated sometimes.
>
> Holy spirit is the presence of God.
> Does the Holy Spirit move, with God. Is God. One with God but independent?
> Some say that the Holy Spirit was created by God to interact with Man. God cannot abide evil or sin. Who is without sin on Earth now?
> Every time, with an exception here and there. Holy Spirit is the spokesperson or presence of God.

My reply:

Having been challenged by what you wrote above, it suddenly came to me.

The person of God is beyond our ability to imagine for He has never been born, can never die and is pure spirit, which means that He has no form as we have visible recognizable physical form. This means that He is not in one place at any time, but everywhere at the same time.

He is not restricted in His ability, knowledge, understanding, wisdom or any other attribute, so that nothing is impossible to Him.

The Father, who is the source of all love which impregnates the

Son and the Spirit, is the decision maker as acknowledged by the Son, to whom He gave birth of Himself, for before the creation there was no one else but Him, and after the creation there was still no one like Him or His equal.

The Son voices the thoughts of the Father (Jn.7:15 – 18) but has no power of decision making of Himself, for He is merely obedient to the will and purposes of the Father. The Son, by that very distinction, is subservient to the Father, but the Father loves the Son as the Son loves the Father and for the moment the praise for our salvation goes to the Son, because of His physical death on the cross in place of mankind for our sin, because He alone was totally pure before His physical birth and during His physical life, and could therefore die for sinful mankind.

It is because He died for man's sins that Jesus attracts the praises of man, but all the praise truly belongs to the Father for as Jesus looked up to heaven said, *"Father, the hour has come. Glorify your Son so He can give glory back to you. For you have given him authority over everyone. He gives eternal life to each one you have given him (see Jn. 17:1 – 5).* Jesus died in place of man so that the Father could be satisfied that the objective of the sentence He imposed on man could be fulfilled, *"You shall surely die"*.

As the Father can never die, the Son will always be the Son of God.

It is also possible that God, who is referred to as the Father and therefore the central figure of the Godhead, needed someone to enact His decision to create the physical things including man, so the Father of Himself provided a Spirit for Himself that was of Himself, who would be the one producing the physical as a result of the Father's spiritual decisions as spoke by the Son.

That is why the Spirit cannot attract praises to Himself, for He is merely being obedient to the will and purposes of the Father according to the word spoke by the Son (Jn. 16:13). He will not speak on His own authority.

The Spirit, has to be an individual person, for independently He created all that exists according to the plan and will of the Father and finally created man in the image of God the Father. When Jesus called for the storm to be stilled, the dead raised to life, the blind to see etc., it was the Holy Spirit who caused it to happen. For such things also happened after Jesus had ascended when the Spirit worked with and through the disciples.

He is also the channel through which man communicates with the Father through the offices of the Son. He is also the barrier between the purity of the Father who cannot look upon sin, hence Him 'turning His back' on His Son as he hung on the cross. So the presence of God that was with man from the beginning is through the Holy Spirit who has dealt directly with sinful man on behalf of the Father.

Because it was the Spirit of God who created all that exists, He is able to see into and understand the workings of men, including all that is happening in their minds and hearts. The heart is understood to be the very centre and hub of a person.

Because of this attribute He was able to tell the Son what the men listening to Him were thinking. It is also He who applies the blood because He witnessed the Son shedding His physical blood on the cross.

Also, because the Son is also a Spirit being who was housed in a human body for a time, as soon as He left the body hanging on the cross, the body died, which is why the soldiers did not need to break His legs.

Whilst in the body the Son experienced what it was like being a human being, and suffered the extreme agony of the pain of hanging on the cross, as any human being would. For that reason, He not only sympathises with our weaknesses (Heb. 4:14- 16), He is also our advocate before the Father (1 Jn. 2:1).

So, although the three separate persons of the Trinity are all members of the Godhead, it is the Father who is the source and inspiration of the other two.

Thus, we have the three members of the Godhead explained. Each an individual in their own way and equal in the Godhead and bound by a depth and intensity of love that man could not possibly understand, but the Father is, and always will be, the source and head of the Trinity.

ABOUT THE AUTHOR

After an electrical engineering apprenticeship in the Royal Navy, Peter went on to serve on a number of ships in different parts of the world, finally being responsible for the weapons maintenance department of a frigate and lecturing to trainee officers on weapon control systems. He also spent two years at the Royal Navy's training college in Fareham, Hampshire instructing on underwater weapon and defense systems.

Leaving the service in 1969, Peter worked as a quality engineer for the British Aircraft Corporation on spacecraft and guided weapon systems before moving to R. A Lister (Diesels) where he became a technical author in 1984. He then worked as a contract author, mostly in the nuclear generation industry, writing operating instructions, maintenance manuals and other instructional and training documentation before finally retiring in 2011. Peter gained membership of the Society of Authors in 1993

For over 20 years, Peter was a Methodist Local Preacher before becoming an official prison visitor and worshipping with his wife at the prison he visited in order to focus on supporting prisoners who wanted to change their lives around. He resigned as a prison visitor in January 2016 after 26 years but continued to attend worship services at the prison chapel until January 2020.

In the prison Peter met a Jew named Derek who had become a Christian in prison. On his release into the local community, Peter was able to help him adjust to a new life of going straight.

It was Derek who first asked Peter to write on scripture. After which Derek's brother Aaron, a rabbi serving in the USA, came under the influence of Peter's writing and became a Christian. Aaron asked him to write first on the book of Revelation and then on the subject of Moses' Tent of the Meeting, which he self-published early 2011. He currently has 29 books available through Amazon worldwide as a paperback or for downloading to an eBook reader.

Peter was married December 1961 and has three sons and six grandchildren. His autobiographical book explaining how he came to write so many books is called "A Tale of Three Men"

MORE FROM

Peter Russell-Yarde

www.ingramcontent.com/pod-product-compliance
Lightning Source LLC
Chambersburg PA
CBHW021610120626
46545CB00001B/157